Praise for
Fire in the Turtle House

"Turtles have graced the seas for hundreds of millions of years. What their future holds, no one can say. *Fire in the Turtle House* is an important book about this wounded world and the people who are trying to set it right."

—Carl Safina, author of *Song for the Blue Ocean*

"A hard-working, sincere and scientifically valuable little book ... a truly menacing and heart-achingly sad tale. [Davidson] is a disciplined and cogent storyteller."

—*Los Angeles Times*

"An elegant ecocautionary tale wrapped in a scientific mystery.... A quick-flowing narrative sparkling with wit.... Readers interested in ecology and animals, as well as those who value strong prose, will be intrigued and troubled by this book."

—*Publishers Weekly*

"*Fire in the Turtle House* is a profound and beautifully written account of the plight of the sea turtle. It is also, surprisingly, a story of hope for the future of these magnificent creatures."

—Jan Cousteau, ocean advocate

"A lucid and disturbing report on grim happenings in the sea-turtle world—and by extension the oceans themselves.... Davidson brings environmental passion, as well as a gimlet-eyed environmental appreciation, to the turtles' predicament."

—*Kirkus Reviews*

"Overhunting, coastal contamination, habitat destruction and global warming have conspired against the world's oldest surviving reptiles, setting the stage for a plague of tumors. Osha Davidson's saga of these 'wise and generous' creatures reminds us that we too are part of the food web and that we too are endangered by the current scope of our own activities."

—Paul R. Epstein, Associate Director, Center for Health and the Global Environment, Harvard Medical School

"Reading like a detective novel, the text draws the reader into the search for the cause of the (turtles') tumors: Is it a virus? Parasites? Marine pollution? Following the strands of evidence, the author reminds us of the interrelatedness of life and the environment."

—*Booklist*

"A masterful scientific detective story, with abundant human interest thrown in for good measure. It is impossible to make the frightening story of green turtle fibropapilloma disease simple, but Davidson has made it highly readable; furthermore, most of the players in his story are my friends and colleagues, and the author has captured their personalities and nuances brilliantly. Every turtle aficionado, professional or amateur, should read this book."

—Peter C. H. Pritchard, Ph.D., Director, Chelonian Research Institute

"Davidson's writing is ... the best kind of journalistic reporting: clear and well-paced, employing individual human experiences—his own as well as those of dozens of people he interviews—to elucidate the global problem. He writes for people who don't have biology degrees in a way that scientists will likely respect, simplifying the science but not the issues. Reads as readily as a detective story...."

—*The Honolulu Advertiser*

Fire in the Turtle House

The Green Sea Turtle
and the
Fate of the Ocean

Osha Gray Davidson

PublicAffairs   *New York*

Book design by Mark McGarry, Texas Type & Book Works
Set in Stempel Garamond

Library of Congress Cataloging-in-Publication data
Davidson, Osha Gray.
Fire in the Turtle House: the green sea turtle and the fate of the ocean /
Osha Gray Davidson
p. cm.
ISBN 1-58648-199-1 (PBK.)
1. Green turtle. 2. Green turtle—Diseases. 3. Endangered species. 4. Ocean.
5. Nature—Effect of human beings on. I. Title.
QL666.C536 D37 2001
597.92'8—dc21
2001031868

10 9 8 7 6 5 4 3 2 1

The most popular Hawaiian turtle legend is that of Kauila. Historian Daniel Akaka, Jr., tells the story this way:

This takes place on the island of Hawaiʻi at a black sand beach called Punaluʻu. Two turtles, the female named Honupoʻokea (White-headed Green Sea Turtle) and the male named Honuʻea (Hawksbill), entered the beach of Punaluʻu and dug out a pond which provided the people of the area with a supply of drinking water. Honupoʻokea left a nest of eggs and when they hatched, all but one of the hatchlings entered the sea and that one hatchling lived in the nearby pond. The people named the baby turtle Kauila, for her shell was the color of a dark-brown native hardwood of that name. This female turtle grew in the pond and was known to possess special powers. She could transform herself into a little girl and would often be seen playing on the beach with the other children. When children were caught in the strong ocean currents while swimming she would go out and save them. When Kauila wanted to retire back to her home pond she would once again transform back into her turtle form. The people of Punaluʻu loved Kauila as the guardian of their children and also for the spring that gave them pure drinking water.

For Kauila and her children

Epidemics are like sign-posts from which the statesman of stature can read that a disturbance has occurred in the development of his nation—that not even careless politics can overlook.

—DR. RUDOLF VIRCHOW, 1848, quoted in Epstein (1997:3)

If an animal goes extinct that is not economically useful, no human is going to care too much.

—JIM SHEEHAN, director of international policy,
Competitive Enterprise Institute, *Toronto Star*, 3 May 1997

Contents

Preface to the Paperback Edition

Not much has changed for sea turtles since *Fire in the Turtle House* first appeared in 2001. These ancient mariners continue to die from the tumor disease called fibropapillomatosis (FP) and from the more established threats posed by commercial fishing and habitat destruction. The ocean itself is still abused as a resource to be exploited without limits and as the end point for our river-borne pollution, primarily nutrients from agricultural runoff and industrial livestock production.

Still, there is progress to report.

George Balazs, of the National Marine Fisheries Service, is finding the first tentative signs that FP may be declining in Hawaii. It's possible that the disease has reached a peak as turtles unable to shake the affliction die off and survivors develop a natural immunity. The federal program of euthanizing severely affected turtles (for research) may have also helped limit the spread of the disease.

Researchers led by Paul Klein at the University of Florida continue to make progress in unraveling the complexities of FP. Klein—whose accomplishments as an FP researcher and as a mentor to others were inadvertently omitted from the 2001 text—and his colleagues are exploring many areas, including similarities between the pathogen linked to FP and another turtle killer, a herpesvirus known as LET (lungs, eyes, and trachea).

It's been known since the mid-1980s that some FP turtles regress, their tumors gradually disappearing. But a recent study by University of Central Florida (UCF) graduate student Shigetomo Hirama surprised many with the finding that 88 percent of lightly infected turtles caught in Florida's Indian River Lagoon were in various stages of regression when recaptured ten months or more later. Hirama's study has its limitations—it provides only a snapshot view of a single site using a small sample size—but his work underscores the importance of research into regression.

In another victory for turtles, nesting rates are increasing for several sea turtle species in the Archie Carr National Wildlife Refuge in Florida, as a variety of conservation measures take hold. The refuge is the most important nesting area for loggerhead turtles in the Western Hemisphere, with as many as 20,000 loggerheads coming ashore to nest annually. The number of green turtles nesting on these same beaches has skyrocketed. When Congress created the refuge in 1989, fewer than 100 green turtles nested there. In 2002 volunteers counted nearly 3,000 green turtle nests. In Hawaii, where the green turtle was once on the verge of extinction, nesting rates have been rising steadily, largely due to the Endangered Species Act's ban on hunting turtles.

But these gains are only a small part of the picture. The outlook for sea turtles and for marine life in general remains as clouded today as it was in 2001, for several reasons. There is growing evidence that global warming is linked to marine epidemics. As the Bush administration continues to resist meaningful reductions in the emission of greenhouse gasses that cause global warming, marine and terrestrial epidemics will likely spread, with new diseases emerging as temperatures rise.

Nutrient-laden runoff may have killed hundreds of sea lions and scores of dolphins off the California coast in 2002. The second largest die-off of marine mammals in U.S. history was linked to a toxic microorganism that thrives in coastal waters polluted with nitrogen from agriculture. Even as I write, there are reports of a new spate of sea lion deaths in California, with the same toxin thought to be the cause.

Commercial fishing remains the single greatest killer of sea turtles. For example, the colossal leatherback sea turtle, the oldest species and the largest, is headed for extinction in the Pacific, a victim of longline fishing. A single longline can stretch up to sixty miles and carry 3,000 hooks. Although longlines generally target swordfish, leatherbacks are among the hundreds of species caught and killed accidentally by this gear (the total "by-catch" of nontarget species in U.S. waters alone is estimated at 2.3 billion pounds annually). Between 1980 and 2002 the number of nesting Pacific leatherbacks plunged 95 percent, a staggering decline that is largely attributable to longlining. In February 2003 hundreds of marine scientists from around the world signed a letter to UN Secretary-General Kofi Annan calling for an international moratorium on longline and gill-net fishing—another practice that kills sea life indiscriminately. The United Nations has not announced a decision on the issue.

Clearly, these are difficult times for those who love the sea. It sometimes seems that everywhere you look you're confronted with the specter of needless death. Dead turtles, dead sea lions, dead fish. Innumerable corpses ride the tides. If you gaze at them too long, you can be consumed by hard emotions: pain, rage, a piercing sorrow. But our salvation lies in the fact that hope is the last emotion to die—and the first requirement for action. Buoyed by hope, we can work. And in working we discover that the planet can be made whole again. It will be difficult, to be sure, but not impossible.

My father-in-law, a devout Catholic, believes in salvation, hard work, and hope's religious cousin: faith. He's also an Irish American with a fondness for Old World blessings. If I could coin a blessing for a new world, it would be this: May your children swim in an ocean full of turtles.

Phoenix, Arizona
May 2003

Acknowledgments

For many traditional peoples, turtles are the embodiment of wisdom and generosity. It must be true, because over the three years I've spent working on this book, the people who have devoted their lives to studying and helping protect these wonderful creatures have demonstrated both qualities in abundance.

First and foremost, I want to thank Ursula Keuper-Bennett for her help and encouragement in every phase of a project that grew like a turtle: slowly, inexorably, and seemingly without limits. She and her husband Peter Bennett have devoted their lives to a particular assemblage of wild turtles, the *honu* (Hawaiian for green sea turtle) of the eponymous Turtle House. I'm under no illusion why Ursula has been so helpful, and she's certainly never attempted to hide her reasons. These can be summed up in her motto: "Think of the *honu* first." Ursula believes that this book may in some way help the *honu* of Honokowai. I applaud her priorities and hope she's right.

Ursula appropriated that motto from her mentor, George Balazs. His official title is Leader, Marine Turtle Research Program, Southwest Fisheries Science Center, Honolulu Laboratory, National Marine Fisheries Service. But anyone who knows George knows that he holds an even nobler station in life: He is the *honu*'s best friend. And if he, too, went to extraordinary lengths to help this project, it was done in that capacity. Again, I only hope his faith proves justified.

There are so many others who have helped, supplying information, sharing memories, answering questions, taking time from busy schedules in order that I could better understand and write about the important and complex world of marine diseases. Most of them, too, have dedicated their lives to sea turtles, or to other creatures in the sea. Of course I appreciate their help. But my primary debt arises from their work itself. They are the protectors of the sea, and if the ocean world is to be saved, it will be because of their efforts and those of like-minded people throughout the world.

I also want to thank my longtime agent Alison Picard and my editor at PublicAffairs, Lisa Kaufman. To family and friends who have supported me in this work, I offer my heartfelt thanks and deepest gratitude.

Prologue

Hawaii

FORTY FEET DEEP in the shimmering waters off the west coast of Maui, I glide through a school of brilliantly colored fish that parts like a living curtain above a field of blue-gray boulders. The water is warm and clear. There had been a strong southward current running dangerously hard for days through the narrow channel separating Maui from the neighboring island of Moloka'i, but sometime before dawn the flow began to slacken. By 10 o'clock, it abated to a gentle tug.

There is nothing subdued about the sunlight, however. It illuminates everything for a hundred feet around with blinding tropical intensity. Clouds of bluestripe snapper hover around a rock the size of a minivan. An eel pokes its sinewy head out of a hole and then slithers back as my shadow riffles over it.

I am entranced watching a beautiful Picasso triggerfish when Ursula taps me on the arm. Ursula Keuper-Bennett is my dive partner. For nine months each year she teaches elementary school in Toronto, Canada, but every summer for over a decade she and her husband Peter have dived these waters, at a place called the Turtle House. She knows every boulder around, every sandy patch, even many of the individual creatures that live here. In a very real sense, it's her neighborhood, and, to carry the metaphor a step further, Ursula is head of the Neighborhood Watch program.

She pulls a laminated sheet from her dive vest and points to an entry: Tutu (since 1990). Tame but respect large comfort zone. Read signals.

I look around and then back at Ursula and shrug.

What, where?

A burst of bubbles races from her regulator to the surface. She's laughing, but I haven't the faintest idea why.

She grabs my wrist with her left hand and with her right she points to a nearby boulder. I'd rather follow the triggerfish, but if Ursula wants me to look at the boulder, I'll look at the boulder. Like many of the rocks around here, the surface is smooth, probably the result of the eroding current. A few large white barnacles grow on it. Maybe it's the barnacles she wants me to observe. I inspect the barnacles. All in all, not very interesting.

I turn back to Ursula and nod.

Okay, I've looked. Very nice rock, Ursula.

She vents more bubbles. I can see her eyes through her mask crinkling in mischievous, though still inexplicable, delight. Ursula shakes her head and points at the rock more emphatically, jabbing her finger at it repeatedly for emphasis.

Look (jab) *more* (jab) *closely* (jab), *dummy.*

I look more closely. It takes a few seconds before I realize that the rock is staring back at me. The regulator nearly falls out of my mouth.

What I would have sworn was a boulder, about a yard long, has a large broad head, twice the size of my fist, which has swiveled to regard me, casting a cool gaze in my direction. In one smooth unbroken motion, the "rock" pushes off from the ocean floor and without looking back hurls itself toward the surface. Its huge front flippers (how did I miss those?) sweep in slow powerful downstrokes, sending it skyward.

I watch awestruck as the creature ascends, silhouetted against the surface ablaze with light. It hurts to stare into that liquid brilliance, but I can't turn away. At the surface, the massive head disappears briefly above the water, where it draws a breath and then quickly reappears. The huge shadow descends, gliding effortlessly down until it comes to rest several yards away, its head turned in the other direction. In a breach of the instructions Ursula had typed up, I had failed to "read signals" and had violated the "comfort zone." That's what caused the animal to leave. "Read signals"? Hell, I had mistaken a giant sea turtle for a rock.

I look back at Ursula, who is still chortling. She points again at the sheet.

Tutu. The Hawaiian word for grandmother. Tutu is a Pacific green sea turtle, a *Chelonia mydas* in scientific terminology, or *honu* in Hawaiian. She is a true matriarch, with metal tags in her rear flippers attesting to the fact that she has nested several times at a site hundreds of miles to the west.

Ursula points to other names on the sheet and then to other boulders. Suddenly, the underwater world shifts before my eyes.

This isn't a boulder field. It's a turtle field.

The change is so dramatic and it occurs so quickly that my stomach drops, the way it can when an elevator plummets too quickly. I'm surrounded by sea turtles. Most of the *honu* lie motionless, dozing on the sea floor as cleaner fish pick at the wisps of algae growing on their shells. A few juveniles, closer to the size of large frying pans than boulders, are more active. They swirl around, nipping and buzzing each other. Sometimes they crash into one of the larger turtles with an audible "*thuuunk*." The larger reptiles generally ignore the antics of their smaller cohorts. But occasionally, an older turtle gets fed up and pushes its bulk into the water above, pirouettes, and comes grumpily to rest a few feet away.

You can almost hear it thinking: *Kids, hrrumph!*

I propel myself into a vertical position so that I can turn slowly and look at them all. They're all over the place.

Ursula indicates for me to follow her. We kick over to an old section of reef, where several turtles lie in shallow depressions. She points to one turtle, not as large as Tutu but not one of the youngest ones, either. We are ten to fifteen feet away when Ursula stops and settles to the bottom. With a wave of one hand she indicates that I am to approach the turtle alone. I creep forward an inch at a time, trying to read her signals this time. (I refer to this turtle as "she" although it's impossible to determine an immature turtle's sex without a full-scale clinical examination.)

Ursula has already explained her theory of signals, a long list of behaviors that she maintains turtles use to communicate. Some biologists I've talked with question Ursula's interpretations of these turtle movements. Others are firm believers. Most seem to fall somewhere in between. Ursula isn't a turtle scientist—as she would be the first to point out. She isn't a marine biologist either, or a scientist of any kind. Yet she is well known throughout the "turtle world," a small but dedicated group of biologists who specialize in these ancient creatures. Although they are laypeople, Ursula and Peter have spent more time with a single wild population of sea turtles than anyone else in the world. Between 1988 and 2000, they have logged more than 1,200 dives in this same area, filming 240 hours of videotape of these turtles and taking 4,500 photographs. Thanks to this ongoing contact, she and Peter were the first people to implement a system for identifying individual turtles using photographs of facial markings. Over the years the couple has identified more than 200 turtles in this one area. Ursula can recognize many of them on sight. She has also been observing turtle behavior more and more systematically over the years. So when she says that *honu* frequently show irritation by making a kind of yawning display, there is good reason to believe she's right.

Bearing this in mind, and alert to any signals, I edge closer to the *honu*. When I am a few feet away, she looks over and tenses her flippers, as if about to push off. I immediately stop and then allow myself to drift slowly backward a few inches. She keeps her head toward me but seems to relax slightly, her body moving back to the ocean floor.

I wait a few seconds and then move a few inches closer and stop. She seems unalarmed.

I creep closer. Still no problems.

But when I'm a couple of yards to her left, she suddenly lifts one flipper, the first stage of what Ursula has called a flipper swipe. According to Ursula, *honu* use flipper swipes—rapidly pulling a single flipper downward across their face—as a sign of intense displeasure. I've watched the maneuver many times on a video Ursula sent me to prepare for these dives. I've seen *honu* swipe when other turtles try to dislodge them from a resting spot, or when Ursula or Peter have gotten too close. One sequence showed a *honu* swiping repeatedly while a nesting wrasse, a highly territorial fish, dashed about trying to get the turtle to leave "its" area. Relating the flipper swipe to human behavior, Ursula sometimes calls it the *honu* version of giving someone the finger.

I've never been swiped before and after my gaffe with Tutu, I don't want to provoke another negative response. I instantly move backward and for good measure lower my head, a sign of submission in many mammals. I have no idea whether turtles use these cues, but I figure it's best not to take any chances.

The *honu* freezes in mid flipper swipe, leaving the flipper raised. Without taking her eyes off me, she slowly lowers the flipper—millimeter by millimeter—to a resting position.

A victory! I've avoided being flipped off.

I wait another minute and then as slowly, abjectly, and humbly as possible, I creep back. I slink like a dog who knows he's been bad and whose only desire is to demonstrate his servility. The *honu* seems reassured. At any rate, she allows me to grovel my way up to her side. With our heads now only inches apart, I look up. We stare into each other's eyes.

Turtles are reptiles and I had expected their eyes to resemble those of snakes, with eerie black slits cut across incandescent golden irises. But the eye looking into mine is startling only in its familiarity. Her pupil is round like mine and surrounded by a light blue-gray iris that is also round. Her gaze is steady, unafraid, and, it seems, curious.

For a modern westerner, an intimate encounter with a wild animal is a rare gift. The remarkable quality of the experience is magnified when the animal is as extraordinary as a sea turtle, a creature revered in the legends and creation myths of many peoples. These marine reptiles have existed since the time of dinosaurs—for at least 110 million years. At first I am overwhelmed and excited. My heart races. As we continue staring at one another, however, I feel my breathing slow down. Without planning to (if I had known what I was about to do, I would have stopped myself), I extend the little finger of one hand and gently touch the turtle's left flipper, my finger sliding smoothly over her scales. Sea turtles are a protected species and it is not only against federal law to touch them, it is also stupid. These aren't pets. They are wild animals. The Park Ranger in my head admonishes me, *If you want to pat an animal get a cat or a dog! Leave the frigging wild animals alone!*

I know all this, and I can offer a variety of rationalizations, but what it all comes down to is this: I couldn't help myself. Okay, I didn't *want* to help myself. And I don't think I did any harm. Certainly the turtle didn't appear disturbed by the contact. On the contrary, with finger and flipper joined, the turtle's eyelids descend. She falls asleep.

A few moments later, still under the spell of the contact, I propel myself gently backward so that I don't awaken the slumbering turtle. I turn to face Ursula, whose eyes shine from behind her mask. She nods in understanding. She points to the air pressure gauge on my dive console. Time to head back.

We haven't gone far before I see it above me, flickering on the edges of my peripheral vision. It is a shadow, shapeless and indistinct. It could be the darkened trough of a wave seen from below, or the tumble of my own hair spilling over the top of my mask. Quickly, however, the shade gathers itself into solidity. It swims down into full view a few yards ahead. It is a turtle, an adolescent, judging by the size. What grabs my attention are the tumors sprouting in clumps under its front flippers. Even more grotesque is the larger and darker mass obscuring one eye. It moves slowly and heavily through the water like death itself, dragging its tumors along. It is a terrifying sight, despite the fact that this is the reason I'm here, to see the disease that has already killed many of the *honu* at the Turtle House. Ursula had written me months before that more than 70 percent of the turtles here are afflicted with this disease, a pestilence that came out of nowhere and now burns through the Turtle House like a wildfire, claiming new arrivals and old friends they had known for years.

"MAN I HATE this @#$#$%ing DISEASE!" reads one of Ursula's E-mails. She calls it an "obscene personal enemy."

It is very personal for Ursula, in part because of Clothahump. Clothahump was the first sea turtle Ursula had seen in the wild, a juvenile: small, playful, and completely unafraid of the Canadian divers when they first met in the waters off West Maui in 1988. Clothahump (named for a turtle wizard from a fantasy story), seemed more like an overeager puppy than a turtle.

"Ursula went nuts over Clothahump," Peter tells me later. "She was totally entranced right from the very first. I wasn't a big reptile person, but even I had no problem falling in love with Clothahump. She was so cute. I mean, you'd have to have a heart of stone not to fall in love with that thing right away."

When they left Hawaii at the end of that summer, Peter and Ursula said a sad good-bye to Clothahump, not knowing whether the little turtle would be around when they returned the following summer. But there she was in 1989, bigger, but just as puppyish and eager to hang around them as they dove. They saw her nearly every day that summer. The same thing happened in 1990, and again in the following year. Clothahump became a permanent fixture of their summers in Maui, a faithful friend who welcomed them each year. But she was more than just a friend to the Canadian couple. She was a teacher of sorts. "She introduced us to the ways of turtles," is how Ursula puts it.

In 1991 tumors started showing up on some of the turtles. In 1992, Clothahump showed possible early signs of the disease: a sprinkling of white and gray spots mostly on her neck and shoulders. During the long Canadian winter that year, Clothahump was never far from

Ursula's thoughts. She told herself that perhaps the spots meant nothing. She wasn't a turtle biologist, after all. Maybe the spots were just a natural part of Clothahump's maturing process. Maybe the spots were temporary, some kind of rash that would clear up by the next summer. Maybe.... But Ursula was whistling in the dark. "I knew all along what we'd find the next summer," she admits.

It was one of the first dives of the summer 1993. Peter was already videotaping when Clothahump appeared. On the video, you can see the turtle approaching. As she comes closer your eyes are drawn to the welter of tumors that sprout from her head, from her shoulders, and that nearly cover both eyes. Their friend makes a single slow looping turn around Peter and Ursula and then heads off, disappearing into deeper water. For several seconds you have a clear view of the sandy ocean floor, the image bobbing as Peter weeps.

It was the last time they saw Clothahump.

The disease doesn't become personal for me even after several weeks diving with Ursula and Peter. That doesn't happen until months later, and several thousand miles away.

The Florida Keys

Sue Schaf is talking to a visitor when, for no apparent reason, she stops in midsentence and casts a suspicious glance at a large green sea turtle named Buddy. To an observer, Buddy seems to be sitting placidly in his blue plastic kiddy pool that has no water in it.

"Don't even *think* about it, Buddy," warns Schaf, the thirty-four-year-old animal director of the Marathon Key Turtle Hospital, the world's only hospital devoted fully to the care of sea turtles. Her voice is friendly but tinged with the steely resolve mothers reserve for mischievous children.

There is a moment of calm as the two regard each other.

Then Buddy makes his move. He lunges toward the edge of the pool and in a flash his powerful right front flipper is already over the side. Using the flipper as a lever, he pulls himself up and is a nanosecond away from hurling himself onto the tile floor. But Schaf's reflexes are too quick. She manages to grab the side of Buddy's large round shell at the precise moment that his center of gravity is shifting over the fulcrum of the pool's edge. Grunting with the effort, Schaf lugs the thrashing turtle, all sixty-three pounds of him, back into the middle of the wading pool.

"Come on, boy!" she pleads, catching her breath. "Don't be so *nuts*."

Buddy does seem a bit nuts for a green sea turtle. Out of the water, most greens are about as impulsive as rocks. But in the three months that Buddy has been in residence at the hospital, he has earned a reputation for rowdiness. Some hospital employees sometimes refer to him affectionately as "Spazz-turtle."

Buddy might well have escaped from the kiddy pool, if it weren't for a major defect in his anatomy: he lacks a left front flipper. It was already missing when Buddy was found bobbing about like a giant cork in Florida Bay, a quarter mile out from shore. There are only a few ways in which turtles as large as Buddy can lose a flipper. A shark can bite it off (although it's usually the *rear* end of the fleeing turtle that gets maimed in shark attacks). Turtles also lose limbs to boat propellers. But it wasn't a shark or a propeller that took Buddy's flipper. Monofilament fishing line, most likely discarded by a thoughtless fisherman, was the culprit. Buddy had white nylon fishing line wrapped all around his head when he was found, with more line coming out of his mouth.

"He probably ate the baited end and got tangled up in the rest," explains Schaf. She strokes Buddy behind his large head to calm him down. "The fishing line around the flipper just got tighter and tighter until it cut the poor thing off," she says.

Buddy exhales, as if in response. The sound is that of a tire deflating.

"Yeah, Buddy's kinda crazy," says Schaf. "But I'd rather have them feisty instead of so sick like Jonathan." She nods toward a small plastic bucket in the corner. Inside the container lies a much smaller turtle, a mere twelve pounds, and just over a foot long. Buddy, who is more than two feet long, is probably in his late teens. Jonathan is the turtle equivalent of a toddler. He, too, was entangled in fishing line but was rescued before the line had a chance to cut deep into his tissues. Unlike Buddy, who was found only a few miles away from the hospital, Jonathan is an "out-of-towner." He comes from the waters off Vero Beach, a few hundred miles to the north, halfway up Florida's Atlantic coast.

Jonathan doesn't look well. He floats listlessly in his small bucket. Occasionally an eye swivels to the rear as if he is trying to see something behind him. A small yellow tube extends from an incision in his neck just above the right front flipper. He is too weak to eat on his own, Schaf explains. She points to the underside of his shell, the part biologists call the plastron. It's caved in, and the skin covering it hangs loosely, like an adult's sweater on a child. "In a healthy turtle the plastron is kinda pushed out," Schaf says, her voice warm and solicitous. "This little guy is starving."

The cause of Jonathan's predicament is obvious, even at first glance. The small turtle is covered with tumors. They grow in dark clumps from his rear flippers. Tightly packed clusters of pink and gray tissue adhere like congealed foam to the skin beneath Jonathan's front flippers. Smaller, dull-white tumors sprout like mushrooms from the corners of his eyes. The largest tumor bulges from Jonathan's right shoulder, nearly as large as his head. It is rounded, completely black, and gives off a vile odor. The surface is ulcerated and bits of dark tissue mixed with blood are constantly sloughing off into the water.

Buddy has tumors, too. They are on his eyes, under his good flipper, above the stump where he lost his other flipper, on top of his neck, below his neck. Along his hindquarters, the tumors grow in an angry-looking line that stretches from one flipper all the way along his tail and then up the other flipper.

These tumors are the reason the two turtles are here today, in the hospital's "pre-op" room, waiting for veterinarian Doug Mader. While there is no known cure for the disease that affects the turtles, Schaf says that if all the tumors are surgically removed the patient often recovers and no more tumors grow back. One permanent resident of the hospital underwent the procedure more than a decade ago, and she has stayed tumor-free ever since. (She remains at the hospital because of another problem. A powerboat cracked open the top part of her shell—the carapace—and the accident left her unable to dive without a three-pound weight strapped to her, a condition that gave her the name Bubble-Butt.)

At a little after nine o'clock Mader strides into the hospital. He is tall and powerfully built, exuding an aura of authority that befits a surgeon (even a veterinary one). Mader isn't just any veterinary surgeon, however. He is something of a superstar in the small but fanatical world of reptile enthusiasts. In his early forties, Mader is recognized as one of the leading reptile surgeons in the country. He edited the standard reference work on reptile medicine and writes a monthly column for *Reptile* magazine. With his close-cropped black hair, neatly trimmed goatee and mustache, and dark brooding eyes, Mader could have stepped out of an Elizabethan drama. You half expect him to perform surgery with a dagger instead of a scalpel.

"Hello, people," Mader says as he walks briskly across the room and immediately begins to examine his patients. He turns to Schaf and inquires, "How are these guys?"

"Buddy's a bit hyper," she says. "As usual. And the little one—he's not doing so good."

Mader leans over and examines each animal for a few seconds. Then he glances at their charts. "Okay," he says. "We'll take Buddy first. Then the little one." He pauses for just a second and then stands up. "Let's get started."

People leap into action. Schaf prepares the operating room. Right behind Mader is Richie Moretti, a former Volkswagen mechanic who—along with his girlfriend at the time, a fishing boat captain named Tina Brown—founded the Turtle Hospital in 1986 to treat injured sea turtles. Moretti seems Mader's opposite. He is short and slim, with a ponytail of wispy brown hair cascading down his back and doelike brown eyes.

Even the slight edge of Moretti's New Jersey accent has been softened by his many years on the island. First appearances to the contrary, however, Richie Moretti is no typical laid-back Keys character. His mellowness is like the calm at the eye of a hurricane: a tranquillity surrounded by 150-mile-per-hour winds.

The team works quickly and efficiently. In five minutes, Buddy lies prone on the surgical table, calmed first by an injection of the sedative Domator, his heart rate stabilized with 3 cc's of Atropine, and finally knocked out with a general anesthetic administered through a tube inserted into his mouth. Now covered by full surgical scrubs, mask, and goggles, Mader is anxious to begin. As soon as the machinery is ready, he steps up to the table and instructs Schaf to lift Buddy's right front flipper. Mader holds an electric scalpel which cuts off the tumors and simultaneously seals the blood vessels around them. Most of the tumors grow on a peduncle, a narrow stalk that connects the growth to the turtle's body. Mader lifts the tumor with tweezers and then traces around the base of the peduncle with the electric scalpel. The scalpel makes a crackling noise as Mader works and leaves behind a blackened trail of charred flesh. Each time a full circuit has been completed around a peduncle, the tumor and the underlying skin come neatly away. Through the exposed hole, dark layers of bulging muscle are clearly visible, covered only by a gossamer veil of connective tissue.

Mader is moving right along. Soon, a large pile of tumors is stacked beside Buddy's head. The growths range in size from the width of a fingernail to the size of your fist. They vary in color, too, from creamy white to salmon pink, and from eggplant purple to jet black. As the tumors grow, they take their pigmentation from the underlying skin. A few tumors have smooth surfaces, but they are the exception. Most are conglomerations of warty nodules that are creased by deep fissures called crypts. Some have tiny projections that look exactly like pencil points. Tiny leeches, barely visible to the eye, crawl over the surface, and even more are found deep within the crypts, feeding on the blood supply that keeps the tumors growing. (One researcher with a strong stomach counted fifty of these bloodsuckers in a tumor section just a half-inch square.) The tumors are also filled with pockets of yellow eggs that come from blood flukes, a parasite commonly found inside the sea turtle's circulatory system. The flukes themselves have never been found in the tumors. But their eggs, each only 1/100th of an inch long, permeate the tissues. Between the blood fluke eggs, the miniature leeches, and the ulcerated tumors themselves, the pile of tissue is about as ugly as anything you can imagine. I try to keep count of the tumors, but after reaching two dozen I give up.

"You have to get every tumor, and every bit of tumored tissue from each one, or they come back," Mader says without pausing or taking his eyes from his work. The acrid smell of singed meat fills the room.

When one side is done, Buddy is turned over carefully, exposing the tumors growing out of the soft tissues below. "I don't think I've seen a turtle this size with so many tumors before," says Mader.

"Nope," says Moretti, positioning the rear paddlelike flippers to make it easier for Mader to reach the tumors. "They're usually dead."

The last to be removed are the tumors on Buddy's eyes. The tumors frequently begin in the corner of a turtle's eyes, or on the conjunctiva—the mucous membrane that lines the inside of the eyelid. Eventually, the growths may move into the eyeball itself, collapsing it. Buddy is lucky. With an ultrasound machine similar to the one used to see developing fetuses in humans, Mader has already determined that the turtle's corneas are intact. His eye tumors haven't spread to the eyeball itself. Soon, these tumors, too, are excised, ever so delicately, and lie in a pile with the rest.

Buddy now appears tumor free. As Mader goes into the other room to prepare the other turtle for surgery, Schaf tapes gauze over Buddy's eyes and then bandages some of the larger surgical wounds. It's hard to believe, but by tomorrow afternoon all the bandages will be removed and Buddy will be swimming in a large saltwater tank in back of the neighboring Hidden Harbor motel, which Moretti runs to finance the hospital. Buddy will live there for a year. If the tumors don't return, he'll be released back into the wild.

Moretti explains this process as he helps clean up the table, placing the ghastly pile of tumors into a container marked biohazard, and moves Buddy onto a gurney. He stands back and admires the large turtle.

"Doesn't Doug do beautiful work?" he asks. And it's true. Thanks to Mader, the large green turtle on the gurney is no longer smothered with tumors.

"Bring in the little guy," shouts Moretti with a satisfied smile.

Mader's voice comes from around the corner.

"I don't think so," he says.

We walk over and find Mader and Schaf standing over Jonathan, his foot-long body resting on a stainless steel table.

Moretti stares down at the turtle.

"He's dead," says Mader without looking up.

"Shit," says Moretti.

"Poor little guy," says Schaf.

No one says anything for a few seconds. We all look at the turtle. His eyes are open but clouded over.

Mader is the first to shake off the pall. "I'm going to necropsy him," he says in a voice that is just slightly too loud. A necropsy is the veterinary equivalent of an autopsy.

Moretti goes silently back into the other room to help with Buddy.

Mader turns Jonathan onto his back, exposing the sunken plastron. Using a small handheld circular saw, the veterinarian cuts around the plastron's edge and then removes the hard lower plate. Reaching inside the body cavity, he uses a scalpel to sever the lungs and pulls out the spongy masses, examining them carefully.

"I'm looking for internal tumors," he explains. Internal tumors are most frequently found in the lungs, but Jonathan's seem free of them. The next most common spot is the kidneys. Mader removes one of the tiny organs, roughly the size and shape of a large cashew, and examines it closely. The organ is shot through with pearly white lumps. "Those are tumors," Mader says. He shakes his head. "It wouldn't have mattered what we did with the external tumors," he explains. "This one was a goner."

Schaf nods in agreement.

Mader ends the necropsy with a small surprise: Jonathan is—was—a female. The surgeon points to the ovaries, which are small and white and filled with thousands of tiny immature eggs. An hour ago each one of those eggs had the potential to become a new turtle. Now they are pinpoints of degenerating tissue.

Mader continues removing the organs until all that remains is a pool of thick dark blood at the bottom of the shell. The head and flippers are still attached, and the tumors seem even more evident on the exposed areas. Her small head is tipped backward against the steel table, her mouth slightly open.

"It's really better like this," says Mader. He peels off his latex gloves and tosses them into another biohazard bag. "She would have just suffered more."

"That's true," says Schaf. "When they get like that, there's nothing you can do. It *is* better this way."

"Yep," says Mader over his shoulder as he scrubs his hands and arms with medicated soap and hot water. "It's better like this."

As the veterinary surgeon leaves, Schaf calls after him, "Thanks, Dr. Doug. Great work!"

Mader doesn't say anything but waves good-bye. He walks across the parking lot and steps into his car. His tires shriek on the hot asphalt as he pulls into traffic on highway A1A.

That night when I return to my hotel room, I try to focus on Buddy, the feisty turtle who made it, thanks to the team at the Turtle Hospital. I imagine him as he will be tomorrow, swimming around his large plastic tank, spazzing with his one good flipper as he begins his recovery. I try to conjure up images of him back in the ocean sometime next year, munching algae and seagrass, growing into an adult, mating, reproducing. But I can't manage it. Instead, Jonathan's slight and spent body fills my imagination. I see her first in the plastic bucket, her eye rolling back, sick but still alive. Then I see her as she was only ninety minutes later, lying on the hard metal table with all her organs scooped out. A shell with a head and flippers: a turtle husk.

It's not surprising that images of the dead turtle crowd out visions of the living one. We are mortals, turtles and humans alike, and death awaits us all. But it isn't just the knowledge of our shared mortality that parades Jonathan's lifeless form before my closed eyes that night, and on many nights since. It's the knowledge that for every "Buddy" saved, there are likely thousands of "Jonathans" who will succumb to this plague.

The disease is called fibropapillomatosis, or FP. Some biologists consider it the most serious epidemic now raging in the natural (nonhuman) world. There are several reasons for this distinction. Most epidemics are localized, striking animals in a single population. FP, however, has been found in turtles from every ocean basin in the world. In an astonishingly short period, FP has changed from a rare disease to an epidemic and from an epidemic to a global pandemic.

The high incidence of the disease also sets it apart from many other epidemics. In some places, more than 90 percent of turtles are affected. And somewhere along the line, the disease jumped species. Until recently, FP had been seen only in green sea turtles. Now FP tumors have been reported in six of the seven remaining species of sea turtles.

Most important, the victims of FP belong to a group whose existence is already threatened. For creatures that have existed for more than a hundred million years, extinction, that black hole of evolution, is a real possibility. The tumors themselves aren't malignant, but the likely fate of a diseased turtle is death—and sooner rather than later. Some turtles will be found tangled in fishing line, their tumors providing plenty of opportunity for entanglement. Others will be blinded by tumors and will starve to death and wash up on beaches. A few may make it as far as the Turtle Hospital before they, too, die. Most, however, will develop the disease and die unseen, far from humans.

Sea turtles aren't the only marine creature falling prey to a mysterious and deadly epidemic. Over the last few decades diseases have been

burning through nearshore waters around the world, with unprecedented lethality. New diseases wipe out entire populations; old diseases
show devastating resurgences. From seagrasses to corals to marine
mammals like dolphins and seals, no form of aquatic life is immune to
this growing epidemic of epidemics. And in nearly every instance, one
finds the fingerprints of man.

Not to take anything away from the heroic efforts of Schaf, Mader,
and Moretti, but the story of FP isn't really Buddy's story at all. It is the
story of Jonathan.

Chapter 1

Discovery

FROM THE MOMENT the guards threw open the massive wooden doors on a crisp December morning in 1896, the New York Aquarium was a smashing success. Gotham's wealthiest citizens—Astors, Goulds, and Vanderbilts—came in a parade of gleaming carriages, sweeping down Fifth Avenue to the elegant building in Battery Park. Immigrant families from the lower East Side trudged over on foot, escaping their dank brooding tenements for a few hours, while those living in the outer boroughs jammed into the newly built elevated trains for a screeching and jostling ride to the very tip of Manhattan. They came by the thousands—30,000 on opening day alone—rich and poor, native and newcomer, to gape at seals, sharks and other marine specimens, and all for no charge.

By 1935, more than two million visitors annually were streaming through the brownstone arch of the remodeled theater and former immigration center, making the aquarium one of the most popular attractions in the city. Many visitors that year came expressly to see the aquarium's latest acquisition, an enormous electric eel. On the hour, Dr. Christopher Coats, the aquarium curator and the world's leading authority on electric fish, reached into the large tank and, using a metal hook, poked the mysterious creature. Instantly, the fish discharged a burst of electric current, causing a neon lamp above the tank to glow. Astonished and delighted by the spectacle, the crowd burst into spontaneous and thundering applause.

Another popular attraction at the aquarium was the large turtle tank, built in the adjacent harbor. Five sea turtles spent most of the time resting on the bottom, periodically rising to the surface to breathe. The marine reptiles held a curious fascination for viewers. Some people were intrigued by the antiquity of the turtle's lineage. The species in the tanks, three green turtles (*Chelonia mydas*) and two loggerheads (*Caretta caretta*) arose over 65 million years ago, sharing the ancient tropical waters with another turtle, *Archelon*, a behemoth fifteen feet long. While *Archelon* went extinct, no one knew how several other species of sea turtles managed to survive when all dinosaurs—including many oceangoing animals—had died out. Other people were attracted by the fact that sea turtles, like whales and porpoises, had started life in the ocean, emerged onto land, and then returned to the sea. Whatever their reasons, New Yorkers flocked to watch the placid marine reptiles glide around their tank, like giant birds skimming currents of air.

In December 1936, Dr. Coates noticed several small warts growing on one of the green sea turtles. Normally, a sea turtle's skin has a rough and bumpy texture, but Coates observed that these growths were unusually large. He kept an eye on the turtle. Soon the warts had grown larger and spread. It occurred to the curator that the turtle may have had a form of cancer. Coates contacted George Milton Smith, a medical doctor who specialized in cancer research at Yale University. Smith had a lifelong fascination with marine biology, and he combined his two interests by studying tumors in fish. He also served on the aquarium's scientific staff as an associate in pathology, and so it was only natural that Coates should consult Smith on the matter.

Our knowledge of what the men found comes from a single source: a brief article about the case written by Smith and Coates that appeared in 1938 in the journal *Zoologica*, the magazine of the aquarium's sponsor, the New York Zoological Society.

They identified the animal as a medium-sized green turtle (150 pounds) that had been shipped from Key West in 1934. The "warts" were all fairly small—none larger than an inch and most significantly smaller—and grew on the animal's soft tissue, on the back of the neck, in its "armpits" (the axilla), and around the equivalent of our thighs (inguinal areas). There were also extremely small growths on the upper eyelids. Smith surgically removed several growths and examined them under a microscope. Later, he and Coates obtained other similar tumors—including a few much larger ones—from the turtle fishery docks in Key West, Florida. After examining roughly 200 turtles in Key West, they found three with growths resembling the ones on the animal at the aquarium. They concluded that the condition, whatever it was, occurred in the wild, but at a low level.

While the growths looked similar at first glance, on closer examination they showed a startling variety of forms. Some tumors were colored and others were not. Then there was the matter of which layers of skin the growths affected. Skin has two layers: the outer, protective surface or epidermis, and the inner layer, richly supplied with blood vessels and nerves, called the dermis. The scientists found that the masses grew out of either layer—and sometimes out of both simultaneously. When these growths involved only the lower dermal layer, they were considered "fibromas." When they grew from the epidermis, they were "papillomas." And when both layers were actively involved in the growth, the two names were fused to form "fibropapillomas." Whatever the name, Smith and Coates determined that the masses were composed mostly of tough, fibrous tissue. The good news, concluded the cancer expert Smith, was that the tumors didn't appear to be malignant. It was true that the growths represented an unusual proliferation of cells. But the tumors appeared to have more in common with warts than with aggressive cancer cells that raged through an organism, destroying it.

The answer to one critical question, the most important question of all, in fact, eluded Smith and Coates: What caused the growths? They offered a few possibilities. Perhaps the intense tropical sunlight somehow triggered the "warts." They pointed out that fishermen in the Keys sometimes developed skin cancer and other strange skin conditions caused by years of exposure to sunlight. Even more likely, the pair concluded, was that the turtle tumors were a response to a parasite or the product of a virus. The authors concluded their article on an upbeat note. "The study of the transmissibility of the turtle papilloma has been begun," they wrote, "and it is hoped to report on this at a later date."

A transmission study was the next logical step. An extract prepared from a tumor would be injected into a healthy turtle and then that animal would be observed to see whether it developed the disease. If it did, the scientists would be one step closer to finding the cause of the tumors. Once the cause was isolated, work on a cure could begin. It sounds like a logical progression, but there are no reports by Smith and Coates on transmission studies. At least, no one has found them. Perhaps the pair never got around to conducting the studies. Or maybe they were unsuccessful in transmitting the disease and chose not to report on an inconclusive experiment.

In 1941, the New York Aquarium was shut down to make way for the construction of a lower Manhattan bridge. Until a new full-sized replacement could be built at Brooklyn's Coney Island (which wouldn't happen for sixteen years), the marine creatures from Battery Park had to share a section of the Lion House at the Bronx Zoo. There was only room in the Lion House for the smaller fish, and so the larger creatures were dispersed to other aquaria. The fate of the original "warty" green turtle remains a mystery. It could have been among the sea turtles shipped by rail to the Belle Isle Aquarium in Detroit. Other turtles were loaded aboard a steamship and sent to Bermuda. Was the diseased turtle among them? Or had it already died? No one knows.

The paper written by Smith and Coates suffered a somewhat similar fate, disappearing into scientific obscurity. "Fibro-epithelial Growths of the Skin in Large Marine Turtles, *Chelonia mydas*," was just one of thousands of similarly esoteric papers published that year. The journal containing the article was dutifully placed on the shelves of university libraries across the country. And there it sat, forgotten and mostly unread, for nearly half a century.

Chapter 2

How Many *Honu?*

ON A LANGUID tropical afternoon in 1969, a young couple carefully edged their thirty-foot ketch into the harbor at Lahaina, a former whaling port on the west coast of Maui, Hawaii. The man was twenty-six years old, tan and fit, with a round Hungarian face that was dominated by a thatch of tousled brown hair, a prominent nose, and an exuberant bottle-brush of a mustache. The woman was slightly younger, tan and athletic also, but with a Modigliani face—long and angular and framed by straight blonde hair cascading to her swanlike neck.

As the couple secured their vessel to the dock, a peculiar sight caught the man's eye. Not far off, a flotilla of skiffs waited at the boat ramp. One at a time their crews were unloading something—he couldn't tell what—into the beds of pickup trucks parked by the wharf. The two columns, of boats and of trucks, converged to form a single assembly line. Curious, the young man walked over to see what was going on. As he approached he was surprised to realize that what the men were heaving into the trucks were live sea turtles, each one weighing a hundred pounds or more. Each boat held at least a half dozen of the marine reptiles.

The young man was outgoing by nature, and he struck up an easy conversation with the fishermen. They told him that the turtles were headed for the row of tourist restaurants that lined Lahaina's main street, where they would be slaughtered and served up as deep-fried turtle fritters and grilled turtle steaks.

If the sight of giant *honu* being slung around like sacks of flour repulsed the young man, the sheer number of turtles being taken concerned him even more. He was a recent graduate of the University of Hawaii with a master's degree in animal sciences, and he knew a bit about population dynamics.

"This looks too easy," he told his wife when he returned to their boat, casting his gaze out to sun-dappled waters where whales were once hunted nearly to extinction. "How many turtles can there be out there?"

In fact, Hawaiian green sea turtles, like the humpback whales of the nineteenth century, were spiraling toward extinction—though no one knew it at the time. It would become the young man's mission to save them.

George Balazs grew up in the Mojave Desert, a harsh and dry environment that is about as different from lush Hawaii as one could imagine. His father clipped turkey beaks at a poultry farm and his mother waited tables at a local restaurant. Balazs's ambition was to be a lineman for California Power and Electric. There were turtles there, however—desert gopher tortoises. As a boy, Balazs would sometimes find one plodding alongside the road and bring it home with him, where the creature would crawl around the family's backyard, chomping on the lettuce leaves George would feed it, before heading slowly back into the desert.

After graduating from high school, Balazs started college in San Diego. But he quickly grew restless after the first year and transferred to a community college in suburban Los Angeles where a group of friends lived. He worked full-time at a dry cleaner and took classes at night. In July 1963, at the age of twenty, Balazs married his girlfriend

Linda (with the Modigliani face). One warm evening the newlyweds went to a local drive-in theater. Before the feature, there was a five-minute travelogue about a hit movie of the previous year, a remake of *Mutiny on the Bounty*, starring Marlon Brando and filmed on location in Tahiti. Inspired by that film, the travelogue featured scenes of the mist-cloaked peaks and turquoise bays of the lush French Polynesian island. By the time the travelogue was over, Balazs was already making plans for getting to Tahiti.

"I just kept thinking that whatever we'd find there would have to be better than the life that was ahead of us in southern California," he says. "I didn't know where we'd end up, or what we were supposed to be doing with our lives, but I figured maybe there was a clue to it in Tahiti."

For the next six months Balazs worked eighty-hour weeks, economizing wherever possible and saving enough money to afford two round-trip tickets to Tahiti. In January 1964, the couple arrived in the capital, Papeete. *Mutiny on the Bounty* had sparked a tourist boom on the island and motel prices had skyrocketed, but through a retired American doctor they met on the island, the couple found a private house far from the tourist areas, which they rented for $45 a month. The place was rustic but beautiful, surrounded by palm trees and with an open-air verandah that caught the trade winds and provided a panoramic view of the lagoon. They easily fell into a languorous routine. They ate French bread on the verandah for breakfast every morning as the sun climbed into the cloudless sky. Then they'd take a dip in the lagoon. Afternoons were spent riding their rented Vespa motor scooter out into rural areas where curious Tahitians would invite the young Americans in to visit.

Balazs had found paradise. "I kept thinking 'Oh, my God, is this real?'"

By exchanging their return airline tickets for cheaper passage on a French cargo liner, they managed to stretch their stay into a seven-month idyll. Finally, they spent their last franc and were forced to

backtrack to the United States. But they had a plan to return to Tahiti
as permanent residents. They would work in California, save their
money and move to Hawaii. There, George would earn a college
degree, allowing him to have a career in Tahiti. Hawaii was to be a steppingstone for their return to French Polynesia.

The first part of the scheme went as planned. Living with his parents
to save on rent, Balazs worked for a local bricklayer, carrying buckets of
mortar up ladders in the desert heat. It was backbreaking work, but it
paid $7 an hour—a good wage for unskilled labor. Nearly all their
money went into the bank. In less than a year, they had built up enough
savings to move to Hawaii. The second part of the plan was also successful. They arrived in Honolulu in 1965. Linda found a job and
George enrolled at the University of Hawaii, studying animal science
and working part-time mowing campus lawns. To save money on housing, and because they had grown to love sailing, they bought a thirty-
foot Tahitian ketch and lived aboard their boat.

Somehow, the final step of the plan, moving back to Tahiti, never
happened. Hawaii, the steppingstone, became instead the cornerstone
for their new lives. After George finished his BS, his professors encouraged him to get a master's degree, which he did.

By 1969 Balazs had had enough of academe. He wanted to clear his
head of all the paper-writing, fact-checking, and laboratory experiments
he had been doing for the past few years, and so he and Linda set sail,
bumming around the Hawaiian islands. Eventually, their travels took
them to West Maui, to the dock in Lahaina where they saw the *honu*
being scooped out of the ocean to feed the tourist trade. Following that
incident, George and his wife continued their wandering existence,
hanging out in the Hawaiian Islands, watching sunsets, catching and eating fish from the surrounding ocean. In early 1971, one of George's former professors showed up at the marina where their boat was docked.
The man, Balazs remembers, "wasn't pleased that I was kicking around
in part-time jobs that had nothing to do with science." He urged George
to apply for a position at the Hawaii Institute of Marine Biology on

Coconut Island, a beautifully situated research station located on Oahu's Kaneohe Bay. It was only a temporary job, working on a marine aquaculture program. Balazs wasn't sure. "Why don't you give it a try?" his former professor said. "You never know what it could build into."

"Why not?" thought Balazs, and took the position. He set to work formulating foods for a variety of commercially raised marine creatures, from shrimp to fish to sea turtles. He needed baby sea turtles for his research and was surprised to find that there was no ready supplier of either hatchlings or fertilized sea turtle eggs. So Balazs decided to just dig up some eggs from wild nesting turtles. He asked around to find out where the turtles nested locally. Again, he was surprised to find that no one knew for certain. Balazs's curiosity now prodded him to find out just what *was* known about the *honu*. He read everything he could on the subject, a task made easier by the fact that there was so little to read. Biologists knew astonishingly little about sea turtles in general.

Eventually, the Fish and Wildlife Service (FWS) provided Balazs with a clutch of eighty-five eggs, taken from a green sea turtle nest in the Hawaiian Islands National Wildlife Refuge, a remote outpost hundreds of miles to the northwest in the area known as the Leeward Islands. Balazs buried the eggs in the sand on Coconut Island, recreating as best he could their original nest environment. On a whim, he buried a microphone alongside the eggs, attaching the device to a small tape recorder. As the turtles matured inside the eggs, Balazs recorded the scratching sounds they made as they first moved around and then began to break out of their shells. He published a small note about the experiment— "Observations on the preemergence behavior of the green turtle"—in *Copeia*, a respected ichthyological journal. That led to a correspondence with Archie Carr, a professor at the University of Florida who was widely recognized as the world's leading sea turtle scientist. Carr urged Balazs to find out more about sea turtles in the Pacific, pointing out what Balazs already understood all too well, that in virtually every area—reproduction, population, ecology—scientists knew next to nothing about the ancient creatures. What they did know, Carr stressed, was that sea turtles of all species were threatened throughout the world. (In addition to the green turtle, there are six species of marine turtles: the flatback, the hawksbill, the Kemp's ridley, the leatherback, the loggerhead, and the olive ridley.)

The three-month study kept getting extended, and the more Balazs worked with sea turtles, the more fascinated with them he became. Word of his interest got out. Soon, workers at the Waikiki Aquarium and Sea Life Park were telling people with questions about turtles to contact Balazs. To respond to people, he was forced to go ever deeper into the subject. The local newspapers ran a couple of feature articles about his work. Grade school teachers invited him to talk to their classes about the strange sea creatures (invitations he always accepted). Before long, Balazs was known throughout the islands as the man to see if you wanted information about Hawaiian sea turtles.

"That's pretty ironic," he readily admits now, "considering how little I actually knew."

Despite the media stories and the phone queries, Balazs still considered sea turtles little more than a fascinating hobby—something that had grown out of his temporary job.

That all changed in November 1972 with a phone call from a friend named Hilde Cherry. Cherry, an activist with many causes and boundless energy, was concerned that nothing was being done to protect sea turtles in Hawaii. She had asked herself the same question Balazs had that day on the docks in Lahaina: "How many turtles could there possibly be?" She had done some reading on the subject and had a gut-level sense that the answer was "Not many."

Once she discovered a problem, Cherry was not the kind of person who could just sit back and do nothing about it. She contacted the state-run Animal Species Advisory Commission (ASAC) and demanded that they hold a hearing on the status of sea turtles in Hawaii. Cherry was insistent. If only to get this woman off their backs, the commission scheduled a hearing.

"Okay, so I got the hearing," recalls Cherry, "but I'm no scientist.

What would I be able to tell them? We needed someone who could speak about the problems facing turtles, a scientist to back up the call for protection with evidence."

Cherry called George. Balazs didn't want to testify.

"What the hell do I know about it?" he complained to Cherry. "I don't have any data on this."

Cherry wasn't impressed. "George, we need you," she said. "You do this right now."

Faced with the force that was Hilde Cherry, Balazs had little choice in the matter. In fact, he had even less maneuvering room than he had thought. Without his permission or even his knowledge, Cherry had already placed Balazs's name on the ASAC's agenda.

At a few minutes past 1 P.M. on 1 December 1972, nine ASAC commissioners convened their meeting in the spacious lieutenant governor's conference room at the Hawaiian state capitol building. The meeting got underway with a three-hour discussion on the status of the Hawaiian green sea turtle. Eugene Kridler, the manager of the Hawaiian Islands National Wildlife Refuge, was the first to testify. He told the commissioners that his agency already protected the *honu* at their refuge breeding grounds. The only change necessary was to prohibit turtle fishing in the leeward waters. That action should be taken immediately, Kridler added. "I don't think we have the luxury of time that some might think," he told them.

Kridler added that Cherry and other environmentalists went too far in endorsing further restrictions. More than 700 sea turtles had been tagged in the refuge, he said, going back to 1964. The manager concluded that calls for a complete ban on the taking of sea turtles throughout the Hawaiian Islands were unwarranted, although he said that more research was needed. In the discussion that followed, one commissioner agreed that a full ban on turtle fishing was unnecessary and called commercial turtle landings in Hawaii "insignificant."

These views were based on an estimate that there were up to 5,200 turtles in the Hawaiian breeding population at the time. This number, while smaller than it would have been before European arrival, still represented a viable population. The problem was that the estimate was wildly inaccurate, based on extrapolations of hit-and-miss surveys done with no regularity or anything approaching scientific precision.

The methodology used to arrive at the figure of 5,200 reproducing turtles does not instill confidence. A 1971 report explained:

In 1965, 86 adult turtles were tagged ... on 3 islands during August; an average of 5 turtles was tagged on each of the 17 days tagging occurred. Thus, if new turtles arrived and departed each day, this would mean roughly 150 using each of the 3 islands during the month, or a total of 450 for these 3 islands for August. But this is a minimum figure for several were lost or missed each day and from 5 to 20 were actually observed each day. Using 10 as a more realistic average, the estimate for these 3 islands then becomes 900. If we consider those using the other 2 turtle islands in the atoll, the August population could range from 650 to as many as 1,300.

The June and July breeding populations are probably higher than in August for as many as 60 turtles have been counted on a single island at one time. The total population using the atoll may be very large. Hendrickson [the author of a 1969 report] discussed the August 1965 estimates and noted that they were "highly tentative," but suggests "that one might assume twice the August number to represent the month of July and take the same increment for the early part of the season. One would then obtain a figure of between 2,600 and 5,200 turtles as the Hawaiian breeding population (1 + 2 + 1 times 650 – 1,300, and ignoring all other island nestings)."

Even Hendrickson cautioned against putting much stock in these numbers. "While it is very important to state flatly that this estimate has little basis and is *not* to be trusted, one can at least say that it does not appear to conflict violently with any other available quantitative information."

But other quantitative information was even more speculative, and the already questionable figure of 5,200 turtles would have included many nonbreeders. Despite their unreliability, these figures were trotted out before the commission as the basis for inaction. Balazs knew that all this was nonsense and he was dumbfounded and infuriated by the discussion.

After Kridler finished testifying, it was Balazs's turn. He was, he would later recall, "scared like hell." Balazs had no speech prepared for the occasion and began by distributing a number of documents; the first was the commercial sea turtle catch statistics for the past few years. In 1963, fishermen reported taking only 380 pounds of sea turtle meat. In 1972, that total had jumped to 25,583 pounds, a 67-fold increase in less than a decade. Struggling to keep his anger in check, Balazs pointed out that these figures reflected something more than the "insignificant" amount one commissioner had alleged. The reason for the skyrocketing rise in the turtle catch, Balazs explained, was due almost entirely to an increase in tourism and the desire of mainland and foreign visitors to eat sea turtles.

The official minutes from the meeting give little of Balazs's testimony, other than to say that he "made a strong plea for the preservation of the green sea turtle."

His recollection of that meeting is that he backed up his call for protecting the *honu* by citing turtle experts from around the world who had done reliable population studies.

"There were clearly sea turtle problems elsewhere, distant from Hawaii," he explains. "Serious ones. Could Hawaii's situation be so different, especially in the face of no protection, no meaningful regulations, and substantial hunting by very efficient methods (use of bullets, scuba, and turtle tangle nets hundreds of yards long)? Or, was it 'simply' that our heads were in the sand, too many other things keeping state and federal folks occupied? I said that you can't exploit them like a copper mine. You can't *mine* them. You've got to *manage* them and harvest them, rationally. Things were wide open in Hawaii. How

on earth could our turtles sustain this without any limits whatsoever?"

Balazs wasn't prepared to expose all the flaws in the rosy population
estimates presented at the meeting, but within a few weeks he submitted
an additional statement to ASAC members pointing out that the 700
turtles tagged by Kridler and his assistant were *not* nesting turtles—and,
in fact, weren't even necessarily females, as some commissioners had
mistakenly believed. Kridler hadn't intentionally misled anyone. The
misunderstanding came about because the term "tagged turtle" is usually synonymous with "nesting female." Elsewhere, turtles were invariably tagged when they came ashore, and only females came ashore, and
then only to lay eggs. Except in Hawaii. Perhaps because the *honu* were
at the northern edge of their range, Hawaiian turtles, both male and
female, regularly came ashore to bask—warming themselves in the sunlight. Virtually all the 700 turtles tagged over the years at the refuge
were daytime baskers, males and females. In that time, a total of just 15
turtles had been tagged in the refuge at night while nesting. No population estimates could be derived from the figures provided, asserted Balazs, certainly none that implied reproductive potential.

Balazs left the meeting angry and exasperated. But in a strange way
he was also excited. When he walked out into the warm Honolulu sunshine, Balazs had already decided what lay ahead. Somehow, he would
go to the refuge that next summer, identify the heart of the *honu*'s
breeding herd, and conduct the first in-depth, scientifically rigorous
population study of the Hawaiian green sea turtle. And if this weren't
ambitious enough, Balazs (who, despite his growing reputation, was
still just a low-ranking temporary employee of the University of
Hawaii) saw this project as just the first step in a systematic, long-term
tagging and monitoring program in the Hawaiian archipelago. As when
he decided to go to Tahiti years before, Balazs wasn't sure *how* he was
going to pull off his plan. He just knew that he would.

Within hours of the fateful ASAC meeting, Balazs was already planning his campaign. Funding was, as always, a critical issue. He turned to

the FWS for support, a logical place to start, since the division controlled the refuge where he proposed to work. But the FWS turned him down. Their reason was that it already had "an extensive tagging marking program" in Hawaii.

Five months later the same FWS division chief would write Balazs asking for information on green turtles. The agency was reviewing the status of sea turtles in general and, the man wrote, "One difficulty we have encountered ... is the lack of rigorous, up-to-date data on the Hawaiian and Pacific populations."

After several frustrating weeks making phone calls, writing letters, and following up leads, Balazs managed to secure a small grant from the New York Zoological Society. The money came through just in time, and at 8:30 A.M. on 1 June 1973, Balazs climbed aboard a red-and-silver twin-engine DC–3 "Gooney Bird" and began the 500-mile flight northwest from Oahu to French Frigate Shoals, a coral atoll composed of ten tiny islands, mere specks of sand and scrub. After passing over the main inhabited islands of the eastern section of the archipelago, the WWII-vintage plane headed out over the open Pacific. Balazs gazed out a small window. As the hours passed, only water—flat and green—slid by below them. Finally, in the distance something appeared that looked like the deck of a small aircraft carrier. It was Tern Island, the only inhabited spot for hundreds of miles. The island measured just 3,300 feet by 600 feet, and nearly all of it was taken up by the runway the Coast Guard used to supply their crew of twenty manning the LORAN radio station there, which broadcast directional signals used by planes and ships.

French Frigate Shoals are equal parts isolation and splendor—although it's the isolation you notice first. Charles Welch, who spent several months on Tern Island, recalls:

Just the name French Frigate Shoals instilled feelings of dread and fear into your mind. There were not many facts known throughout the Coast Guard about French Frigate Shoals, mostly rumors and innuendo. It was spoken of only in whispers or as a threat. No one actually knew anyone who was stationed there to ask questions of. But a friend of a friend knew someone who once did a tour of duty on French Frigate Shoals and they were allegedly never the same after returning from what was known as: The Worst Duty Station in The Coast Guard. However, those few fortunate ones, or maybe unfortunate ones, who served a tour of duty there would probably say today that they would not trade their experience for a few days on the beach with beautiful girls.

Another "Coastie," who served at Tern Island in the late 1960s, called French Frigate Shoals the ultimate isolated duty, the destination used when threats were made to send someone to the middle of nowhere. As the men assigned there climbed off the plane they were greeted by a sign reading: WELCOME TO FRENCH FRIGATE SHOALS INTERNATIONAL AIRPORT. POP. 20. ELEVATION 6 FT.

Balazs was accompanied on this first visit to French Frigate Shoals by David Olsen, the acting wildlife administrator of the refuge who had actually done most of the turtle tagging over the previous years, and by John Wheeler, a volunteer student from the University of Hawaii. For Olsen and Balazs it was the beginning of a long-term friendship. The refuge worker wasn't much older than Balazs and he shared George's love of turtles. That first night on Tern Island the trio went out at sunset and began looking for nesting turtles. They found none, nor any on the next night. This wasn't much of a surprise despite the fact that historically hundreds, if not thousands, of turtles had nested each year on the beaches of Tern Island. Many had been slaughtered by commercial fishing ships over the years. The final blow to the breeding aggregation came, ironically, when the military *expanded* the island to build the runway there in 1942. Through dredging and landfill operations, the eleven-acre island grew to cover fifty-seven acres. But the resulting shoreline was made of coral gravel and hard-packed sand—an environment unsuitable for turtle nesting. Balazs determined that nearly 20 percent of Hawaii's total turtle nesting habitat was destroyed in the expansion.

On 3 June a Coast Guard boat ferried them over to East Island, six miles southwest of Tern. As small and desolate as Tern Island was, it must have seemed like a spacious resort compared to East Island. The place Balazs would call home for the next several months was only one-fifth the present size of Tern, covering a mere twelve acres. The only structure on the island was a single wooden pole rising bleakly from the shrub- and grass-covered sand, a relic of the Coast Guard's old LORAN station there. East Island did have a significant population, however. Of birds. The place was packed with more than 70,000 screeching sooty terns. Even the constant trade winds couldn't dispel the acrid stench of ammonia coming from the mass of bird droppings, an eye-watering smell. The men pitched their tents, and a few minutes before sunset they began looking for turtles coming ashore to nest. In the spreading darkness, Olsen was leading the way with a flashlight strapped to a band on his forehead. The light spooked a masked booby bird, which took flight. Blinded by the light, the bird flew straight into Olsen's head, its beak piercing his scalp. Olsen wasn't hurt badly, but blood from the laceration flowed freely down his face. Balazs took one look at his bloodied friend and wondered: "Oh my God, is this what it'll be like on East Island?"

Once they patched Olsen up, the men continued their "turtle walk." Later that night they encountered, measured, and tagged their first nesting turtle. It was a historic first for Balazs.

The next day, it was time for Olsen to move on. The two men said good-bye, and Olsen climbed aboard a boat and sped away. Balazs and Wheeler were left alone on the tiny island. They had a couple of small tents, a supply of food and drinking water, a barely serviceable walkie-talkie (for raising the Coast Guard station on Tern Island in case of emergencies—such as the tidal waves that periodically washed over the tiny, low island), and materials for tagging turtles. It was during this period that Balazs developed what might be called a Pop-Tart® addiction, comfort food for the long difficult days on the isolated island. The scorching Pacific sun made it impossible to sleep during the daytime inside the stifling tents. At night, sleeping in their clothes, Balazs and Wheeler awakened every hour and a half to walk a complete circuit around the island. Despite their exhaustion, sleeping between walks was nearly impossible thanks to the birds, which seemed to shriek just as the men started drifting off.

In later years, Balazs would spend the entire summer on East Island by himself and would come to think of the tiny island as both a paradise and a prison. There were gorgeous nights when the young researcher was enthralled by the tropical night sky with no lights around to dim the fiercely burning stars and was lulled by the rhythm of the pounding waves. But at other times he suffered from insomnia, anxiety attacks that sent his heart racing uncontrollably and a sense of isolation so profound that he would sit on the shore looking out at the Pacific and weep into the sand. He faced southeast, toward his family. At such times, his thoughts took a morbid turn, musing on the possibility of someone dying on the island. "I think it likely," he brooded in his writings. "What a God-awful place to die, if alone. Buried here, ok, or ashes. But not dying."

The bad times, the lonely times, weren't always improved by the presence of others. Some individuals provided companionship and a respite from the overwhelming isolation of the place. Others, however, had full-scale breakdowns on the island during which they were certain that ghosts walked the atoll. Some believed the island itself was a malevolent presence. Still others were convinced that strangers were going to land on the island in the dark in search of buried treasure and murder them.

When Balazs returned from East Island late that summer, he brought with him treasure of another sort: scientific data on the size of the *honu* breeding herd. Instead of thousands of females crawling ashore to lay their eggs at French Frigate Shoals (as others had estimated), over the course of the summer Balazs had counted just 67 nesters. While a few turtles nested on two other islands at French Frigate Shoals, Balazs determined that over half of the breeding herd used East Island as their nesting site.

The essence of Balazs's study at French Frigate Shoals was this: the fate of the *honu* population throughout the entire 1,500-mile-long Hawaiian archipelago depended upon fewer than 150 individual females nesting each year.

Balazs wasted no time in spreading the word about the precarious status of the *honu*. His new goal was to get legislation passed to protect the turtles, and as soon as possible. Over the next several months Balazs testified at numerous public hearings, wrote articles both for scientific journals and popular environmental magazines, wrote countless letters to the editors of Hawaiian newspapers, and hounded state legislators. He also worked behind the scenes, acting as an unofficial adviser to the ASAC. Even before his summer at East Island, Balazs had written a draft for legislation protecting sea turtles, a document that became the basis for the first state law banning the commercial killing of *honu*. Within days of his return to Oahu from his turtle monitoring on East Island, Balazs, now armed with scientific data to back up what he already believed to be true, was the key expert witness at a public hearing on the new law.

Bruce Benson, a respected science writer for the *Honolulu Advertiser*, became an ally in the battle, writing several articles on the plight of sea turtles. Benson's 23 September 1973 article about that first public hearing highlighted Balazs's findings.

Green sea turtles in Hawaiian waters are destined to become a rare and possibly extinct species if they continue disappearing from the ocean and into the bellies of tourists, a scientist said in a public hearing at the Bishop Museum last night.

George H. Balazs of the Hawaiian Institute of Marine Biology said turtle catch statistics revealed that "extremely large increases" have occurred in the turtle catches of recent years, linked closely to the rise in tourism.

"It is interesting to note that the pounds of turtles taken since 1963 follows increasing trends of tourism, and that much of the incentive to exploit turtles is provided by restaurants and hotels that depend on tourism for a large portion of their business," Balazs said.

"If this is the case, it then logically follows that a few fishermen are eroding a unique Hawaiian resource to provide an exotic luxury food for short-term Mainland visitors. It is unfortunate that those to suffer the most from this practice will be the low-income, less fortunate residents of Hawaii.

"The turtles that could have been captured for home use to provide additional meat will now be all the more difficult to find."

Letters began pouring in from people sharing their concerns about the dwindling number of turtles. A helicopter pilot wrote Balazs that since 1966 he had been making informal counts from the air of the sea turtle population at Na Pali, a relatively remote part of the island of Kauai. "I could sum up a ten year, almost daily observation of Na Pali, with one statement," the man wrote. "The population of sea turtles has declined by at least 90 percent."

Another individual wrote, anonymously, revealing how he had witnessed many turtle hunters killing up to fifteen to twenty turtles a day using power heads—explosive charges shot from spearguns. "The turtle population on Kauai has been depleted to a point where something has to be done to curb the greed of these few fishermen," urged the informant.

Balazs cited these letters at public hearings and in his many letters to the editors of newspapers. Hawaiian public opinion began to shift toward protection. The manager of a large grocery store chain selling turtle meat wrote Balazs thanking him for his work and promising not to order any more turtle flesh.

"We will sell out our present stock of 25–30 pounds," he wrote, "but will not advertise this remaining stock as planned in recognition of your work."

Not all reaction was positive, of course. Angry turtle hunters made their feelings known, too, and Balazs even received a letter from an obviously confused Canadian seafood broker who wanted to know if George could supply them with frozen turtle meat.

By early 1974, public opinion was clearly on the side of protecting the *honu*. In May of that year, the state's Department of Land and Natural Resources, Division of Fish and Game (DFG), adopted a landmark measure called "Regulation 36." The centerpiece of the regulation was a ban on the commercial exploitation of green turtles in Hawaii—the first such protection in over a century of slaughter. While many individuals and groups worked hard for Regulation 36, the measure owed its existence to one person: George Balazs. On its own, the DFG wouldn't even have considered such a regulation, much less adopted it, for the division knew little about sea turtles and seemed to care even less about protecting them. Acting on his own initiative, the temporary worker at Coconut Island conducted the scientific work proving the need for the regulation (drumming up the funds needed for the work himself), drafted its framework, and galvanized public support for it.

But Balazs didn't have time to celebrate adoption of the regulation. He considered Regulation 36 merely a step in the right direction, a holding action. Almost from the beginning of his efforts to protect sea turtles, Balazs had his eyes on a larger prize. He wanted the *honu* protected under the far more comprehensive and formidable federal Endangered Species Act (ESA). Three species of marine turtles had been included in the ESA of 1973: Kemp's ridley, hawksbill, and loggerhead sea turtles. Balazs had already started his campaign to add the green turtle to the list—writing letters, building networks, and always continuing and expanding the turtle tagging and monitoring program at French Frigate Shoals, which supplied the scientific evidence needed to back up any new protections.

Even while he was hard at work on this front, Balazs was also pursuing creative strategies to protect sea turtles from commercial exploitation. In late 1974 he noticed $500 turtle-skin purses for sale in an exclusive Honolulu store that catered to tourists. He immediately wrote the store manager, pointing out that the sale of items made from the three turtles listed under the ESA was illegal. "No indication was given on the purses as to which type of sea turtle had been used," Balazs wrote. "If you are unable to adequately show that it is *not* one of the three I have mentioned, you could very well be in violation of federal criminal statutes." Just to make sure the store did the right thing, Balazs sent a copy of the letter to the federal government agent in charge of enforcing the ESA in Hawaii. Nor was this an isolated incident. Balazs wrote many such letters during those years. Honolulu was still a growing community at that time with a small number of specialty shops. Storekeepers must have learned to recognize Balazs (his picture was in the paper more and more often) and shuddered when they saw him coming if they were selling contraband turtle items. It's easy to imagine store employees scurrying around as Balazs approached, frantically shoving turtle purses and jewelry into boxes below the counters.

Nor did he limit his activism on behalf of turtles to Hawaii itself. When he spotted an article in *Vogue* magazine about a formal White House dinner at which Green Turtle Soup was on the menu, Balazs wrote directly to First Lady Betty Ford, politely pointing out that the turtle was threatened worldwide and that the government was currently considering listing the animal under the ESA. "Hopefully," he wrote Mrs. Ford, "you will ... see fit to substitute the genuine Green Turtle soup on your menu with one of the equally nutritious imitation turtle soup recipes."

If neither the threat of legal repercussions nor moral suasion was the right tool for a given situation, Balazs used other strategies. In 1976 he ran across an advertisement in a surfing magazine for a waterproof skin lotion containing turtle oil. He fired off a letter to the magazine's editor:

> By running this advertisement, you are, in essence, encouraging surfers and other readers active in ocean sports to use a body lotion which contains sea turtle oil. I question the wisdom of such practices. Sea turtles are known to be a dietary component of large sharks, especially the tiger shark. For example, in a shark control and

research program conducted by the State of Hawaii in 1971, 18 percent of the tiger sharks captured were found to have turtle parts in their stomachs.

In 1974, his science-driven activism led to his appointment to the Marine Turtle Specialist Group of the most prestigious international conservation organization, the International Union for Conservation of Nature and Natural Resources (IUCN). Within two years Balazs was named cochair of the group, an unprecedented appointment for someone who still signed his letters "Junior Marine Biologist."

Despite these other activities, working to get the green turtle protected under the ESA was always Balazs's top priority, aside from scientific research itself. Bureaucracies work slowly, however, and it took four years to win that battle. The National Marine Fisheries Service in particular dragged its feet, drawing out what should have been a short process. Finally, in September 1978, the *honu* was officially listed as "threatened" under the ESA and afforded the penultimate level of protection possible under U.S. law (only a listing of "endangered" brought more stringent controls). Many others were involved in this larger battle, but Balazs was the central player in the fight to get the *honu* listed.

"George almost single-handedly saved the Hawaiian sea turtle," says Mike Salmon, an eminent sea turtle biologist and conservationist in his own right. "He's one of the true heroes of the conservation movement."

With the increased protection provided first by Regulation 36 and then the ESA, the number of nesting turtles in Hawaii, which had declined to a critical level, slowly began to grow. Annual nesting figures at French Frigate Shoals provided by Balazs showed that nesting took place in cycles, with most of the turtles returning to lay their clutches every two years (some took three years, others even longer). So while there were "down" years in which few turtles came to French Frigate Shoals, these were balanced by "up" years with ever-increasing numbers. In 1978 (the years the *honu* won protection under the ESA, and also, coincidentally, an "up" year in the turtles' reproductive cycle), slightly more than 100 nesters were counted at French Frigate Shoals. In 1981, the next "up" year, nearly 200 females returned to French Frigate Shoals to lay eggs. In 1984, Balazs counted nearly 300 nesters.

The overall trend was encouraging. Once teetering on the edge of extinction, the *honu* were on their way back. At least that's how it appeared until FP showed up.

Chapter 3

The Turtle Sea

How inappropriate to call this planet Earth,
when clearly it is Ocean.

ARTHUR C. CLARK

TO GET A SENSE of just how profound and longstanding our ignorance about the sea is, it's helpful to visit a room in the British Museum.
Enter the building's imposing entrance on Great Russell Street and take
an immediate left. Hurry past the unobtrusive book-and-poster shop
and turn right when you come to an immense pair of winged bulls.
You're not likely to miss *them*. Once the guardians of an Assyrian
palace, the jet-black statues weigh several tons apiece and have implaca-
ble human faces with towering crowns above and magnificent flowing
beards below. Continue past the flocks of schoolchildren flitting about
the Rosetta Stone (the ancient carving that allowed archeologists to
decipher Egyptian hieroglyphics) and turn left at the first opportunity.
Keep going past treasures from nearly every great civilization that rose
and fell on earth, and eventually you will enter a final massive wing.
This section, which is the size of small museum in itself, is known, with
typical British understatement, as Room 8.

Many argue that the contents of Room 8 are the jewel in the crown
of the British Museum. They have a good case. Fastened to the walls are
the colossal marble figures of sublime beauty that once adorned the out-

side of the Parthenon, the most famous structure in all of Western civilization. Built of blindingly white marble 2,500 years ago, the Greek temple perched like an extraordinary bird high above ancient Athens on the sacred ground of the Acropolis. A large sign on the museum wall refers to these magnificent carvings as the Elgin Marbles, named for the seventh Lord Elgin, who took them piece by piece over the course of a decade beginning in 1801. Elgin's workmen pried the carvings off the Parthenon's walls (he also took several statues from the interior and even yanked out a full column), crated them up, and shipped them off to London—"for safekeeping" claim his defenders, who maintain that Lord Elgin was a hero who rescued the exquisite marbles from certain destruction in Ottoman-controlled Greece. His detractors, and there were many, branded Lord Elgin a craven imperialist thief who looted the treasures to add to his personal art collection. At any rate, the British government eventually paid the hero/villain £35,000 for the carvings and placed them in the museum for public display (where their presence remains a source of enmity between Greece and England).

It is tempting to linger in the doorway and allow oneself to be mesmerized by the procession of carvings encircling the room: sleek chariots pulled by muscular snorting horses, gods—alternately vain and sober—strolling musicians, and endless phalanxes of triumphal soldiers. The great marble frieze that once encircled the outer wall of the Parthenon now marches completely around the inner wall of Room 8. Resist the temptation to peruse these gorgeous carvings and head to your right until reaching a smaller room (merely the size of your average bungalow) that holds the carvings that once filled the east pediment, the large triangular area on the end of the Parthenon. There, you'll find two headless, yet still beautiful, female figures. They emanate eroticism, their tunics emphasizing rather than covering the voluptuous bodies beneath. On one figure, the top of the robe has slid down to reveal an exquisitely soft shoulder and the rise of one breast. "A luxuriously reclining figure rests in the lap of her companion," reads the explanatory text on the wall. Experts disagree over the identity of the pair, but one school maintains that the upright figure is Gaia, goddess of the Earth. The reclining figure is Thalassa, goddess of the sea.

Though Gaia's name is invoked today to include all the Earth—land and sea together—in the classical era she was most closely associated with dry land, which explains why Thalassa, the sea goddess, is shown as a separate entity—separate but unequal. On the Parthenon pediment Thalassa is supported by the goddess of land, a relationship made even more explicit in the back, where Gaia's strong left arm cradles Thalassa, keeping the sea goddess from slipping indecorously to the floor.

But surely the Athenians had it backward; it's the *land* that rests in the lap of the *sea*. Thalassa, not Gaia, is the guardian of life on the blue planet. A simple, albeit apocalyptic, experiment suggests Thalassa's power. Destroy all life on land; the ocean creatures will survive just fine. Given time, they'll even repopulate the land. But wipe out the organisms that inhabit the oceans and all life on land is doomed.

"Dust to dust," says the Bible, but "water to water" is more like it, for all life comes from and returns to the sea. Our ocean origins abide within us, our secret marine history. The chemical makeup of our blood is strikingly similar to seawater. Every carbon atom in our body has cycled through the ocean many times. Even the human embryo reveals our watery past. Tiny gill slits form and then fade during our development in the womb.

The ocean is the cradle of life on our planet, and it remains the axis of existence, the locus of planetary biodiversity, and the engine of the chemical and hydrological cycles that create and maintain our atmosphere and climate. The astonishing biodiversity is most evident on coral reefs, often called the "rain forests of the sea." Occupying less than one-quarter of 1 percent of the global ocean, coral reefs are home to nearly a third of all marine fish species and to as many as nine million species in all. But life exists in profusion in every corner of the ocean, right down to the hydrothermal vents on the seafloor (discovered only in 1977), where more than a hundred newly described species thrive around superheated plumes of sulfurous gasses. The abundance of organisms in the ocean isn't surprising given that the sea was, as already mentioned, the crucible of life on Earth. It is the original ecosystem, the environment in which the "primordial soup" of nucleic acids (which can self-replicate, but are not alive) and other molecules made the inexplicable and miraculous leap into life, probably as simple bacteria, close to 3.9 billion years ago. A spectacular burst of new life forms called the Cambrian explosion took place in the oceans some 500 million years ago, an evolutionary experiment that produced countless body forms, the prototypes of virtually all organisms alive today. It wasn't until 100 million years later that the first primitive plants took up residence on *terra firma*. Another 30 million years passed before the first amphibians climbed out of the ocean. After this head start, it's not surprising that evolution on that newcomer—dry land—has never caught up with the diversity of the sea. Of the thirty-three higher-level groupings of animals (called phyla), thirty-two are found in the oceans and just twelve on land.

This is what is threatened today: the ancient, living, sacred sea. A sea which provides the primary source of protein for millions of poor people throughout the world. A sea which has deep spiritual, as well as practical, importance. Our children may inherit an impostor ocean, a sickly ghost, drained of animal life and crowded with pathogens. The turtle plague of fibropapillomatosis is a flashing red light alerting us to marine problems.

This transformation is taking place at a fast pace and with little public outcry and inadequate government response. But the *Homo sapiens* capacity for devastation has always outstripped our ability to master or even imagine our fatal powers. How many times have we extolled something—a species or a habitat—as "limitless" only to obliterate it in a few generations? Since we're terrestrial creatures, most examples come from the land. The American prairie, a quarter-billion acres of grass and flowers—a place unique on the planet, so big it was dubbed "the inland sea" by early settlers—was largely plowed under or paved over in not much more than a century. The vast buffalo herds of the plains were reduced to relic populations in an even shorter span—over the violent objections of those who had inhabited the area with no negative impact for some 10,000 years. Then there is the passenger pigeon, native to North America, and perhaps the most egregious example of our destructive capabilities.

The sleek, brightly colored bird (which only slightly resembled its cousin, the urban-dwelling European immigrant, the common pigeon) was once the most abundant bird on the continent, accounting for 25 to 40 percent of the entire bird population of the United States. John James Audubon wrote that when a flock of pigeons passed, "the light of noonday was obscured as by an eclipse." He later observed the aftereffects of the great flock's roosting: trees, with trunks two feet in girth, had collapsed under the weight of so many birds. It looked, he wrote, "as if the forest had been swept by a tornado." Like forest fires, such intermittent damage was probably an important component in keeping the forests healthy, clearing out deadwood and allowing for new growth.

Even the "inexhaustible" flocks of passenger pigeons disappeared almost overnight, in evolutionary terms. An estimated 5 billion birds were reduced to a single flock of some 250,000 individuals by the end of the nineteenth century. A group of hunters found the brood in April 1896 and by the end of that bloody day only around 5,000 individuals remained. By 1909 the number of living passenger pigeons totaled just three—two males and a female, housed in a cage in the Cincinnati Zoo. The males died in the following year. For four years, the female named Martha was the last of her species. The crowds that passed before her cage were looking at a living fossil. On September 1, 1914, at approximately 1 P.M., she died, and the passenger pigeon was gone. In the span of a single person's lifetime, a species had gone from a population of several billion to extinction.

The fate of the passenger pigeon is remarkable only because of the large number of individuals involved. In all other respects the story is actually quite commonplace. And that's what makes the demise of the passenger pigeon so alarming—its very banality. We are living in an age defined by human-caused mass extinctions. Such events have occurred without human assistance only a handful of times in the planet's history. Paleontologists have identified five major cataclysmic events worthy of the title mass extinction since life evolved into a large number of complex forms in the Cambrian explosion. The most recent was the Cretaceous extinction of 66 million years ago, when the dinosaurs perished, and, along with them, three of every four species living at the time.

Since then, and for millennia, one or two species have gone extinct each year—what scientists call the normal "background rate" of extinction. Creatures began to disappear at an ever-accelerating pace after humans walked onto the stage. Today, estimates of extinctions range between 1,000 and 50,000 species annually. It is difficult for most of us to step out of our own time, to see how anomalous, how calamitous, this massive biological destruction is. Because we lack the perspective of a larger time horizon, we view the ongoing carnage as humdrum: "Another day, another extinction." We live in a charnel house and call it home, because in our lifetimes most of us have known nothing else.

Geography also plays a role in our complacency. Most of us live in cities where the number of visible wild species was long ago winnowed down to a few dozen. The sight of anything wilder than a sparrow, pigeon, or a squirrel makes the hearts of urban dwellers soar like the eagles we nearly exterminated. Those of us in the developed world are insulated, for the time being, from the newer, more widespread devastation occurring in the more pristine regions, where humans have only recently begun to have a major effect.

The extinction figures cited above are only for that fraction of life that makes its home on land. But what we do to the land, sooner or later, we do to the oceans. Marine extinctions and extirpations (localized extinctions), like those on land, are due to a variety of human activities, and over the years, our understanding of the extermination process has become subtler. The most direct method, hunting, was the first to be recognized. Which only makes sense—when you target a single species, and then proceed to shoot, trap, bludgeon, or net it every chance you get, and when everybody around you is doing likewise, it's pretty hard to miss the causal relationship between your activities and the complete disappearance of your prey.

In the ocean, Steller's sea cow was the first to go. The story of this strange and magnificent creature—from discovery to extinction—is short and cruel.

THE SEA COW

When the fog lifted briefly on the morning of 4 November 1741, the forlorn sailors on the Russian brig the *St. Peter* let out a cheer. In the struggling fall sunlight rose salvation: land.

"It is impossible to describe how great and extraordinary was the joy of everybody at this sight," wrote Georg Wilhelm Steller, the expedition's young German-born naturalist, in his journal of the voyage. "The half-dead crawled up to see it, and all thanked God heartily for this great mercy." The men broke out the dregs of their brandy and cried and drank toasts to the snowy peaks of the great Kamchatka peninsula that burned a pale-lemon in the Siberian morning light. They had been at sea for five months, on a reconnaissance mission for a planned expansion of the Russian Empire into the new lands of America. Nearly all of them suffered terribly from scurvy. By November, one or two men died each week from the excruciatingly painful disease. Their gums grew soft and spongy and brown, swelling up over their teeth, which loosened and fell out. Internal hemorrhaging caused shooting pains to course down their legs, making it impossible for many of the crew to stand. The *St. Peter* had been meandering for days, separated from their sister ship, the *St. Paul*, during a storm. The *St. Peter* was lost in what would later be called the Bering Sea, named after their captain, Vitus Bering. Bering himself lay near death in his cabin, the victim of scurvy and an anal infection that had turned gangrenous. It was already cold, and the subarctic winter would begin in earnest at any time. Every man aboard knew the dreadful finality of remaining at sea under those conditions. But that knowledge made the sight of Kamchatka all the sweeter. Soon, they congratulated each other, they'd be back in their own homes, warming themselves before a fire, reunited with their families and gorging on salmon-stuffed dumplings called *pelmeni* in the port town of Petropavlovsk.

Georg Steller wasn't so sure. He secretly wondered if what they had glimpsed was, in fact, Kamchatka. The landmarks he saw to the west weren't noted on his maps of the peninsula. If the mountains were part of an uncharted island, as Steller believed, then the situation was beyond desperate. Winter was almost upon them. Fresh water was nearly gone. The sails were in tatters. A ship's officer called the *St. Peter* "a piece of dead wood." There weren't enough healthy crew members left to man the brig, even if the ship were in good condition, and even if they knew where they were going. If this weren't Kamchatka, they would have no choice but to wait out the winter on the island until they could build a more seaworthy vessel by cannibalizing their ship and attempt a return to Petropavlovsk in the spring.

Fearful that the *St. Peter* would fall apart at the next wave, Steller made sure he was part of the initial landing party. The men rowed the ship's longboat to the closest beach. As the 32-year-old naturalist climbed out, he looked around and took stock of the place. It was a forbidding spot. A few feet from the beach the land became rock-strewn, bleak, and desolate, with high jagged cliffs. Steller saw no plants taller than the tawny grass that covered the hillsides. On the other hand, there was fresh water, rivers burbling under a thin layer of ice, and plenty of wildlife. Arctic foxes were everywhere, and they were completely unafraid of humans. Fat ptarmigans and other game birds exploded from behind rocks at every turn. Sea otters by the hundreds frolicked in the frigid waters. Well, thought Steller, if this were an island and not Kamchatka, at least they wouldn't starve there.

Two days after arriving, Steller was exploring the area south of the rough base camp when he heard a sound he described as "a snort such as a horse makes in blowing his nose." There were no horses in Kamchatka at that time. Besides, this sound was coming from the water. Steller turned and looked out to sea. He was shocked to see a group of immense creatures with their giant brown backs thrust above the surface. Every few minutes one would raise its head from the water to exhale and take another breath (which accounted for the sound he had heard). Steller crept closer to observe the creatures. They were feeding on the leaves of a seaweed that grew in tangled brown masses where rivers entered the sea. The animals had large tails, "like mermaids," wrote Steller, and short, paddle-shaped front limbs. He watched, awestruck, as they ate.

"As they feed they move first one foot and then the other, as cattle and sheep do when they graze, and thus with a gentle motion half swim and half walk.... When their stomachs are full some of them go to sleep flat on their backs, and go out a distance from the shore that they may not be left on the dry sand when the tide goes out."

Steller identified them as sirenians, members of an order of tropical marine mammals that includes manatees and dugongs. But these animals were double the size of its largest known relatives—up to 25 feet long and weighing as much as ten tons, twice as heavy as the largest bull elephants, which are a distant relative. And what were these normally tropical creatures doing in the cold waters of the north Pacific? Steller had plenty of time to observe and study the massive "sea cows," one name common at that time for manatees. He was right about the land not being Kamchatka. It was an island, twenty-five miles long and three miles wide. The men named it Bering Island, in honor of the captain who died only a few days later, and the shipwrecked survivors would spend the next nine months there. Steller, who endured his period on Bering Island only to drink himself to death just four years later, left behind a detailed record of the sea cow. It was is a good thing, too, since he would be the only scientist to see one alive.

Steller's document, *De Bestiis Marinis* (*The Beasts of the Sea*), is particularly striking given the dreadful conditions he had to work under.

Much of his time on Bering Island was spent just trying to survive: gathering water and firewood (no trees grew on Bering, so the men had to walk long hours in search of driftwood), hunting and preparing meat and keeping their flimsy shelters from falling in. As a physician, Steller was also in charge of nursing the sick men back to health. (A task that he accomplished with unprecedented success, curing the men of scurvy with a diet that included large servings of a plant rich in vitamin C, a treatment he had learned from the native peoples of Siberia.) When he finally found the time to work on his scientific journals, he had to battle the elements, and, frequently, the incompetence and reluctance of his assistants.

Reading *The Beasts of the Sea* conjures up a vivid picture of the awful conditions Steller endured on Bering Island. It's easy to imagine the naturalist dissecting the huge creature in a freezing drizzle, slipping on the rain- and seaweed-slickened rocks, fingers numb. Packs of arctic blue foxes were a constant nuisance. Dissecting was a race with the foxes, which showed no fear of humans and swarmed over the sea cow, snapping at each other as they fought to devour the creature even while Steller tried to identify organs and make accurate measurements of bones. "The droves of blue foxes would spoil everything with their teeth," he wrote, "and steal from under my very hands; they carried away my maps, book, and ink when I was studying the animal."

The Russian sailors he hired with bits of tobacco were nearly as destructive as the foxes. "In their ignorance and dislike for the work they would tear everything to pieces," Steller complained.

Here, Steller writes about dissecting the animal's small intestines: "The thin intestines are smooth, rolled up in a great amount of fat; they are round and 6 inches in diameter. If only a very slight aperture should be made with the point of a knife, the liquid excrement (a ridiculous thing to behold) would squirt out violently like blood from a ruptured vein; and not infrequently the face of the spectator would be drenched by this springing fountain whenever some one opened a canal upon his neighbor opposite, for a joke."

Poor Dr. Steller; he had the misfortune to have been shipwrecked with the Russian naval counterparts of Larry, Curly, and Moe.

Despite his many difficulties, the document he produced is a fascinating first, and last, look at a marvelous animal, *Hydrodamalis gigas*, known today by the common name Steller's sea cow.

More than its neighbors the whales and porpoises, at first glance the sea cow still bore signs of its land origins. As Steller remarked: "Down to the navel it is comparable to a land animal; from there to the tail, to a fish." Its skull resembled that of a horse, but its powerful tail, over six feet wide and lying in a plane perpendicular to its body, could easily have been mistaken for the fluke of a whale. Nearly everything about the sea cow was huge, as its Latin name *gigas*—giant—implies. It measured twelve feet around at the shoulders and swelled to more than twenty feet in circumference at its massive belly. Inside was a stomach that Steller described as "stupendous." It was, he wrote "6 feet long, 5 feet wide, and so stuffed with ... seaweed that four strong men with a rope attached to it could with great effort scarcely move it from its place." Just past the giant stomach was an intestinal tract which, when uncoiled, measured 500 feet—approximately the height of a 40-story building. The sea cow's heart weighed 35 pounds and was two feet long. When Steller described the sea cow's penis, which was nearly a yard long, the scientist (who had been educated in a religious German university) felt compelled to add that he found the giant organ "obscene to look upon." Parts of the sea cow seemed disproportionately small, however. The immense animal had eyes "no larger than a sheep's," wrote Steller, and cars so small as to be invisible, lost in the deep folds of the animal's rough, barklike skin.

Its proportions aside, the sea cows were unique in three important respects. First, they completely lacked teeth, using instead bony plates to mash the kelp they fed on. The second difference was in their front flippers. While other marine mammals (and even marine reptiles like turtles) had flippers, Steller's sea cow alone lacked the interior "finger" bones that marked terrestrial creatures that had returned to the sea. Instead, the bones inside the sea cow's flippers ended abruptly, like that of an amputated limb, observed Steller. Finally, the giant sea cow spent its life floating at the surface—the only marine mammal incapable of diving.

Steller wondered about the origins of this strange creature, but it wasn't until two centuries later, beginning in the 1960s, that Howard University paleontologist Daryl Domning slowly pieced together the "family tree" of Steller's sea cow, using fossilized sirenian skeletons found scattered around the world. This group first appears in the fossil record over 50 million years ago as a grass-eating land animal, no larger than a pig. Domning described its unlikely appearance as "something like an otter crossed with a hippopotamus." Sirenians returned to the ocean in Europe when that region was covered by a body of water called the Tethys Sea. Over the next several million years, the creatures spread and evolved into two major families—the *Trichechidae* (which would become the manatees that are still found in the Caribbean) and the *Dugongidae*, which includes the present-day dugongs in the Pacific and Indian Oceans.

Somewhere in the range of 30 million years ago, the family *Dugongidae* began splitting into several different smaller groupings, called *genera* (the singular is *genus*). One by one, most of the branches tapered off into extinction, evolutionary dead ends. But Domning traced the evolution of one branch as it continued to adapt to changes in its environment. One creature that lived in the waters off present-day Santa Barbara approximately 12 million years ago piqued Domning's interest. While this ancient Dugongid differed from Steller's sea cow in several ways, it appeared to be evolving in the direction of the giant creature Steller discovered. Judging by the roughened surface at the back of the skull, the way the muscles attached to the neck was closer to Steller's than any other fossil Domning had seen. Even more important was the fact that while this animal still possessed teeth—unlike Steller's sea cow—the fossilized remains from different individuals showed a wide variation in size—something you'd expect if teeth were losing their functional importance. But why should teeth become less necessary?

Noting that ocean waters were cooling at that time, Domning reasoned that the sea cows were adapting from a diet of tough sea grasses (which grow in warm tropical waters), to reliance on kelp, a cold-water alga that is closer to gelatin in consistency than to sea grass. The new colder habitat also explained the giantism found in Steller's sea cow. The creatures needed more insulation—blubber—to conserve body heat in the increasingly frigid waters.

In 1966 workers at a construction site south of Los Angeles uncovered the fossilized remains of what looked at first like a whale. But it was something far more interesting. It was a sirenian, well over thirty feet long, and one that, for the first time, lacked teeth. It was the first *Hydrodamalis* to be found, a member of the same genus as Steller's sea cow, and only 3 to 7 million years old. In time, other ancestors of Steller's sea cow were found, from California and across the Pacific to Japan. The fossils indicated a rarity in evolution—a linear descent from the sirenians of nearly 20 million years ago to the strange creatures bobbing in the waters off Bering Island in 1741.

As Domning summed up: "the lineage of Steller's sea cow had not branched at all, but consisted of a simple temporal sequence of species, one evolving into the next." Steller's sea cow, the result of 20 million years of evolution, was the last of its kind. And more: the population of *Hydrodamalis gigas* at Bering Island wasn't just the last of its species, but the last of an entire genus, its ancestors going back 20 million years. The sea cows were much more than a branch on the tree of life; they might be said to have constituted an entire limb.

Even before the arrival of the *St. Peter*, the sea cow was in an extremely precarious position, in evolutionary terms. Only between 1,500 and 2,000 of the creatures lived in the waters around Bering Island. What's more, *H. gigas* had the long gestation period typical of mammals. *Any* fluctuation in population could spell disaster. One additional factor sealed its fate. Humans found nearly all parts of the animal to be delicious.

Steller's account is full of glowing descriptions about the culinary values of the sea cows. He likened the taste of young sea cow meat to veal; older animals tasted like beef. The female's milk, Steller wrote, "is very rich and sweet." Steller even found fluid from the animal's thyroid gland to be "sweet to the taste."

But it was the fat of the sea cow that Steller praised most highly. "The fat of this animal is not oily or flabby but rather hard and glandular, snow-white, and, when it has been lying several days in the sun, as pleasantly yellow as the best Dutch butter. The boiled fat itself excels in sweetness and taste the best beef fat, is in color and fluidity like fresh olive oil, in taste like sweet almond oil.... We drank it by the cupful." Not only were sea cows delicious, but each one provided enough meat and fat to feed the entire group for two weeks.

Unafraid of humans (a species they had never seen before) and, because of their high buoyancy, unable to dive out of harm's way, the sea cows were easy pickings. Once harpooned, the chief problem was hauling the huge creatures in to shore. With forty men pulling on a rope, however, the job was manageable. It was not a pretty business. One of the expedition's surviving officers described the process in his journal: "Those in the boat were equipped with rapiers, bayonets and spears, with which they thrust at the animal until they had pierced it through and through, and then hot blood spurted like a fountain. Sometimes the boat's crew was a whole hour stabbing at a sea-cow before its strength began to fail."

As with many social animals (including the passenger pigeon), an attack on a sea cow produced a frenzy of activity among the group. Steller wrote that after impaling a sea cow with a large hook:

> some of them try to upset the boat with their backs, others bear down upon the rope and try to break it, or endeavor to extract the hook from the back of their wounded companion with a blow from their tails, and several times they proved successful. It is a very curious evidence of their nature and of their conjugal affection that when a female was caught the male, after trying with all his strength, but in vain, to free his captured mate, would follow her quite to shore, even

though we struck him many blows, and that when she was dead he would sometimes come up to her as unexpectedly and as swiftly as an arrow. When we came the next day, early in the morning, to cut up the flesh and take it home, we found the male still waiting near his mate; and I saw this again on the third day when I came alone for the purpose of examining the entrails.

Before judging the crew too harshly for killing these gentle and affectionate creatures, it should be remembered that the men had suffered disease and privation for a year, losing nearly half their shipmates to scurvy, and were in a battle for their own survival. To the shipwrecked and sickly men, the presence of the slow-moving sea cows seemed providential.

"It was evident," wrote Steller, "that all who ate it felt that they increased notably in vigor and health. This was noticeable especially in some sailors who had relapses and had been unable to recuperate up until now.... [B]y means of sea animals it pleased God to strengthen us human beings who had suffered shipwreck through the sea."

When Steller and his surviving castaways at last sailed from Bering Island in the late summer of 1742 in the small boat built from the remains of the *St. Peter*, they carried with them several barrels of sea cow meat. The taste was so appealing that even after they arrived back in Petropavlovsk, many of the men preferred to eat sea cow rather than to dine on the foods they had been missing nearly a year.

Back in Russia, the late captain-commander of the expedition, Vitus Bering, was eulogized as the Christopher Columbus of Imperial Russia. For all the disasters of the journey, he had, like the Italian mariner sailing for Spain, successfully sailed from his home port to the New World. Bering had merely sailed east instead of west like Columbus. During their absence, however, times had changed in St. Petersburg. Peter the Great's dream of Russian expansion into the American lands was no longer a priority of the new court under Peter's daughter, the Empress Elizabeth.

But back in Kamchatka, a different group of men listened attentively to the tales of discovery told by the *St. Peter*'s crew. They weren't interested in the glory of an expanding Imperial Russia. They had more immediate and practical concerns. They were *promyshleniki*, fur hunters, and the reports of uncharted islands teeming with sea otters, blue arctic foxes, and fur seals had them nearly salivating with greed. Furs had been a mainstay of the Russian economy for centuries, and the quest for beautiful pelts was the reason Russia had conquered Siberia in the first place. Unfortunately, Russian hunters had never heard of conservation management, and they were continuously forced to make their way east, trapping and shooting everything they could, wiping out entire populations. By the end of the seventeenth century, the *promyshleniki* were desperate for new hunting grounds.

The hunters wasted no time. In the spring of 1743, only a few months after the reconstructed *St. Peter* came limping into port, the first hunting expedition landed at Bering Island. Thirty men spent eight months there and when they returned to the mainland they carried with them the pelts of 1,600 sea otters, 2,000 fur seals, and 2,000 foxes. Such a wholesale slaughter must have turned the rocks of the island red. Word of the new hunting grounds spread throughout eastern Russia, and fur hunters by the hundreds poured into Kamchatka, lashed together crude boats, and headed for Bering Island and the Aleutians further to the east. There was no commercial market for the sea cows, but the huge, docile creatures made perfect provisions for the hunters. In the pursuit of rubles (many fortunes were made in the process), the *promyshleniki* had, in effect, declared war on the fur-bearing creatures of the subarctic, and the men proceeded to wipe out the enemy with unrelenting, methodical, and well-honed skill. One island after another saw its population of otters, seals, and foxes annihilated. Steller's sea cow was, in modern parlance, merely "collateral damage" in this war.

In the first years of plunder, most hunting expeditions stopped first at Bering Island to load up on the delicious sea cow meat, taking on enough meat and fat to last the entire crew for a year or more. That was in addition to the hunting groups that spent the season on Bering Island itself, whose method of catching sea cows was stunning in its inefficiency. A lone hunter would sneak up on a sea cow grazing close to shore and impale the huge animal with an iron-tipped harpoon. The wounded animal would flee out to the open ocean, where it usually died. If the body drifted back to shore, the hunter was set for provisions for months. If, on the other hand, the dead sea cow simply sank or floated farther out to sea, well, there were other sea cows around. Perhaps the next attempt would be more successful.

This kind of wastefulness, combined with the sheer numbers of *promyshleniki* slaughtering sea cows for provisions, made extinction inevitable. The hunters didn't take long to accomplish the deed. In 1768, just twenty-seven years after the scurvy-wracked crew of the *St. Peter* was shipwrecked on Bering Island and a startled Georg Steller heard his first sea cow exhaling into the frosty air, the last of the species was harpooned and butchered on the barren shoreline. Discovery to extinction in less than three decades. It must be some kind of a record.

COLUMBUS AND THE TURTLES

The sea turtle itself is one of the more notorious examples of the ability of humans to wipe out huge populations of marine creatures in a relatively short time. It's true that no species of sea turtle has gone extinct—but each of the seven species is today either endangered or threatened. It's also true that the destruction of sea turtle populations hasn't happened with the extreme rapidity that saw the exit of Steller's sea cow—but the time frame in which turtles have gone from common to nearly extinct has been short, a biological wink of the eye.

When he sailed into the waters of the New World for the first time in the fall of 1492, Christopher Columbus entered an arm of the Atlantic Ocean so filled with turtles that he might have logically named it the Turtle Sea. (Certainly that would have made more sense then the name

"Caribbean," derived from a single warlike people, the Caribs, living on a few islands on the eastern boundary of the sea at the time of the Spanish incursion.) Wherever he traveled on his four voyages to the New World over the next decade, Admiral Columbus encountered huge numbers of turtles. At times there were so many turtles that his small fleet had to stop dead in the water for hours to allow the migrating animals to pass. At another point the water was so thick with turtles that a member of his crew remarked that, although the ship was still a mile offshore, a man might be able to walk to land on the backs of the turtles gathered there.

On his trouble-plagued fourth and final voyage to the Americas, Columbus stumbled upon the largest rookery of green turtles anywhere in the world, on what is today known as the Cayman Islands. There is no mention of this discovery in the admiral's logs or letters, but that's hardly a surprise given the dire circumstances of his expedition at the time. Columbus and his crew had just barely survived a hurricane, a multitude of illnesses, and near-starvation. Eight months into the voyage the sailors were so hungry that, as Columbus's son Ferdinand (who accompanied his father on this last voyage) wrote, "what with the heat and the dampness even the biscuit was so full of worms that, God help me, I saw many wait until nightfall to eat the porridge made of it so as not to see the worms." While the insect larvae were eating the Spanish provisions, a variety of wood-eating worm was devouring the admiral's small fleet. Worms had chewed so many holes in the four ships that before long the *Capitana*, the *Santiago de Palos*, the *Galega*, and the *Vizcaina* resembled sponges more than seagoing vessels. Not a single ship would make it back to Spain. On top of these problems was the fact that the indigenous peoples were now less docile than Columbus had found them back in 1492. After his first meeting with the people of the New World (the Arawaks of the Bahamas), the Italian mariner marveled at their friendliness and lack of guile. He wrote "With fifty men we could subjugate them all and make them do whatever we want." Eleven years later, after they had suffered mass killings and enslavement at the hands of the Europeans, the "Indians" had grown less hospitable. While searching for gold in Panama in 1503 the captain of Columbus's flagship, Diego Tristán, was sent ashore to collect fresh water. A few hours later Tristán's body came floating downriver with a spear wound through the eye and carrion birds picking at the corpse. The sight was rightly taken as an evil omen by the rest of the men, who frantically made their way back to their ship. As soon as weather permitted, Columbus turned his ships homeward, making for the Spanish settlement on the island of Hispañola. But an argument soon arose between Columbus and his pilots. The men charged with navigation believed that Hispañola lay due north. No, Columbus argued, they were still a few hundred miles west of the island. If the admiral were wrong, the pilots insisted (with the support of the crew), by the time they turned north the expedition would be well into the open Atlantic, and they would all die of starvation before reaching port—assuming the worm-eaten ships didn't sink first. Columbus feared inciting a mutiny if he didn't give in. This wasn't an idle fear. Mutiny, or the threat of it, had stalked Columbus every league of each of his voyages, starting with the very first journey of exploration in 1492, when, just thirty days out from Spain, his crew feared they were about to sail over the edge of the world and demanded that their captain turn the ship around. Columbus had managed to talk his way out of that encounter, but this time he relented and the ships headed due north. Columbus was right; the ships were directly below Cuba. And so, on May 10, 1503, the beleaguered ships made a discovery that would open the Caribbean to long-term settlement by Europeans.

Ferdinand Columbus recorded the event with a brief entry: "We sighted two very small low islands full of turtles (as was all the sea thereabouts, so that it seemed to be full of little rocks); that is why these islands were called Las Tortugas [the turtles]."

The crew cared little about the discovery at the time. After the months of travails that had reduced their number by one-quarter, they had had their fill of lush tropical isles. More than half the crew was made up of boys between the ages of twelve and eighteen who wept for their mothers at night. All they wanted was to see once again the grand Moorish buildings of their home port of Cádiz back in southwestern Spain and to return to their familiar whitewashed villages surrounded by olive groves in the dry and dusty Andalusian countryside. But despite this early lack of enthusiasm, the Cayman rookery was the answer to the starvation that plagued Columbus's voyages. Every summer, green turtles migrated by the millions from foraging grounds all across the Caribbean to mate in the Cayman waters and then nest on the beaches. Out of the water, the huge creatures were essentially helpless. Turned onto their backs, the turtles couldn't right themselves. Sailors from the European countries scrambling to establish footholds of empire in the New World sailed into Cayman waters, rowed to shore, and flipped over the slow-moving creatures. Then, at their leisure, the men could drag the turtles down to the shore, load them onto boats, and transfer them to the decks and holds of ships. There, the turtles lasted for weeks at a time, without food or water, until the ship's butchers were ready to carve them up as needed.

Ships' logs and journals from various New World voyages are filled with odes to the toothsome turtle. "They are very good and wholesome meate," wrote one early seventeenth-century explorer, who continued, "None of it bad, no, not so much as the very guts and maw of it, for they are exceedingly fat, and make as good tripes as your beastes bellies in England." The oil made from turtle fat was used for frying and baking and was described as being "as sweete as any butter," and as for the eggs, these were "sweeter than any Henne egge." The turtles, he wrote, were also plentiful, adding that they "doe abound as dust of the earth."

The sheer number of turtles in the Cayman rookery was astounding, even a century after Columbus's discovery. In 1642 an English captain remarked about the Caymans: "Hither do infinite numbers of Sea Tortoises yearly resort to lay their Eggs upon ye Sandy Bay, which at this time swarmed so thick."

In 1642 the plundering of the Cayman rookery hadn't yet begun in earnest. Barely a decade later the British wrested Jamaica from Spanish control and turned to the nearby Caymans as the major source of animal protein for their most important New World possession. Within a few years the intense but sporadic hunting of sea turtles in the Caymans had been transformed into a methodical pillage. By 1688 some forty British sloops worked the beaches of the Caymans, each hold filled with up to fifty turtles a night. When the turtles weren't nesting, the turtle fishers plied the waters of southern Cuba, harpooning the turtles in shallow water. Besides providing food for colonists, slaves, and sailors, the green turtles of the Caymans became a status food for the British upper classes in the late 1700s. The animals' calipee, a cartilaginous section of the plastron, was the basis of a clear green turtle broth, a delicacy that quickly became the *de rigueur* first course at any respectable dinner party. Some 13,000 turtles (mostly nesting females) were caught and eaten each year. Even at this stupendous rate of killing the British harbored the illusion that the supply of turtles was, as one late eighteenth-century writer put it, "the exhaustless source of profit to the British empire." He continued, "the inhabitants of all these islands are, by the gracious dispensation of the Almighty, benefitted in their turn; so that, when the fruits of the earth are deficient, an ample sustenance may still be drawn from this never-failing resource of turtle, or their eggs, conducted annually as it were into their very hands."

Even so, there had been early warnings that the gracious dispensation of the Almighty might have its limits. In 1620, the Bermuda Assembly had passed an act that neatly summarized the growing problem.

In regard that much waste and abuse hath been offered and yet is by sundry lewd and improvident persons inhabiting within these Islands who in their continual goings out to sea for fish do upon all occasions, And at all times as they can meet with them, snatch & catch up indifferently all kinds of Tortoises both young and old little and great and so kill carry away and devour them to the much decay

of the breed of so excellent a fish the daily skarringe of them from of
our shores and the danger of an utter destroying and loss of them.

The "Act against the Killing of Our Young Tortoises" prohibited the
taking of green turtles smaller than eighteen inches long, at the penalty
of having to turn over to the crown a large quantity of tobacco. However well-intentioned the act may have been, it was doomed as a conservation measure, since it allowed the unrestricted slaughter of larger,
older, and therefore reproductively mature turtles. Within a few
decades, no turtles nested on the sandy shores of Bermuda and the ones
feeding in underwater pastures were gradually eliminated. In the early
days of European settlement forty full-grown turtles were taken from
Bermuda's waters each day. Two centuries later, that would represent a
successful catch for the entire year.

No restrictions of any kind were imposed on the Cayman rookery
until 1711, and even then the ban on collecting turtle eggs wasn't
enforced. The result was inevitable. By the late 1700s, the Cayman
rookery had collapsed. In June 1802 (at what should have been the heart
of the nesting season), a report to the governor of Jamaica stated that
few turtles were seen on the shores of Cayman. The Cayman Island
turtlers—now reduced to a fleet of just six or eight ships—had turned to
other waters, primarily to small islands to the south of Cuba, to supply
sea turtles. Soon those hunting grounds were also depleted. The turtle
sloops traveled to ever more distant waters in search of new turtle
aggregations. One by one, first the nesting areas and then the foraging
pastures where large numbers of the sea turtles gathered to graze were
discovered and picked clean.

Last in the long line of plunder by the Cayman sloops were the
Miskito Cays off the eastern coast of Nicaragua. Archie Carr once
described this area as "a cluster of keys where fresh water could be got,
a shallow sea set with bars and rocks, miles and miles of blade-grass
flats, and turtle herds that looked to the Cayman captains like home in
their grandfathers' day."

The irony here is that this last hunting ground for the Cayman turtlers is where their grandfathers (or, more likely, their great-great-grandfathers) learned their trade. When Columbus's rotting ships limped past the Caymans in 1503, the islands were uninhabited. There was no native population there from which the Europeans could learn the art of turtle hunting. And there is an art to it—certainly not in flipping nesting turtles on the beaches, but in pursuing and capturing the swift-swimming creatures in their native element, the water. Following Sir Francis Drake's raiding parties on Spanish settlements in the region in the late 1500s, British adventurers, buccaneers, and traders began regularly visiting the Miskito Coast. By 1633—twenty-two years before the British took control of Jamaica and the Caymans—the first permanent British trading settlement was established on the Miskito Coast and an alliance was struck between the British and the Indians living there, based on their mutual detestation of the Spanish.

Turtles of several species were important to the indigenous peoples living throughout the Caribbean. Green turtles were prized both for their meat and for their eggs, while the hawksbill's beautifully mottled gold-green and brown shell was made into jewelry and used in trade. These and other species also played a role in the spiritual life of pre-Columbian peoples; in Florida archeologists have uncovered the skulls of loggerhead and Kemp's ridley turtles in ancient burial mounds.

Between 1815 and 1822, a British adventurer named Orlando Roberts traveled extensively throughout Central America, writing about the people he encountered. The importance of turtles to the traditional peoples there is apparent from the fact that rarely does Roberts write for more than a few pages without some reference to turtles. The people he encounters on his travels are always doing *something* with turtles, whether it's catching them, or buying and selling them, eating them, or simply out looking for sea turtles. In the San Blas islands off present-day Panama, for example, Roberts describes how the Kuna people never touched the eggs of the hawksbill turtle but used their shells for jewelry and ornamentation.

But it is the Miskito Indians who lived, then as now, along the eastern coast of Nicaragua that Roberts wrote about most. The British traveler went out with Miskito turtlers many times, and he described the practice of turtle hunting as it had been practiced for generations.

During the months of April, May, June and July, the green turtle comes from various kays, and places a great many leagues distant, to several parts of the Mosquito Shore, especially to the sandy beaches in the vicinity of Turtle Bogue [in Costa Rica], to deposit their eggs.... The handle of the spear with which the Indians strike the turtle, is made of very hard wood; the head is a triangular-shaped piece of notched iron, with a sharp point; a piece of iron is joined to this which slips into a groove at the top of the spear handle, and has a line attached to it which runs through eyes fixed, for that purpose, to the shaft of the spear to which a float is fastened. The Indian, when near enough to strike the turtle, raises the spear above his shoulder, and throws it, in such a manner, that it takes a circular direction in the air, and lights, with its point downwards, on the back of the animal, penetrating through the shell, and the point becoming detached from the handle, remains firmly fastened in the creature's body; the float now shows on the surface of the water which way the turtle has gone; and he is easily hunted up, and secured, by means of the line, which has remained attached to the spear head.

For centuries, the bulk of protein in the Miskito's diet came from the green turtle. But that is just the beginning of the relationship between the Miskito and the turtles that once thrived in the pastures of turtle grass growing around the islands of Nicaragua's eastern shore. Cultural geographer Bernard Nietschmann called green turtles "the pivotal resource around which traditional Miskito Indian society revolved." First comes the hunt, the central activity of Miskito men. Hunting requires skills and ecological knowledge of turtle habits, information that is passed from one generation to another, linking Miskitos to their ancestors and to the land and sea around them. After butchering, women distribute the meat among relatives and friends, in accordance with firmly established social patterns. The whole process, which may appear simple to residents of "developed nations," undergirds Miskito society. As Nietschmann explained:

> Between the sea and the table turtle meat moves along a chain of cultural levels where each transformation increases its symbolic value.... As the meat moves from animals to hunter, from males to females, from individuals to kin and to larger society, it is increasingly imbued with symbolic significance. In the end, the item is no longer simply meat but a cumulative symbolic record of relationships between nature and people, men and women, and the individual and society. Thus, turtling and turtle meat are for the Miskito a means by which part of the structure and organization of society is maintained and their place in their world is defined.

But those complex relationships depended on the subsistence hunting out of which they arose. When the Miskitos entered the market economy, and turtles became increasingly a commodity to be sold to outsiders for cash (which could be kept rather than distributed), the process began to erode not just the Miskito's relationship to turtles, but Miskito society as well.

No one gave any of that much thought in the early days, of course. Among the Europeans, the Miskitos quickly developed a reputation as the greatest seamen in the Caribbean. The seventeenth-century French buccaneer Raveneau de Lussan, no landlubber himself, praised the Miskito as

> the boldest in the world in braving the perils of the sea and are without dispute the most dextrous in fishing. They go out to sea in small boats that the average sailor would scorn; in these they remain three or four days at a stretch as unconcerned, despite the weather, as if

they were part of the boat. Once a fish is sighted, no matter how far under the water, they never fail to get it so great is their skill.

British captains soon came to rely on Miskito "strikers" to provide their crew with food. Captain William Dampier, a contemporary of de Lussan, wrote that "one or two [Miskitos] in a ship will maintain 100 men, so that when we careen our ships we choose commonly such places where there is plenty of turtle or manatee for these Miskito men to strike; and it is very rare to find privateers destitute of one or more of them."

Though it would take a century or more to complete the task, the turtles of the Miskito Coast were probably doomed from the moment they were "discovered" by the Cayman sloops. The Miskito Coast was home to a great number of green sea turtles, but the population almost certainly never matched the size of the Cayman rookery. And hunting pressures increased as time went on and other turtle fisheries were decimated one after the other.

In the United States, the place that became synonymous with the turtle industry, Key West, looked to the Miskito Coast for its supply of turtles early on—although the manufacturer of "Key West Genuine Clear Green Turtle Consommé" tried his best to downplay that fact. By the opening of the twentieth century, the Keys, like the rest of Florida, had largely run through its own once plentiful turtle population. Reminders of the former rookeries and foraging grounds are still found in place names—most famously the Dry Tortugas, some eighty miles to the west of Key West, and named, it's said, by the Spanish explorer Juan Ponce de Leon, who took 160 green turtles from those shores in a single night in 1513. Turtle meat and live turtles had already been shipped to northern cities for years when a French-born chef by the name of Armand Granday moved from New York in 1896 to open a turtle soup cannery in Key West. Granday hoped to capitalize on the newly emerging American snob appeal. "What champagne is to other wines," declared the Frenchman's soup label, "green turtle is to other meat." Granday attempted to give upper-class diners in New York, Philadelphia, Baltimore, and other upscale markets the impression that the turtles were locally caught. According to his label, "The quicker the turtle is cooked after leaving its element, the more delightful the flavor. For this reason, we put up our soups in Key West, where the green turtle is at its best and thrives on the wonderful supply of food that Nature has there so abundantly provided for its benefit. Caught in the neighborhood, the turtles are taken from the sea directly to our kettles."

In addition to being a renowned chef, Granday was apparently a pretty good tightrope walker, for in his claims he trod a very fine line between blatantly false advertising and mere puffery. The turtles used in his soup were "caught in the neighborhood" only if you allow a liberal definition of "neighborhood," one that stretches to the opposite side of the Gulf of Mexico, a voyage of close to 1,000 miles, to the Miskito Coast and to the nesting beaches of Costa Rica, where nearly all the turtles processed into soup were caught.

Shipped alive on the decks and in the holds of Cayman schooners, the turtles were taken first to Grand Cayman, and from there to Key West, where they were kept in pens—called "kraals" (from an Afrikaner word)—in the ocean by the cannery, as many as 800 of the marine reptiles at a time, until workers were ready to slaughter them. A U.S. Fisheries report described in detail the process of turning green turtles into turtle consommé.

Turtles that are used for canning purposes are slaughtered on the turtle dock. Each day during the greater part of the year five or six are killed at 3.30 P.M., at which time an inspector is present to see that the butchering is done in a sanitary manner. No turtles are killed until the desired number has been removed from the pens and laid about 1 foot apart on the dock. Then one person takes a sharp ax and strikes the head and four flippers off each turtle, going from one to the other with great rapidity. In each case the appendages are almost completely severed, allowing the animals to bleed freely. Immediately after the axman finishes, two men commence cutting away the plastron and then remove the entrails. During the operation sea water is thrown over the carcasses to wash away the blood and slime. The edible portions of the turtle are removed in four large pieces, each of which contains one of the flippers. The flesh is cut away from the carapace and thrown into a barrel of sea water, where it is thoroughly washed. It is then taken to the cannery, where it is hung on hooks and allowed to remain over night for use the next day. The following day a small portion of the meat may be sold for local consumption, but the greater part is used in preparing canned turtle soup.

Like everything else in Florida in the 1960s, the turtle business began gradually to assume a touristic element. While vacationing families were kept away from the gruesome process described above, tourists paid a fee to climb a tower erected next to the kraals. From up top they got a bird's-eye view of the giant turtles swimming placidly in their pens. When they came down, the visitors were encouraged to purchase turtle steaks, turtle burgers, and turtle soup. Of course there was a gift shop at the Turtle Kraals (as the site was now officially called). In addition to the usual bins of cheap marine trinkets—seashell bracelets, coral rubble that had been dyed lavender, green, and brick red, coconuts carved to look like monkeys—visitors could take home turtle shells, sold for a quarter apiece and advertised as unique "oven-proof baking dishes."

The business of turtle slaughtering in Key West also continued, with none of the tourists knowing that what they were witnessing was the crash of the last great turtle population in the Turtle Sea. A single Cayman-built schooner, the thirty-year-old, twin-masted *A.M. Adams*, continued bringing its live cargo of Central American turtles back to the Turtle Kraals in Key West. These last turtle roundups continued to be celebrated with thoughtless brio—as in the caption below a 1966 *Miami Herald* photograph showing green turtles on their backs, flippers fastened with thatched cords, heading down a rolling conveyer. "Down the ramp to the turtle kralls [sic] of Key West go future steaks and soup makings," prattled the caption. "These large denizens of the briny blue sea will be kept alive and healthy until 'duty,' in the form of a turtle butcher, calls to carve them into appetizing morsels for the dinner table. There's a lot of eatin' packed in those oversized shells."

Commercial turtling in Key West effectively ended on 23 March 1971, when a new regulation went into effect banning the killing of sea turtles with shells less than forty-one inches long. Although Governor Reuben Askew claimed that the law would save the turtle industry by protecting those animals large enough to breed, the regulation pretty much guaranteed the closure of that industry. Few green turtles, of any age, were longer than 41 inches. Archie Carr, a supporter of the regulation, hinted as much when he told a reporter that "I know it is quite a blow [to the industry], but the green turtle is in foul shape all over the world."

By chance, the *A. M. Adams* arrived in port at Key West on the same day the regulation took effect. Out of the 135 turtles she carried, just five met the new length requirement. Some of the turtles were released into the open ocean, others were kept at the Turtle Kraals for a time as a tourist attraction, and the eight man crew from the *Adams* was sent home to Grand Cayman Island.

Where migrations of turtles once prevented ships from passing for hours at a time, it is a lucky sailor who today encounters more than one or two individuals while cruising the same waters. Vessels lost in fog or haze could once steer their way to the Cayman Islands by the sound of a vast bale of turtles making for the same shore. Today, only a handful of *Chelonia mydas* nest in the Caymans. The greatest assemblage of turtles the world has ever known has been methodically wiped out. While no one can say with anything approaching scientific certainty exactly how many green turtles are left in Caribbean, it is possible to make an educated guess. Based on extrapolation from nesting data, sex ratios, and a number of other factors, an estimate of perhaps 60,000 adult green turtles is not unreasonable. That may sound like a lot of turtles, and if you saw that many adult greens swimming in one area it *would* be a

large number. But understand that this is the scattered remnant population of a once vast empire of turtles which numbered somewhere
between 60 million and 600 million adults in pre-Colombian times. The
word decimate, which comes from the ancient Roman punishment of
killing every tenth man in a line of soldiers, doesn't begin to capture the
enormity of this slaughter. Think about it another way: In 1990 there
were 8.5 million people, fifteen years old and older, living in what's
called the New York City Metropolitan Statistical Area, covering the
five boroughs of New York City, Long Island, and parts of northern
New Jersey and Connecticut. (I chose the age of fifteen somewhat arbi-
trarily as a general onset of reproductive maturity.) If some catastrophe
were to befall the area, inflicting the same kind of losses suffered by
green turtles at human hands, only 850 to 8,500 adults would be left
alive in all of New York City and environs. That is the magnitude of
devastation we have dealt the green turtles of the Caribbean Sea.

For all the damage done, overhunting is just one way humans can wipe
a creature from the face of the earth. Targeting certain species such as
the passenger pigeon on land or Steller's sea cow or green turtles in the
ocean is not, in fact, how most modern anthropogenic (human-caused)
extinctions have taken place. By the late nineteenth century and early
years of the twentieth century, biologists began to understand that,
without even trying, humans were sending more creatures to their
doom than they were by more direct methods.

   Not overt greed, but ignorance and indifference drive this newer,
more efficient engine of biological collapse: habitat destruction.

Chapter 4

Lessons of Cannery Row

JOHN STEINBECK based the novel *Cannery Row* on the life of his quirky friend Ed Ricketts, a scientist who collected and sold marine creatures plucked from the waters of Monterey Bay, California. In the book, Ricketts was called "Doc."

Steinbeck wrote:

> Doc was collecting marine animals in the Great Tide Pool on the tip of the Peninsula. It is a fabulous place: when the tide is in, a wave-churned basin, creamy with foam, whipped by the combers that roll in from the whistling buoy on the reef. But when the tide goes out the little water world becomes quiet and lovely. The sea is very clear and the bottom becomes fantastic with hurrying, fighting, feeding, breeding animals.

Steinbeck continues his lyrical description of the teeming life in the Great Tide Pool of Monterey Bay for another five hundred words or so. We're introduced to starfish, mussels, eels, crabs, shrimp, anemones, octopus, barnacles, and algae. It sounds like an underwater Eden, pristine, undefiled by human interference, and that's likely how Steinbeck saw the "little water world" back in the 1930s.

He would have been surprised to read an angry letter to the editor of *Nautilus*, a scientific journal devoted to shellfish. "Monterey as a collecting ground is already greatly injured," rages the letter writer, "and will probably be nearly ruined before long, on account of the Hotel del Monte, the new town of Pacific Grove and the increased population of old Monterey, all the sewage of which is turned into the bay in front of town. Beaches which formerly would afford several hundred species are now nearly bare, or offensive with stinking black mud. Old collectors will learn this with regret."

This isn't the grousing of a modern environmentalist, or even a Steinbeck contemporary. The letter was written in 1892—a half century before *Cannery Row* was published. And there is no question that the letter writer knew his stuff. William Healey Dall was one of the most qualified naturalists of his day; he was trained by the great Louis Agassiz at Harvard. Dall's career spanned more than five decades, during which he published a staggering 1,600 scientific papers, based on field research that took him around the globe.

Lush as it was, Steinbeck was writing about an already diminished ecosystem. Biologist James Carlton has written extensively about the tendency to be blinded by the radiance of the present moment, a phenomenon common even among scientists, dubbed the "shifting baseline syndrome."

"Without a framework of study and a deeper appreciation for marine environmental history," points out Carlton, "our sense of history often defaults to viewing the step on which we are standing as the second step of the staircase, no matter how far down the staircase we have gone."

Although Dall only mentioned it in passing (and in a letter to the editor at that), he was writing about what biologists consider the greatest threat to biodiversity: habitat destruction.

The notion that humans were endangering species more through indirect activity than through direct means took some time to become common in the scientific community. In the introduction to the 1969 *Red Book*, the recognized authority on endangered and threatened species, there is a chart of extinctions and "rarities" among birds and mammals since the year 1600. The chart is designed to compare human complicity in species loss versus natural decline. Under the heading of human causation, the authors broke down the totals into more specific categories, including hunting and habitat disruption. For known extinctions between 1600 and 1969, the authors found that 24 percent of species went extinct due to natural causes. A whopping 42 percent of avian (bird) extinctions were caused by hunting. Habitat destruction accounted for only 15 percent of bird extinctions. The figures were roughly the same for mammalian extinctions, with 25 percent dying out from natural causes, 33 percent from hunting, and just 19 percent because of habitat disruption. But the coming shift is seen in the section of the chart dealing with "present [1969] rarities," what are classified as "threatened" or "endangered" species. Hunting is still the dominant threat to mammals, accounting for 43 percent of rarities, compared to 29 percent attributable to habitat destruction. (Natural causes has dropped to just 14 percent.) With birds, however, things had changed. While 32 percent of avian rarities are deemed threatened by natural causes, now hunting accounts for just 24 percent of the total. Habitat disruption has jumped to the top of the human-caused list, up to 30 percent. Later in the same volume, this theme is made more explicit. In the section dealing with plants, the authors state that "The preservation of plant species can be satisfactorily achieved only by conserving the habitats in which they live."

By 1975, a standard college environmental textbook makes the point that "Loss or alteration of habitat is the major cause of ... extinction." The idea would take another decade or two to gain widespread acceptance. In their 1981 book, *Extinction*, ecologists Paul and Anna Ehrlich felt it necessary to drive the point home, writing that "Many people realize the dangers of overexploitation, but the much more general threat of habitat destruction is lost on most—including those who should know better."

The primacy of habitat, and the need for preserving it, wasn't definitively accepted by the public until the 1986 National Forum on BioDiversity, held in Washington, D.C. It was largely as an outgrowth of that meeting that the concept of biodiversity itself was firmly established in the public mind. A group of biologists at the forum held a press conference at which they announced that "The species extinction crisis is a threat to civilization second only to the threat of thermonuclear war." And what was driving that crisis? In the opening paragraph of *Biodiversity*, the best-selling book based on the forum, biologist E. O. Wilson proclaimed "Much of the diversity is being irreversibly lost through extinction caused by the destruction of natural habitats."

It may seem a bit surprising that it took some time for that realization to sink in, given that humans' ability to alter the environment has long been recognized as one of the defining characteristics of *Homo sapiens*. But what is "shaping the environment" to one species (humans) may be "destroying habitat" for countless other species.

The relation between habitat destruction and loss of biodiversity is much more than just a question of perspective, however. It is primarily a matter of population growth—human population growth, that is. When there were just a few hundred thousand or even a million *Homo sapiens* roaming around chopping down trees with stone axes, not much habitat was destroyed. But then hunter-gatherers began using fire to drive animals out of forest undergrowth, and, later, between 10,000 and 7,000 BC, discovered that burning grasslands produced open and fertile areas. Agriculture, the cultivation of plants and the domestication of animals, had begun. It was the first great technological revolution of humankind and it sprang up at many different sites all around the world at about the same time. There were two primary effects: humans had an enriched and more dependable food supply (capable of supporting greater population), and the habitat of more and more species was destroyed. *Homo sapiens* had begun nibbling away at the edges of habitat and, so, biodiversity.

To see the link between a burgeoning human population and declining biodiversity, one need only compare graphs of the two phenomena laid side by side. As the number of humans increases, that of species plummets. Consider: In 1400 AD, there were only 350 million people on the planet—roughly the population of the former Soviet Union on the eve of its collapse. It took the next three hundred years for the population to nearly double—up to 680 million. In 1700, human population began what researchers have called an "explosive growth cycle," rising to a billion in 1800, to 1.6 billion in 1900, to 5 billion by 1986, and to 6 billion just a decade later. Even with projected growth rates falling, there will likely be a staggering 10 billion humans on the planet by the year 2050.

But habitat destruction isn't merely a numbers game. There are also qualitative forces at work, forces that are connected to, but different from, the steep upward slope seen on population graphs.

In the mid 1700s, another revolution got underway—one with implications even more profound than the development of agriculture. With its use of complex machinery, powered by previously untapped energy sources, and the new social, political, and economic organization it was both shaped by and helped to form, the Industrial Revolution, in less than three centuries, has transformed the world and human's relationship with everything in it—including the habitats of virtually all the planet's creatures.

Monterey Bay—cited by John Steinbeck and William Healey Dall—is a good example of these changes, of their complexity, and of their impoverishing effect on marine environments.

After visiting Hawaii in 1786, the French explorer Jean François de la Pérouse continued to North America, sailing down from Alaska to Monterey Bay, where he marveled at the profusion of animals, writing "There is not a country in this world which more abounds in fish and game of every description."

This soon changed. The indigenous people had been living along the bay for more than 10,000 years, and although they regularly harvested shellfish and finned fish and practiced limited agriculture not far inland, the ecosystems of Monterey Bay seem to have remained relatively stable for millennia.

Early Spanish settlers disrupted the local habitats to some degree by increased farming and rearing livestock in the area, but the Industrial Revolution was the real engine driving the larger changes. As cities grew on America's industrializing east coast, the demand for whale oil launched a fleet of New England whalers around Cape Horn at the bottom of South America and back up to the Monterey area, where humpback and gray whales were found in large numbers. New technologies for extracting gold combined with a growing market economy to fuel the California Gold Rush. The immigrants needed food—a large quantity of which came from Monterey Bay. Steam-powered locomotives rushed fresh fish from Monterey Bay straight up to San Francisco by the 1860s, further depleting the bay. The great wealth accumulated by industrial titans sought new outlets. Tourism was the rage. The sprawling, opulent Hotel del Monte, which Dall blamed in his letter to the editor for discharging sewage into the bay, became famous as the first major resort on the west coast and one of the premier hotels in late nineteenth-century America.

The bay was also changed dramatically by large-scale agriculture further inland, as new farming technologies (tractors, and then fossil-fuel-based fertilizers), allowed for more and more acres to come under the plow. Today, agriculture is a billion-dollar industry in Monterey County. The region proclaims itself the "Salad Bowl of the Nation." The county produces nearly all the lettuce grown commercially in America, a majority of the broccoli, and huge quantities of other crops. While the destruction of habitat is fairly obvious where grasslands and forests are converted to fields, the damage to distant coastal waters is harder to see. But it is every bit as real. Nearly 6,000 square miles of land drains into Monterey Bay, mostly through the Salinas River. Once a clear-bottomed waterway teeming with life, the Salinas flows through some of the richest agricultural land of California and in the process has been turned into a 150-mile-long liquid conveyer belt, dumping large quantities of eroded soil, nutrients, and agricultural chemicals into Monterey Bay. In one small wetland adjacent to the Bay—draining less than 200 square miles (about 3 percent of the total drainage area for Monterey Bay)—172,000 tons of agricultural sediment are trapped annually. The soil buries marine organisms, radically altering the bottom habitat.

Agricultural chemicals also have a host of harmful effects, few of which are currently well understood. (No one claims that these chemicals are *good* for sea creatures, however, and only agribusiness flacks contend that chemicals designed to kill plants and animals can safely be assumed to be benign.) A federal employee who worked on a project mapping water-quality data from rivers in the Monterey Bay drainage area in the mid 1990s described Monterey County as "the most intensive agricultural area I've seen in the world." The county waterways were put into three categories, based on their level of contamination with agricultural chemicals: good, intermediate, and impaired. Because the most highly contaminated category had such an innocuous label, I asked the researcher what "impaired" really meant. "I'll tell you this," he replied after a pause, "you wouldn't want to swim in it, you wouldn't want to drink it, and I probably wouldn't eat a fish that came out of it. But people do all three."

Perhaps even more disconcerting than what researchers found in the water was the question mark that still hangs over the quality of the waterways in Monterey County, *after* the results were in.

"I'll tell you what alarmed me when I went out there to work on this watershed management stuff," says the researcher. "It's that these state water-quality agencies don't really *know* what's in the water. I was talking with the people who actually do the monitoring, and they couldn't tell you what was going on with the vast majority of compounds that were being used. They didn't know how much was in the water, what the levels were, if any. That's what I found surprising. But there are so many things that could be in the water that they have to choose to measure either what's most toxic or most heavily used or some combination. A lot of things go totally untested."

The net effect of the nation's salad bowl on the nearby marine environment was summed up in a report by the Monterey Bay National Marine Sanctuary (MBNMS), which concluded that "Agricultural operations have [caused] precipitous reductions in coastal ... biodiversity."

The effects of overfishing are the most obvious threat to biodiversity, here as elsewhere, and Cannery Row itself is a good example of the problem. The ramshackle canneries clustered along the shoreline of southern Monterey Bay were built to pack the billions of sardines caught by Sicilian immigrants beginning in the early years of the twentieth century. Here's how Steinbeck described the scene in those boom years:

> In the morning, when the sardine fleet has made a catch, the purse-seiners waddle heavily into the bay blowing their whistles. The deep-laden boats pull in against the coast where the canneries dip their tails into the bay.... Then cannery whistles scream and all over the town men and women scramble into their clothes and come running down the Row to go to work.... They come running to clean and cut and pack and cook and can the fish. The whole street rumbles and groans and screams and rattles while the silver rivers of fish pour in out of the boats and the boats rise higher and higher in the water until they are empty.

Steinbeck was writing during the peak years of the sardine fishery. By the time the book describing this raucous scene was published, many packing plants had already closed and the rest would soon shut their doors, one by one, and the whistles that brought people running down to the Row would cease to blow in Monterey. The sardine fishery had crashed. Where once there had lived an enormous population of fish, with a biomass (the scientific term for the total weight of the population) estimated at over 3 million tons, the years of plunder had reduced the fishery to a fragment, weighing just 5,000 tons.

When later asked where the "silver rivers" of fish had gone, Steinbeck replied, "Into the cans."

"We have not learned everywhere the lessons of Cannery Row," President Bill Clinton observed at the National Oceans Conference, two days of speeches and discussions about the state of America's oceans, held in Monterey in 1998. From a podium on the ocean's edge, at one end of Cannery Row, Clinton told the crowd, "More than two-thirds of the world's fisheries are overexploited."

Calamitous as overfishing is, there are indirect effects of fishing methods that may be even more harmful in the long run. Examples are blast fishing, using dynamite or homemade bombs on coral reefs; divers squirting cyanide solution to stun tropical fish (and in the process killing hundreds of other nearby organisms) to supply the aquarium trade; and what some fishery experts believe is the most devastating activity of all, trawling, an old form of fishing that, thanks to new technology, has vastly increased its ability to capture fish—and to level huge areas of the seabed.

The principle behind trawling is simple: A boat pulls a funnel-shaped net—open on the leading edge, closed on the trailing one—through water until the net is full. At that point, the net is hauled to the surface and the contents are dumped onboard. It's not known exactly how long fishermen have engaged in the practice known as bottom trawling, using weighted nets pulled along the sea floor. The earliest known reference to the technique comes from 1376, when some members of England's House of Commons attempted to have a trawling device called a *wondyrychoun* banned from use on the River Thames. Even at that primitive stage, the concern was over the method's potential effect on underwater vegetation. In truth, relatively little harm was done by fishermen in a rowboat dragging a small net behind them. But neither were they particularly successful in catching fish with this method, and most English fishermen, like other Europeans, continued using the traditional fishing gear, primarily other forms of nets, for several centuries.

It was the Industrial Revolution that remade commercial fishing. The invention of the "beam trawl" in eastern England in the late 1700s was the first step. The beam was just that—a long section of wood, placed horizontally—to keep the front of the trawl net open as a large sailboat pulled the net through the water. Weights were placed along the beam to keep the net where most of the target fish lived, on or near the bottom. By the mid 1800s, the British beam trawler was a frequent sight in the North Sea and throughout the English Channel. In the 1880s, the British fishing fleet adopted the steam engine, allowing trawlers to pull even larger nets and travel to more distant fishing grounds, establishing England as the unrivaled fishing power of Europe.

Technology has raced ahead. Today's bottom trawlers, some longer than a football field, are powered by 5,000 horsepower diesel engines. The beam has largely been replaced by large vertical plates, one on either end of the net's mouth, weighing more than a ton each. The giant nets themselves, attached by thick steel cables, can be anywhere between thirty feet and several hundred feet across. Metal weights are fixed to the bottom of the net's leading edge, each one weighing up to hundreds of pounds. These massive devices, into which the old British beam trawlers could have easily fit, are dragged along the ocean floor, where they swallow everything in their path. The type of terrain in which bottom trawlers can operate has changed dramatically in the past few years—again, thanks to new technologies. Until recently, trawlers were forced to keep a respectful distance from corals, boulders, or anything else that could leave their nets in tatters. That left sandy bottoms and mud or seagrass meadows. It is important not to minimize the biodiversity and ecological importance of these seemingly humble habitats. The muddiest or sandiest bottom is often home to many species, almost certainly many not yet described by biologists. And seagrass beds are famous for the multitude of life they support. Trawlers can now operate in virtually any marine habitat thanks to a device called a rockhopper, which allows the weighted nets to bounce off rocky bottoms.

Because trawling takes place deep underwater, scientists never got around to assessing its impact with any precision. For most people, including most biologists, it was the old "out of sight, out of mind" phenomenon at work.

But not for Elliott Norse.

Norse is one of the leaders of the still emerging field called conservation biology, especially that part of it involving genetic diversity in the oceans. His round face, framed by close-cropped graying hair and a beard, and his voice—articulate and warm even as he discusses the ongoing degradation of the oceans—may be familiar to some Americans from his appearances on talk shows and environmental specials. As founder and president of the Marine Conservation Biology Institute (MCBI) in Washington state, Norse is one of the leading and best-known advocates for preserving marine biodiversity.

In 1971, however, Norse was still a graduate student in marine ecology at the University of Southern California, researching his dissertation on the common blue crab. He had never been aboard a trawler before, but Norse leapt at the opportunity when he heard that a professor needed an assistant to go out on a Mexican shrimp trawler bound for the Sea of Cortez in Baja California. Although Norse was researching blue crabs in the Caribbean, the opportunity to visit the subtropical east Pacific was too good to pass up.

As the boat put out to sea from the port of San Felipe, Mexico, Norse wondered how they'd actually manage to collect crabs from a shrimp trawler. The professor assured him that this was, in fact, a good way to collect all sorts of things (a claim that Norse quickly learned was an understatement).

After their first trawl, the crew lifted the large nets, spilling the contents onto the deck. The young graduate student was shocked by what he saw.

"Something like 95 percent of what they had caught wasn't shrimp," he recalls. "It was what is technically referred to as 'by-catch.' Shrimpers in the U.S. call it 'trawl trash.' Today, I'd call it biological diversity."

Norse allows that his first reaction to the mass of dead or dying species spread out on the trawler's deck wasn't outrage. As a student, gathering samples for his dissertation was foremost among his concerns. "Wow," he thought, "what a great way to collect blue crabs!" But later, as he watched the crew shoveling mounds of dead creatures overboard, the future marine ecologist had a second thought: shrimping sure killed a lot of other organisms.

"If you think about it for a moment," says Norse, "there were a lot of shrimpers just in San Felipe alone. And there were even more in Puerto Peñasco. And then there were all the other shrimpers working out of all the other ports in Mexico and the U.S. and everywhere else in the world." In Norse's mind, all that "trawl trash" surely added up to a huge amount of marine life destroyed—hundreds of species, probably—inadvertently killed so that wealthy people could have shrimp cocktail as an appetizer. It was remarkable in its wastefulness. Still, Norse was struggling to complete his dissertation, and so he didn't pursue the topic. But he didn't forget it, either.

After receiving his doctorate, Norse spent the next twelve years building a distinguished career as a marine biologist. He worked at the Environmental Protection Agency in Washington, D.C., and was later named as staff ecologist of the President's Council on Environmental Quality. He left government and worked for a variety of environmental organizations. In the mid 1980s, Norse helped forge the scientific movement of conservation biology, which is devoted to maintaining genetic variation among plants and animals. Norse turned his attention to forests because, as he explains, "forest biologists understand relationships between species and their habitats in more sophisticated ways than my fellow marine biologists. After all, it's much easier to observe wildlife in their habitats on land than in the sea. Indeed, many marine biologists (and almost all fishermen) work from boats or ships on the surface and never actually see fish where they live. In contrast, almost every forest biologist knows that structure—the living trees, snags, fallen logs, shrubs, and small plants that cover the ground—determines the forest's suitability as habitat for wildlife." He wrote two seminal books on forest conservation biology.

But Norse's heart lay in the ocean realm, and he eventually became chief scientist with the Center for Marine Conservation (CMC), a non-profit environmental group based in Washington, D.C. There, Norse began thinking again about what he had seen on the deck of the Mexican shrimp trawler as a graduate student some twenty years earlier. In the spring of 1990, he was talking with a biologist familiar with the large fishing grounds for brown shrimp found in the Gulf of Mexico. After doing some rough calculations, the pair estimated that on average, any given location in the fishery was trawled three times every year. For the first time, it occurred to Norse that, as bad as it was, deaths due to trawler by-catch wasn't the only threat to marine biodiversity. If the heavy trawling gear were dragged across the same area of ocean bed three times a year, what, he wondered, was the physical effect on the seabed, the habitat of countless creatures?

The question nagged at Norse as he worked on other issues. Science is a labyrinth built of questions, and a single researcher is able to creep down only a few passageways in his or her lifetime (and only a short distance in each one). Norse was committed to exploring issues already on the agenda at the CMC. One project in particular consumed a tremendous amount of time — editing the first book on marine biodiversity. It was a mammoth undertaking that kept Norse frantically busy for months. While working on that project, Norse corresponded with a fish ecologist from Connecticut named Peter Auster. As it happened, one of Auster's primary research areas was the effects of trawling on the sea floor. That got Norse's interest. He asked Auster to tell him more. Auster told Norse how once, using SCUBA gear, he had dived down to the seabed so that he could watch a scallop trawl (called a dredge) pass by. After the dredge had disappeared, Auster swam directly into the swirling clouds of sediments left in its wake. Through the murk, Auster saw a seascape radically altered. "What was once a complex of sponges, shells, and other organisms," he reported, "was smoothed to a cobble-stone street."

Norse read some of the papers Auster had written on the subject and he became convinced that "this could be big, important stuff." Still he had the book to finish and other projects ongoing at CMC. Finally, in 1995, Norse moved to Redmond, Washington, to found his own organization, the Marine Conservation Biology Institute. One of the first things he did there was to begin organizing a workshop on the effect of bottom trawling on marine ecosystems. In June 1996 seventeen marine scientists from around the world gathered at the University of Maine for that purpose.

"I think the results of what we produced are extraordinarily shocking," says Norse. "We calculated that bottom trawling is 'plowing' an area of seabed that's equivalent to half the area of the world's continental shelf every year."

The result of that meeting was a special issue of the journal *Conservation Biology* devoted to the topic in December 1998. The seriousness of the scientists' findings was underscored by the unusual flourish of a news conference held to coincide with the journal's publication.

Ted Danson, the movie and television actor who is also an activist for ocean causes, spoke at the news conference, but it was Norse who gave reporters the bottom line: "Trawling is the greatest single disturbance of the world's seabed." He also provided the "hook" for most of the stories generated by the news conference.

"Comparing the fishing techniques to forest clear-cutting," began one such article, Norse "warns that the living structures of seabeds are being destroyed at a rate much greater than the current rate of destruction of the earth's forests."

Clear-cutting is a widely condemned technique that uses heavy equipment to denude entire mountainsides of everything but the smallest shrubs. Norse and other scientists provided evidence that bottom trawling, especially when done repeatedly over the same terrain, has much the same effect on the seabed. The rockhoppers and other trawling gear pulverize whatever is in their path—leaving a path of devastation where a complex community may have existed before.

The scale of the destruction surprised even Norse. Just two years earlier he had thought he was going out on a limb when he told a reporter that "We're talking about destruction of marine habitat that is, if not equivalent, at least in the ballpark with clearcutting forests on land."

The reports published in *Conservation Biology* showed that trawling was far more extensive. According to United Nations estimates, each year clearcutting ravages approximately 62,000 square miles. A huge area to be sure, equal to the size of the state of Indiana. But it is 1/150 the area that Norse and his colleagues estimate is pummeled by bottom trawlers each year—an area roughly double the size of the lower forty-eight states combined.

And if anyone doubted that the analogy to clearcutting was accurate, two photographs on the cover of *Conservation Biology* made what was, for many laypeople at least, a more convincing case than all the articles inside. The cover shows two views of the seabed, 275 feet down, at Georges Bank, off the northeastern coast of the United States. The top photo shows an impressive collection of creatures, including ethereal tubeworms, long-armed brittle stars, and colonies of featherlike hydrozoans. The second picture was taken a quarter-mile away after a trawler had passed. In it, you have to search hard to find any signs of life. It looks like someone had gone down to the local building supply store and snapped a picture of the gravel bin.

Back on land, conservation biologists now warn of a new threat to biodiversity. Like habitat destruction, this danger comes from "unintended consequences." Around the world, hundreds of species are being overwhelmed by invaders: nonindigenous species brought by humans to new lands, where, lacking natural enemies, they are so successful that they crowd out native species. The problem earned a chapter of its own in the government study published in 1998: *Status and Trends of the Nation's Biological Resources*. The authors of that report discuss some of the havoc caused by just a handful of the estimated 6,500 nonindigenous species that have become established in the United States, concluding: "This continued homogenization of the world's flora and fauna, which represents at least millions of years of separate evolutionary histories, is an ecological holocaust of major proportions."

Science writer Robert Devine covers much of the same ground, but in greater and graphic detail, in his 1998 book *Alien Invasion*, a fascinating and horrifying examination of killer bees, kudzu, and feral pigs. Devine makes a convincing case that nonindigenous species may ultimately pose a more serious threat to biodiversity than even habitat destruction.

Although a few exotic freshwater fish and mollusks are examined in these descriptions, relatively little research has been focused on the effects of nonindigenous species in the marine environment. And given the combined effects of trawling, blast and cyanide fishing, eutrophication, pollution, and the other assorted human activities both on land and on sea, it's easy to see why habitat destruction is still considered the primary threat to marine biodiversity.

But we may be on the cusp of a new understanding about the human impact on marine life. The problems of overfishing, habitat alteration and nonindigenous species remain. But there is evidence of a new and potentially even more devastating problem. We may be transforming the ocean, especially coastal waters, into a breeding ground for disease.

Chapter 5

Outbreak

THE PHONE CALL was like so many others: a stranger on the other end of the line telling George Balazs that a sea turtle needed help. Ever since beginning his crusade to save the *honu* two years earlier in 1972, distress calls increased in frequency, until now they were a regular part of his job. A vacationing snorkeler would find a turtle with a flipper tangled in monofilament line and then somehow track down Balazs in his tiny office on Coconut Island. Or a local surfer would spot a turtle with an ugly fresh gash across its carapace—likely the work of a boat propeller—and Balazs's phone would ring. The junior biologist responded promptly to every call. After all, he *had* started the campaign to protect the turtles and now he couldn't very well say no when people sought his help for injured *honu*. So when the phone rang on that morning in early 1974, Balazs had no clue that the call would mark a major turning point in his life. The caller merely reported that a sea turtle had washed ashore on Waikiki Beach. Would Balazs please come take a look at it? Of course, he replied.

Balazs took a small skiff over to the mainland, hopped into a rusted-out State of Hawaii pickup truck, and drove the scenic, winding road from Kaneohe Bay over to Waikiki. Amid the mainland sun-seekers on that most famous of Hawaiian tourist destinations sat a large green turtle, immobile on the golden sand. The man who had telephoned told Balazs that the turtle had been blowing around like a balloon in the water. Then he pointed to the turtle's neck. "What the heck is *that*?"

Balazs stooped down to get a closer look. A fist-sized tumor grew beside the turtle's head. Balazs straightened up, astonished. He had no idea what the growth was. With the help of a couple of the onlookers, Balazs loaded the turtle into the back of his truck and headed back to Coconut Island, where he placed the animal in a tidal pond. The creature bobbed on the surface, unable to dive. Balazs wasn't sure what was wrong with the turtle, but he sensed that the problem was related to the horrible-looking growth on the animal's neck. He longed for someone to turn to for advice, but there was no one for him to call. *He* was supposed to be the turtle expert in Hawaii. So Balazs started combing through journals, new and old. He quickly found the 1938 article by Smith and Coates, "Fibro-epithelial Growths of the Skin in Large Marine Turtles, *Chelonia mydas*," describing the tumored turtle at the New York Aquarium. The authors used the word "wart" to describe the growths. That pretty much fit what he saw on the *honu*'s neck. But if this were a wart, thought Balazs, it was a huge one.

As he searched through the journals, Balazs found other references to the condition. A short paper published in the same year as the Smith and Coates article described growths found in a female green turtle caught off Florida's southwestern tip. The article was written by a cancer researcher named Balduin Lucké, and although his focus was cancer, Lucké was interested in all forms of neoplasms—the medical term for tissue growths that serve no physiological purpose. Cancer is a particular kind of neoplasm, a virulent growth that continues to spread to surrounding tissues and even throughout the entire system. By studying neoplasms in lower organisms such as turtles, frogs, and fish, Lucké hoped to gain better insight into just how cancer worked.

The turtle Lucké examined was covered with tumors. "They were located on the edges of both anterior flippers," he wrote, "in the axillary regions, the neck, on the eyelids, the corneal surfaces, and on the tail." The pathologist didn't know what caused the tumors. But he observed that humans and other animals developed similar growths and many of them were caused by viruses. Perhaps a virus was also responsible for the turtle growths, Lucké mused.

Balazs found a long article from the early 1950s on sea turtles in Malaysia, written by John Hendrickson, a name already familiar to him. Hendrickson was one of the top sea turtle biologists of his generation, and Balazs also knew of him as the author of the 1969 study that had overestimated the size of the Hawaiian *honu* breeding population—but only because it was based on the flawed data of other researchers.

In 1953 Hendrickson was a young professor of zoology at the University of Malaya, Singapore, who had recently graduated from the University of California–Berkeley and was conducting research on green turtles of the South China Sea. Balazs nearly jumped when he read an excerpt from Hendrickson's field journals, dated 16 March 1953.

> Found a turtle with a large, mushroom-shaped, leathery growth on its carapace.... This growth, measuring about 10 cm. by 15 cm. [4 inches by 6 inches], was attached by a relatively small stalk and I was able to remove the mass in its entirety. The growth was rooted very strongly through the carapace plates into the underlying bone, and the root was highly calcified. The mass contained a number of the burrowing barnacles seen before. When the mass finally came away from the turtle's carapace, it left a hole about 2.5 cm. [an inch] in diameter and about 2 cm. deep.... Is this a sample of a relatively successful host reaction to the parasites, isolating them off in a stalked tumour where they receive minimal blood supply, etc.?

Balazs quickly flipped to a series of black and white photographs accompanying Hendrickson's report. There it was, in the middle of the last page: the ugly, lobed tumor the young professor had cut off the turtle nesting on a Borneo beach. From the description and the photograph, it appeared that the Waikiki turtle suffered from the same condition as the one in Borneo had—and the others from Florida.

Balazs's research was productive, but it was also frustrating. The disease was known, but only in the sense that others had encountered it before. Beyond a physical description of the tumor, there was precious little information. Most important, no one knew what caused turtles to sprout the tumors. Not that there was any lack of hypotheses—everything from exposure to sunlight to a virus to a reaction to burrowing barnacles had been suggested.

Balazs ran across an early paper that proposed yet another scenario. Tiny leeches had been found in many of the tumors. The leeches could be opportunists, feeding off the blood vessels that crisscrossed the tumors. (Hendrickson was wrong about the tumor's "minimal blood supply"—there was plenty to keep the leeches happy.) A parasitologist named Ross Nigrelli, working with George Smith, the coauthor of the very first description of the tumors, suggested that the leeches could actually be helping the tumors to grow. To keep its food supply flowing, the leeches produced a compound called hirudin that prevents blood from clotting. Perhaps the increased blood flow caused by hirudin "fed" the tumor cells, allowing them to proliferate and grow.

One more plausible theory, sighed Balazs, closing the old journal.

In the course of his research, Balazs discovered an institution that would prove vital in his work. It bore the uninspired but utilitarian name: the Registry of Tumors in Lower Animals (RTLA). The RTLA was a division of the Smithsonian Institution in Washington, D.C., and was less than a decade old, the brainchild of a Clyde Dawe, a researcher at the National Cancer Institute. Like Lucké, Dawe believed that pathologists could learn about cancer by studying tumors in less complex organisms. The RTLA conducted some studies and published information about what it learned, but its most important contribution was, as its name denotes, to serve as a home for tumor samples. Starting in 1965, zoologists from universities, veterinary clinics, and wildlife agencies began sending samples of tumors they had found in invertebrates and cold-blooded vertebrates. It was the only collection of its kind in the world. Balazs wrote the RTLA's director, John Harshbarger, asking if he had information about the tumors of sea turtles. Harshbarger responded that, yes, the registry had samples of the kind Balazs described and promised to send Balazs a copy of the most recent tumor inventory, which was then in preparation. The director added that "extraneous material of plant or animal origin is usually present" in the tumors and offered his opinion that this material "initiates the growths." Of course, he pointed out "this would have to be proven experimentally."

Without knowing what caused the condition, Balazs had no idea how to treat the turtle he had brought to Coconut Island. Each day the creature grew more listless. Balazs stood by, powerless to stop its decline. The turtle refused to eat, or perhaps it couldn't eat, and its plastron gradually collapsed, caving in as it starved. When the animal died a week later, a sense of inevitability pervaded its death. That didn't make the loss any easier for Balazs, but he tried to comfort himself with the thought that he was fortunate to have seen a case of this extremely rare disease. Over dinner that night Balazs told his wife, "Well, I'll probably never see *that* again, thank God."

In June 1974, a few months after seeing his first FP turtle, Balazs returned to East Island to continue the tagging program he had started the year before. He was encouraged by the fact that in his weeks on the isolated island 124 turtles came ashore to nest—more than a 50 percent increase over the previous year's total.

But Balazs made a more ominous discovery on East Island that year: 10 percent of the turtles had tumors.

Some of the growths were only the size of a nickel. Others were massive. The largest was nearly a foot in diameter. Balazs was startled to find so many turtles with tumors, especially since he had observed no tumored turtles at the nesting grounds the summer before. One possible

explanation for that omission is that in his first year of the tagging program, Balazs had been so preoccupied with all the effort of beginning
such a project—getting used to the island itself, figuring out the best
procedure for tagging the turtles, etc.—that he missed spotting the
tumors on the few turtles affected. After all, with only 81 nesting turtles
observed in 1973, a 10 percent tumor rate would mean just eight turtles
with growths.

But Balazs rejects the idea that he could have missed spotting
tumored turtles. "I was very meticulous recording things that first
year," he insists. "And later on [too], but especially that first year."

Reading through his field notes from that first summer, it's hard to
imagine that Balazs missed *anything*. From the moment he set foot on
the islands of French Frigate Shoals, Balazs kept scrupulously detailed
records of virtually everything he saw, heard, or even thought. He was
like a sponge, soaking up everything around and then transforming it all
into scribbled descriptions on dozens of blue-lined pages. Balazs
scrawled the names of the birds that crowded those coral islands, along
with entries describing them: "Noddy Tern—gray; Sooty Tern—
black/white, Red Foot Booby—in trees, Laysan Finch—male yellow."
He made detailed maps of the islands, including what few buildings
were there. (He even roughed in floor plans for those still in use.) He
kept track of the weather by the hour ("10–11 pm: Light rain showers—
hot during night, wind shifted west to north"). He made countless notes
to himself on everything from how to improve his census ("Count eggs
when falling into pit when convenient") to reminders of biological eti-
quette ("I would rather *not* get info on sex of baskers or tag present if it
means making animals retreat into water").

And, most important, Balazs recorded anything that had to do with
the *honu* that was out of the ordinary. These notations usually involved
injuries, the work of the sharks that gathered in frightening numbers in
the waters surrounding the islands. One turtle, he recorded, had a
"healed bite in shell." Another was missing "[fr 1/2] right hind flipper."
Others comments included anomalies as modest as "distinctive barnacle
right side of carapace."

Given this attention to details, it's hard to believe Balazs could have missed something as obvious as tumors growing on 10 percent of the turtles at French Frigate Shoals. The most likely explanation for why he recorded no FP in 1973 is that there were no tumors to see. But this raised an even more perplexing question in Balazs's mind; namely, what accounted for FP's sudden appearance at French Frigate Shoals in 1974? The question baffled Balazs and drove him to learn more about the condition.

He still hadn't received the report from the RTLA with the inventory of sea turtle tumors, and so as soon as he returned to Oahu at the end of the summer, Balazs wrote John Harshbarger and reminded the RTLA director that he was keenly interested in learning about the registry's collection. Two weeks later he received the report. He tore open the envelope, giddy with anticipation. He quickly scanned the pages. The RTLA had over 400 tumor specimens in its collection. Most of them came from fish, but there were also neoplasms cut from mollusks, frogs, and several species of reptiles. Researchers had also submitted anomalies that turned out not to be tumors at all, but inflamed masses of tissue called granulomas, produced by the body as a reaction to an infection or a parasite. These samples came from starfish, corals, sponges—in one case, even from a fungus—in addition to the many creatures mentioned above.

Wading through this information, Balazs at last found the short section on sea turtles. There were only three samples. Two had been submitted from turtles caught in Florida. The first had been sent to the registry's founder, Clyde Dawe, back in 1963, even before Dawe had started the RTLA. A virologist at the Variety Children's Hospital in Miami had been vacationing in the Florida Keys when he had spotted a turtle with tumors on its neck and flippers. The researcher, named Glenn Waddell, removed samples of the tumors and sent them along with photographs of the turtle to Dawe. In a letter accompanying the material Waddell explained that he had begun a transmission experiment, transplanting some of the tumored material into young turtles. But as with Smith and Coates's mention of a similar intention, there was no record of any further study.

There was a second tumor from a Florida turtle, also from the Keys, and although the date listed in the registry for the tumor was 1972, that was the year the sample was processed. The material was actually obtained from a turtle off Marathon Key in the mid-1960s, by a graduate student studying parasitology at the University of Miami.

The only non-Florida record was entry #121. It consisted of three samples, each coming from a separate turtle, but otherwise, information about the tumors was nearly identical to that of the others in the registry. It had been submitted in 1967 by a young medical doctor named Al Smith, who had known Harshbarger when the two had been at the University of California–Irvine. The tumors resembled the others from Florida, both in gross appearance and under the microscope. Like the researchers in New York, and Waddell in Miami, Smith had wanted to do more experiments on the tumors. A grant application for this project was rejected, however, and he was forced to abandon the idea.

It was the location of entry #121 that got Balazs's attention. The tumored turtles had been given to Dr. Al Smith by a turtle fisherman working the waters of Hawaii.

A "baseline" is crucial to biologists, and the search for it is the first step in any scientific journey. That's because data without their context are, at best, meaningless. At worst, data ripped from the fabric of time and space lead to conclusions that sound reasonable and possess an irrefutable internal logic—but that may be completely wrong.

There is an old joke that relies on just this circumstance.

A medical researcher is studying longevity. The next subject walks in, bent over but apparently still getting around well with his cane. The man lowers himself slowly into a chair and says, "Well, doc, I can tell you right off the secret to my good health."

"Okay," says the doctor. "Go ahead."

"I smoke two cigars every day, without fail," says the man. "I drink a shot of cheap whiskey with every meal. And I chase women all night long, seven nights a week."

The doctor looks up from his chart, shocked.

"My God, that's amazing!" he says. "You smoke, drink, and carouse without let-up, and yet you appear to be in excellent health. That's simply amazing. How old are you, anyway?"

The man leans back in his chair and says, "Thirty-three."

Okay, it may not be a great joke, but it illustrates the need for a reliable baseline.

The quest to establish a baseline was behind George Balazs's tagging and monitoring program at French Frigate Shoals, and it was the starting point for his work on FP as well. When was the condition first seen? Where? What was the prevalence of the disease as far back as could be determined?

A baseline is just the beginning. By itself, a baseline is like a foundation with no building above it. Once a baseline was established, however, it could be compared to the current data Balazs was collecting. Out of this combination would emerge something akin to the Holy Grail for biologists: a trend. That was the key, finding FP's trend among the *honu*, and Balazs went after it with the same fierce determination that marked his other efforts at turtle conservation.

But first, the baseline. When did FP first show up in the Hawaiian Islands? That was one of the primary questions Balazs hoped to answer, and in seeking it he followed several different avenues. He corresponded with countless biologists and researchers. He continued combing through the scientific literature, extending his search to the so-called "gray literature," reports, studies, and field notes that had never been published or widely distributed. And he questioned local fishermen and wildlife officials whenever he got the chance. Over time, all three methods yielded results of varying quality, a mishmash of hard evidence, tantalizing clues, and dead ends. The RTLA records proved that FP was present in Hawaii in 1967. The disease was likely there before Al Smith sent his tumor sample to the registry, but how long before, exactly, and on what islands?

Balazs found a partial answer while searching through the gray literature, in an unpublished report prepared for the U.S. Fish and Wildlife

Service (FWS) by Eugene Kridler, the manager of the Hawaiian Islands National Wildlife Refuge. This was the same Gene Kridler who had angered Balazs in 1972 by testifying before Hawaii's Animal Species Advisory Commission against a full ban on the taking of *honu*. For his part, Kridler resented the suggestion that the upstart junior biologist (who was 24 years younger than Kridler) had begun the tagging and monitoring program in Hawaii. Kridler liked to point out that while working first as the refuge biologist and then manager, he had tagged hundreds of *honu* (in addition to 800 monk seals and thousands of birds) between 1964 and 1973. But despite his best efforts, Kridler's tagging operations were of limited scientific value. As usual, the biggest problem was money. For many years Kridler was the sole FWS administrator for U.S. territories in the Pacific, a domain that included more than 2,000 islands spread across 3.5 million square miles. The Hawaiian Islands Wildlife Refuge itself stretched some 800 miles, and Kridler had to hitch rides on U.S. Coast Guard and Navy vessels for his census trips. He was finally given an assistant, but the workload was still enormous, far beyond what two individuals could reasonably be expected to accomplish. Their tasks included (in addition to tagging turtles, monk seals, and birds) posting and maintaining refuge signs on all islands, conducting plant surveys on land and fish surveys in the sea, interdicting illegal trade in protected animals, and cleaning up mountains of trash left on the islands by the military.

Another problem involved the tags themselves, standard cattle ear tags made of an alloy that included copper and nickel. The tags were fine for land animals, but they corroded quickly in the tropical saltwater of Hawaii. (Balazs noticed this limitation right away and helped develop a long-lasting alloy still used for tagging turtles.) Given all these difficulties, it's not surprising that Kridler was unable to maintain reliable data on the sea turtles he encountered. Nor is it surprising that he took out some of his frustration on Balazs, who was, in essence, the new kid on the block.

But the younger man didn't allow any hard feelings to get in the way of his research on the turtle tumors, and he set about reading Kridler's many unpublished field reports. Balazs was going through a write-up of a 1969 trip to Pearl and Hermes Reef, a remote location over 1,000 miles northwest of Oahu, when he read: "Large growths, similar to cysts, were noted on the necks of two turtles. These growths were surgically removed, and although the turtles bled profusely for a few minutes it appeared that the cuts would eventually heal up."

Asked about the incident today, Kridler laughs about the phrase "surgically removed."

"By pocket knife," he explains. "That's all we had."

Neither turtle had been tagged previously, and Kridler doesn't remember whether he tagged them after the "surgery." But he recalls having seen the growths before and has a photograph of one *honu* with a severe case of the tumors, taken at Pearl and Hermes Reef in September 1966. That pushed back the date when FP was confirmed in Hawaii by more than a year.

Balazs's big break came unexpectedly. While chatting with an NMFS fisheries biologist, Balazs mentioned that he was interested in a tumor disease that afflicted green turtles. He asked biologist John Naughton if he had ever seen anything like it.

"Yeah, I've seen that," Naughton answered casually.

"Do you remember where and when?" Balazs asked.

Naughton said he could do better than that; he had a photograph of the tumored turtle at home, with the date the turtle was caught written right on the back. Balazs nearly grabbed Naughton by the collar and demanded to see the photograph.

It was the kind of snapshot you could find in any family album—grainy, slightly out of focus, the black-and-white emulsion faded with age. Six teenaged boys posed in a ragged semicircle, standing on a grassy area just in front of a beach. They all wore shorts or swimming trunks. Most of them were bare-chested. The photograph was taken on Oahu, on the shore of Kaneohe Bay. The bay appeared in the photo as a nearly white, featureless glow in the background.

The boys had just returned from fishing in the bay. In front of them lay a row of a dozen fish, arranged from smallest to largest, the scales still glittering in the tropical sunlight. Even across the years you could sense the life fading from the fish. Beside the fish was a smaller row of lobsters. A few of the boys looked directly at the camera. The others, by their gaze, drew the viewer to what was obviously the reason for the photo. The last two boys on the right held between them a large juvenile green sea turtle. Each boy gripped a front flipper. The carapace was perhaps two feet long. Balazs had to look closely before noticing the tumors. They were dark, nearly black in the photograph, a welter of fist-sized blobs bubbling along the left flipper. The boy holding the tumored flipper had his thumb carefully positioned near, but not touching, the tumors. That was John Naughton, who was sixteen when the picture was taken. The date on the back of the picture was 25 January 1958.

Balazs insisted that Naughton tell him everything about the turtle and the circumstance in which he found it.

There wasn't much to tell, insisted Naughton. The larger truth was that he was embarrassed to discuss it. As a fisheries biologist (who would later become the Pacific Island Environmental Coordinator for NMFS), Naughton wasn't especially proud of the fact that he had spent his high school years with his buddies plundering Kaneohe Bay.

Like most kids growing up in Hawaii, the group had spent much of their youth out on the water. Naughton and his friends found they could pick up some extra money while having fun, by selling fish to local restaurants and a few regular customers. It was an after-school-and-on-weekends activity. The group sometimes used the new technology of SCUBA, but that was rare. More often, they'd simply free dive from a small boat and take fish with a speargun. Turtles and lobsters they'd grab as they found them. The turtle in the picture was the first tumored one that they had seen, which was why they deemed it worthy of a picture. It was caught at the southern end of the bay, near where the reef crest separates the sheltered waters from the open ocean, and not far from where sewage was released into the bay.

They tried to sell the turtle, but none of their usual customers would buy it. Everyone thought it had cancer. The boys tried to give the turtle away, but there were no takers. In the end, they killed the turtle, kept its shell and threw the rest away.

Of course, Balazs was thrilled to have the photograph. Although the fishermen he questioned said they had on rare occasions seen turtles with tumors years earlier, January 1958 stands as the earliest documentation of FP in the Hawaiian Islands.

Over the next few years, Balazs saw several FP turtles. He took some samples of the tumors, preserved them in a fixative, and sent them off to John Harshbarger. In fact, all five FP samples submitted to the RTLA during the 1970s were collected by Balazs. The first came from an adult female, found bobbing in the surf in May 1975 off Waikiki Beach—the same general location where Balazs had seen his first FP turtle just one year earlier. This turtle had numerous tumors, inside and out. There were dark blobs of tissue on both sides of the animal's head and on her neck and a massive tumor hung from her right shoulder. Tumors had invaded her intestines, and they grew from her right lung and deep within her throat.

The next sample came from a small adult female that had washed up, weak and emaciated, on Kailua Beach on the southeast side of Oahu in April 1977. In addition to tumors on her jaw and right front flipper, large growths covered both the turtle's eyes. She died within hours, probably the result of starvation.

A few months later, in November 1977, Balazs found another tumored turtle, this one in Kaneohe Bay, in what was essentially his back yard. The turtle was smaller than the others—a little more than a foot long and weighing just 27 pounds. It, too, was more dead than alive, with multiple tumors, including growths that covered both eyes. Balazs euthanized it.

In March 1978 the head of a dolphin research center in Honolulu decided it was time to do something about a young adult turtle that had been in a display tank for several years and had, over time, grown a large stalklike tumor on its left front flipper. Balazs was called in. Since the animal appeared otherwise healthy, Balazs arranged to have the tumor surgically removed. After recovering from the operation, the turtle was tagged and released near Diamond Head, that famous peak overlooking Waikiki Beach and all of Honolulu. It was never seen again, but, then, most tagged turtles aren't, and so there's no way of knowing whether the animal survived.

The last sample Balazs collected during the decade of the 1970s was significant because it came from a turtle found on an island other than Oahu. The *honu* was an adult male, with two small neck growths, found basking on tiny Trig Island in French Frigate Shoals in June 1979. Balazs carefully removed the tumors with a sterile scalpel and tagged and released the turtle. Harshbarger's microscopic analysis of the samples made it official: fibropapillomatosis was indeed present in Hawaii, and far away from Oahu.

The decade ended with Balazs concerned by the high incidence of FP among the Hawaii *honu*. Smith and Coates had found the disease affecting just 1.5 percent of the turtles they examined in Florida. Why was the rate so much higher among Hawaii's nesting turtles? The higher prevalence was doubly troubling given the *honu*'s already extremely low population. The last thing the sea turtles needed was a major epidemic. But FP wasn't yet a major focus of Balazs's life. Between his tagging and monitoring program and his attempts to gain legal protection for the overhunted green turtles, the junior biologist had his hands full.

Besides, although the disease seemed serious locally, Balazs had no reason to believe that the tumors were a significant problem anywhere else in the world.

Chapter 6

The Cayman Hotspot

GRAND CAYMAN ISLAND, 1980

THE PROBLEMS BEGAN with the turtles from Isla Mujeras, a small island off the Mexican Gulf Coast. First it was leeches. There was no proof that the Mexican turtles had brought the parasites with them when they had been reprieved from a slaughterhouse in 1977 and flown over to the Cayman Island Turtle Farm. But because thousands of the tiny bloodsuckers first appeared soon after the arrival of the Mexican turtles, the outbreak would be forever linked to these turtles. At least that's how it seemed to Jim Wood, the director of the Cayman Island Turtle Farm.

There was always some health problem to deal with at the Turtle Farm—even before the arrival of the Mexican turtles. Not that the problem was unique to the facility. Wood, a trained zoologist, knew that diseases and the perpetual fight against them was a fact of life for "ranching" of any kind. Placing a large number of animals (of a single species) into a small area is a prescription for outbreaks of all sorts. This is especially true when that environment in question is artificial, as at the Turtle Farm, where the turtles lived in large concrete tanks resembling swimming pools. The number of factors that needed to be controlled in order to keep the turtles healthy was nearly incalculable. Water just a couple of degrees too warm favored the growth of numerous pathogens. If the water were allowed to get too cold, the turtles' immune systems could be compromised, leaving them prey to the many other microbes that lived in the water or resided inside the reptiles' own bodies, waiting for just such an opportunity. And there was the matter of diet. In the wild, young green turtles ate jellyfish and other floating animals and began to switch over to turtle grass or algae when they were a few years old. But in captivity, it wasn't possible to provide those things, and researchers had developed special feed for hatchlings. A few years before Wood's arrival, the farm's owners had tried to cut corners by using a cheaper feed designed for pond catfish. The effort to save a little money had turned into a disaster. Wood was never told exactly how many hatchlings had died back then, but rumors were that the mortality rate was extraordinarily high. The cheap feed was low in niacin, a vitamin which, it turned out, spelled the difference between life and death for the young turtles.

That was just the beginning of the list of infections, infestations, and assorted maladies that periodically swept through the Turtle Farm. A fungal-caused pneumonia left turtles with collapsed and ruptured lungs, killing scores of the reptiles. A herpesvirus was considered the culprit in "gray patch" disease, another potentially fatal condition that had only been seen in farm-reared turtles, never in wild ones. The skin disease struck nearly 100 percent of hatchlings sometime in their first six months of life and either caused a few small bumps or, in more serious cases, a spreading gray blotch of ulcerating and dying skin. With their protective layer of skin gone, many small turtles succumbed to secondary bacterial infections.

And now there was something new to worry about in addition to the leeches. A disease had suddenly appeared in several turtles. It was named LET, an acronym for the parts of the turtles' anatomy that were affected: lungs, eyes, and trachea. Sometime between a year and two years of age, the turtles began to exhibit strange symptoms. They'd gasp noisily for air. Many had problems diving, and an ugly yellow substance

with the consistency of cheese clotted their eyes. Many died, and during
the necropsy Wood found that their tracheas and lungs were full of this
same substance. The farm had experienced periodic outbreaks of LET
since 1975, especially during the colder winter months, but when an
unusually large number of turtles came down with the illness in 1980,
Wood, who was both a good scientist and a prudent manager, realized
that whatever was happening, the situation was beyond him. It was time
to call in an expert. As far as Wood was concerned there was only one
person to call. The director of the Turtle Farm went into his tiny office,
picked up the phone, and dialed Elliott Jacobson.

Reptile enthusiasts tend to be a bit .... unusual. And why not? Anyone can love a dog or a cat, but it takes a special kind of person to have
warm feelings about cold-blooded creatures. The very term "cold-
blooded" is viewed negatively. Where most pets have soft fur that seems
to invite the probing attentiveness of human fingers, reptiles are covered
with scales, flinty and cold. Domesticated animals walk or run about on
four legs. Most reptiles slither or soundlessly scurry as if they are per-
petually stalking you (which is, in fact, often the case). There's something about the crimson flash of a snake's forked tongue or the
now-you-see-it-now-you-don't flicker of a lizard's nictitating membrane, the clear film that acts as a third eyelid, that gives most people the
willies—and thrills a select few.

Certainly no other group of creatures comes with so much negative
cultural baggage. Of course, there is the snake in Genesis, who beguiles
Eve into eating the forbidden fruit, causing mankind's expulsion from
Eden. Even God—who created the snake in the first place and so was, at
least at first, presumably a reptile enthusiast—turns snake-hater, thundering: "Because thou hast done this, thou art cursed above all cattle,
and above every beast of the field; upon thy belly shalt thou go, and
dust shalt thou eat all the days of thy life." The first creature to be
cursed by God—talk about inauspicious beginnings. And there are the
secular phrases that reflect the low regard given reptiles. Calling someone a "snake in the grass" or a "lounge lizard" is no compliment.

Given this background, it's not surprising that those who love reptiles appear quirky in all sorts of ways. Even when they become scientists or veterinarians specializing in reptiles, they are often a breed apart from their peers. One general-practice veterinarian recalls a conference at which he happened to look in on a session about reptile diseases: "I stuck my head in the door and the audience of veterinarians looked like a scene from the *Star Wars* bar," he says. "They're some pretty crazy and wild individuals who get involved with reptiles."

The vet could easily have been describing Elliott Jacobson, the man Jim Wood turned to in 1980 following the outbreak of LET. Jacobson, the scientist, is widely respected by his peers. When asked to describe him professionally, the words "brilliant," "nimble-minded," "rigorous," and "pioneer" are frequently employed. He is invited to give lectures on reptile medicine at prestigious institutions around the world. He has published 200 scientific papers, most of them appearing in the top veterinary journals, and has written chapters for thirty books. In 1986 alone, Jacobson's name appeared on sixteen journal articles and three book chapters.

Despite Jacobson's eminence in his field, there is no way around the fact that he shares some of the unusual characteristics common to reptile enthusiasts. The most obvious is his striking appearance. Jacobson's eyes are so icy-blue that they seem to fade into the white background, giving the distinctly unsettling impression that he lacks irises altogether. The fact that his large Fu-Manchu mustache calls to mind the fangs of his favorite creatures only adds to the effect.

Many reptile lovers have a fondness for high-performance motorcycles ("it's probably the danger of both activities," suggests one insider), and Jacobson shared this trait. For years, he roared around the University of Florida campus on his beloved BMW motorcycle. Jacobson once totaled his bike in an accident that left him seriously injured. For many bikers, that's the end of the sport. But not for Jacobson. As soon as he was ambulatory, Jacobson limped out and bought another BMW.

Born in 1945, the grandson of Russian immigrants, Jacobson grew up in the tough working-class neighborhoods of Bensonhurst, New

York. Although he left there in 1967, his accent still betrays his origins, and he refers to himself as a "card-carrying New Yorker." Asked when he first became interested in biology, he answers, straight-faced, "at the age of three." He explains that he "started collecting insects in the back-yards of New York City ever since I could crawl around." By the ripe old age of six he had already decided on a career in entomology. A couple of years later he received a turtle as a pet and switched allegiance to reptiles.

In his early years at the University of Florida (where he began his veterinary residency in 1977), Jacobson was well known as a bon vivant who loved parties, played intricate and frequently off-color practical jokes, and both got along, and quarreled, with people of all kinds. His more conventional scientific colleagues, those who knew Jacobson only as a meticulous researcher and dedicated teacher, were often amazed when they'd attend a party at Jacobson's house and find the rooms packed with people who seemed strange and even disreputable: chop-per-driving, tattooed and bearded snake lovers who drank heavily, laughed loudly, and didn't even know how to pronounce the word "tenure." The first time one of his colleagues came to a get-together at Jacobson's house, the man wondered whether a motorcycle gang had crashed the party. And then he spotted Jacobson in the middle of it all, laughing and swapping stories about his most recent snake bite, show-ing off the fresh puncture wounds, and thoroughly enjoying himself.

Over the years, Jacobson has accumulated a collection of wounds. The most significant are the fine dimples on his left hand that he got in a tussle with a fifteen-foot-long reticulated python he had raised since birth. He was feeding it a rat one night in the early 1980s when the snake struck, grabbing not just the rodent, but Jacobson's hand as well. With its fangs deeply inserted into the joint space of the vet's little fin ger, the snake had a good hold of its prey. It quickly threw coils around Jacobson's body, trapping his other arm behind his back. The snake began inching up his body, throwing coils higher and higher and mov-ing toward Jacobson's neck where it could suffocate him. In the end,

Jacobson got lucky. The snake let go on its own, "probably because it was exhausted from the effort," says Jacobson. Minutes later, a colleague spotted Jacobson walking down the hallway, lacerations covering his hand.

"What happened to you?" asked the horrified man.

"Oh, one of my big snakes got me," replied Jacobson casually as he continued on his way to his lab.

All in all, it's safe to say that Elliott Jacobson is a complex fellow.

Of course, it was for his expertise in reptile diseases, rather than for his personality, that Jim Wood called on Jacobson in 1980. The Florida vet had been to the Turtle Farm before, first in 1978 to diagnose and treat turtles with what turned out to be fungal pneumonia. This time, he went right to work, performing necropsies on several turtles that had died from LET. It was while Jacobson was taking a break from this grisly work that Wood asked if he'd like to take a look at an ailing female Mexican turtle. Why not? Jacobson replied.

The turtle had tumors. Although none were large, the growths were numerous. They sprouted from the corners of the turtle's eyes, from its eyelids, and from the skin where the creature's limbs attached to its body.

Jacobson wanted to know whether any other turtles had similar growths. Yes, said Wood, some did. The manager had first noticed them on a couple of the turtles brought from Mexico in 1977 and had watched as others from the same group developed tumors over the next couple of years. The trend wasn't exactly encouraging.

Jacobson recognized the tumors as the fibropapilloma growths described by Smith and Coates in 1938. But as George Balazs had already learned from his research in Hawaii, this diagnosis meant little more in 1980 than it had more than forty years earlier. The cause of FP was still unknown, and there had been no long-term studies on the course of the disease. Given the lack of information, any thought of a cure was premature. Jacobson's first thought was that the disease was caused by a virus. In his head, the veterinarian quickly reviewed what was known about viruses and similar growths. The early work in the area had, of course, been done on humans, beginning in the golden age of germ theory, ushered in by Louis Pasteur's studies of microbes and their role in disease. In 1891, a London doctor with the Dickensian name of Payne, took a scraping from a child's wart and inoculated himself with the material. Small tough growths sprang from the inoculation site, and Payne announced that the common wart was caused by microbes of some sort. Another physician, one G. Giuffo, took a giant step toward discovering the type of microbe that resulted in warts when, in 1907, he forced a mixture of ground up warts and water through a fine filter and injected himself with the resulting liquid. Like Payne, Giuffo developed warts. Since the holes in the filter were too small to allow bacteria through, he concluded that viruses, which are much smaller than bacteria, had to be the cause of warts. Positive confirmation of Giuffo's hypothesis had to wait until the invention of the electron microscope. In 1949 researchers used the electron microscope to observe the virus itself, which was named the human papillomavirus (HPV). It is a spectacularly diverse family; more than 100 strains of HPV have already been described.

The papillomavirus isn't limited to humans. Far from it. Ever since a researcher isolated a papillomavirus from a rabbit in 1933, virologists have been finding related viruses almost wherever they looked. Papillomaviruses have been positively identified in cattle (six separate strains have been isolated), deer, horses, dogs, rodents, and birds. Other forms of the papillomavirus are suspected of causing abnormal growths in sheep, coyotes, wolves, opossums, antelopes, beavers, bears, monkeys, chimpanzees, giraffes, elephants, whales, and land turtles and are implicated in afflictions of cats, guinea pigs, gerbils, elk, dolphins, pigs, goats, rhinoceroses, camels, skunks, badgers, lemurs, caribou, armadillos, newts, and snakes. Jacobson had good reason to suspect that if a virus were the cause of FP, then a papillomavirus was the culprit.

But assuming this was true, how was the virus transmitted from one turtle to another? Wood thought leeches were the key. His reasoning was simple: The Mexican turtles were the first to show tumors, and the outbreak of leeches coincided with the arrival of the Mexican turtles. It was possible, and perhaps likely, that the virus used the leeches as a vector, or carrier of the disease. Such a strategy is quite common in the viral world. While some viruses can move directly between host organisms, others need a vector, a third organism, to carry them inside the target host. The vector rarely appears sick. In fact, it wouldn't make a very good vector if the presence of the virus slowed it down. The whole purpose is for the virus to hitch a ride into a new host—it likes its vector healthy and aggressive.

Searching for a vector would be skipping a step, Jacobson knew, for there wasn't any proof that the tumors were caused by a virus. The first step was to find out if the condition were even transmittable. It was always possible that the turtles sprouted growths not because they were infecting each other, but because they were subject to identical environmental factors. The hatchling die-off that preceded Wood's arrival at the Turtle Farm was a good example of this dynamic. The fact that many turtles were dying at about the same time seemed to suggest a disease spreading through the facility. But in that case, the cause was traced to the turtles' food. No disease. No vectors. Just a poor diet.

So Jacobson started the first real transmission study since Smith and Coates's mention of such an experiment. It was, as he recalls, a "very crude" study. He removed a tumor section from the Mexican female and, essentially, blended it with saltwater and injected the concoction into several two-week-old turtles. The turtles were left at the Turtle Farm, and Jacobson never heard anything more about them.

It was a missed opportunity to get a handle on FP at the very early stages of the epidemic. But the lack of interest in the study didn't surprise Jacobson.

"LET was the major disease that we were working on," recalls Jacobson. "This [FP] was just incidental—they didn't want to put a lot into it. But that's typical of lots of farms. They love other people to come in and work things up. They'll provide you with all the material you want. But they don't want to put money into it. Veterinary medicine and disease is often the last thing that is supported in most farming operations. They don't see the long-term worth. 'How's this going to save me money?' Some farms have been completely devastated by pathogens. It's a real naïve way of looking at things."

Without funding, Jacobson had to abandon the FP work he had begun at the Turtle Farm. Jim Wood did what he could to track FP at the farm on his own, but without the financial support of the farm's owners, any experimentation involving FP was impossible. The Turtle Farm's role in the history of this epidemic would likely have ended here, if it hadn't been for a controversial initiative begun by the farm in 1980. The whole notion of turtle ranching had been marked by controversy since its inception in the late 1960s. Some turtle experts believed that raising turtles in captivity would reduce hunting pressure on dwindling sea turtle stocks in the wild. Others argued that ranching increased the demand for sea turtle meat and so encouraged hunting. Opponents also argued that the interbreeding of turtles from distinct wild populations would lead to genetic mingling with unforeseeable consequences. George Balazs weighed in as an early and vocal critic of the Cayman Island Turtle Farm. In this, he was on the other side of the fence from Elliott Jacobson. In 1978 Jacobson praised the farm in a letter submitted to a U.S. government agency, concluding that "I feel that Cayman Turtle Farm offers a unique situation to scientifically study the green sea turtle in captivity, and information gathered on biology, disease, and medicine should contribute to the success of wild turtle populations." Later, Jacobson would distance himself from the Turtle Farm.

The debate was sometimes rancorous, with biologists trading charges of emotion over rationality, commerce over good science, and rash action—rushing into turtle ranching—over a more prudent approach. The issue strained friendships within the sea turtle scientific community.

One of the many objections to the farm was the possibility of introducing diseases into the wild when farm-reared turtles were released. For several years this argument was moot, because the farm released few turtles—they were too busy building up their stocks for breeding or butchering. But in 1980 the farm's breeding animals were so prolific that the owners needed to do something with the "excess" turtles. Rather than kill the endangered animals, it seemed to make more sense to release them into the waters surrounding the island. These releases (which became annual) also gave the farm greater legitimacy as a conservation program, rather than as a purely commercial enterprise. And visitors to the island were delighted to watch cute turtle hatchlings scrambling down the beach and paddling into the water. Soon the Turtle Farm was making more money as a tourist attraction than as a supplier of turtle meat. In the first decade of the release program, nearly 27,000 turtles were dispersed into the wild. Most of the turtles found permanent homes in the waters surrounding Grand Cayman Island, but a tagging-recapture program determined that other turtles made their way to Cuba, the United States, Honduras, Nicaragua, Belize, Venezuela, and Mexico. The owners of the farm argued that this proved their operation was a significant conservation operation, bringing new life to all parts of the Caribbean. If the farm-reared turtles had a transmittable disease, however, then wherever they traveled they carried within them the potential not just for life, but for illness and death as well.

During the 1980 FP outbreak, the concern over the disease spreading into the wild seemed purely academic. Wood hadn't yet heard about the outbreak in Hawaii, and, even if he had, the Pacific archipelago was too distant to be linked to problems at the Caribbean island. And Elliott Jacobson, who kept abreast of any epidemics involving reptiles, knew that no one had reported an increase in the disease in nearby turtle populations. But that was about to change.

Chapter 7

Turtleheads

To a visitor, there are few places in Florida more beautiful than the Indian River Lagoon. The Indian River Lagoon isn't a river and it's not exactly a lagoon, either. Stretching more than one hundred fifty miles, the Indian River Lagoon is an anthology of coastal waterways: rivers, streams, creeks, canals, sloughs, mangrove islands, sandbars, lagoons, ponds, inlets, swamps, marshes, embayments, sounds, coves, mud flats, and estuaries, all forming a gradual segue between the flatlands to the west and the wide Atlantic ocean to the east. The water within the Indian River Lagoon shows its hybrid origins. Freshwater flows into the Indian River Lagoon from rivers and creeks and it percolates through the ground, mixing with the saltwater that is carried by the tides through a handful of small inlets, breaks in the sandy barrier islands and clumps of mangroves that are the continent's last tremulous and shifting redoubt before giving way to the sea.

At first glance, the Indian River Lagoon appears to be an unlikely candidate for ground zero in a devastating epidemic. But if the modern scourge of FP can be said to have an epicenter in Florida, one could make a reasonable claim that it is here, in the brackish waters of the

Indian River Lagoon. It's possible to be quite precise about the location. On a map, the coordinates read 27° 54' 30" North, 80° 29' West, a place known as Mullet Creek Flats. One can even fix the epidemic's origin in time: 1 July 1982 at 10:20 A.M.

At dawn on that date, three bleary-eyed individuals, a young woman and two young men, climbed aboard a seventeen-foot single-engine Boston Whaler and headed out onto the Indian River Lagoon in search of turtles. They were members of the University of Central Florida's Marine Turtle Research Group. That was their official title. Paul Raymond, a former group member, puts it another way. "We were Turtleheads," he says, using a term that conveys something of the character of that zealous and merry band. "Turtleheads through and through."

They were a disparate group, including undergraduates, graduate students, and some individuals who didn't fit in either category. What they had in common was an obsession with sea turtles. The Turtleheads would stay up all night, observing female sea turtles as they crawled out of the surf to dig holes in the sand and lay their clutches of gleaming white eggs. Before the turtles headed back to sea, the Turtleheads would tag them with small, numbered metal tags, fastened to the turtles' flippers. Exhausted, they'd return to their base of operations, a seedy motel named (with no apparent irony) "Holiday Haven." The Turtleheads would crash for a couple of hours, crawl out of their sleeping bags at dawn, and go netting for turtles in the Indian River Lagoon. The afternoons were invariably spent repairing the three-wheeled motorcycles with which they patrolled the beaches. It was exhausting work, and for their efforts they were paid subpoverty wages—when they were paid at all. But the experience was intellectually and emotionally stimulating beyond what any of them had known. The ardor wasn't entirely due to the considerable and undeniable charms of sea turtles. The Turtleheads were, after all, healthy young men and women. Romantic attachments arose and collapsed—sometimes quite noisily—with the tides and seasons.

Paul Raymond, now a senior law-enforcement official with NMFS, fondly recalls those days. "There was this tremendous camaraderie among us," he explains in a voice honeyed by nostalgia. "We loved, lived, and died for the sea turtles."

The three Turtleheads who climbed into the boat on the morning of 1 July 1982, were Becky Bolt, Rick Smith, and Bill Redfoot. A notation on their data sheet for that day describes conditions as being "sunny, hot; 20% chance of rain." Hot and muggy. A typical Florida summer day. The trio headed for Mullet Creek Flats. When they arrived, they set out their "tangle" net, over 200 yards of twisted nylon twine with an eight-inch square mesh. In addition to turtles, both Becky and Rick studied fish. At around 9 o'clock they tossed out a much smaller device, a monofilament gill net with a three-inch mesh, only a hundred feet long, to see what kind of fish they could catch in the lagoon. Then the crew sat back and chatted, trying to stay cool in the growing heat, while they waited to check the net. All three got along well. Becky and Rick were dating at the time (one Turtlehead romance with staying power; they were married a few years later). Redfoot was older than the couple and wasn't a student at the time. He had earned a master's degree in education a decade earlier and was teaching at a nearby community college. But he loved sea turtles and leapt at every opportunity to help out with any research that involved them.

At around 10 o'clock the crew hauled in the tangle net. It was empty.

At 10:20, Rick and Becky decided to examine the gill net. As they tugged on it, they instantly felt resistance.

"There's something big down there!" called Becky.

When they yanked the net into the boat they were surprised to find, not a fish, but a green sea turtle. That was extremely unusual. The turtles nesting out on the beaches were mostly loggerheads. In the lagoon, loggerheads were also the most common species, although the individuals were nearly always juveniles or subadults. This green turtle was small and young, nearly perfectly fitting the metaphor biologists use to describe turtles of this age: dinner-plate sized. It was less than a foot long and weighed just under nine pounds; about the size and weight of a healthy human baby.

"Whoa," said Rick, when he had extracted the turtle from the gill net. "What are *those*?"

They were tumors. The small turtle had large masses of pink cauliflowerlike growths completely covering the area where its rear flippers emerged from between the plastron and the carapace. It also had close to a dozen smaller tumors in front, on its neck and around the front flippers.

"We kept asking each other, what do you think this is?" remembers Becky. "We were trying to figure out if it was a growth, or a parasite, or if it had an injury. We touched it and thought, 'Yuck! We probably shouldn't be touching this thing. Wash your hands, wash your hands!'"

Rick recalls that the tumors resembled coagulated popcorn.

"It's like if you were to take popcorn and get it wet," he explains. "It would still maintain a mass but the surface would be very rough, going up and down and all around. I'd never seen this before or even heard of anybody describing this in class. We made all these guesses, but the truth was that we really had no idea of what it could have been."

When a turtle was caught in the lagoon, it was standard operating procedure to record its vital statistics, clip on metal flipper tags and then release the animal back into the lagoon. This time, however, the group decided that they had to show this turtle to their professor, who, they knew, would be waiting for them back at the boat dock. They started up the whaler's engine and headed in to shore. They pulled up to Honest John's Fish Camp at around 11 o'clock. Standing on the dock were Paul Raymond and Professor Llewellyn M. Ehrhart.

No one called him Professor or Dr. Ehrhart. He was referred to as Lew, or, more often, by his nickname, "Doc." Forty years old in 1982, Ehrhart was already recognized as one of the top sea turtle biologists in the field. He had received his doctorate in vertebrate zoology at Cornell University in the 1960s and had a decade of field experience under his belt with articles published in several prestigious journals. Despite these impressive credentials, Ehrhart's primary position was that of chief Turtlehead. He had an easygoing demeanor and a knack for awakening the "Turtlehead" slumbering within students. A large man, a former high school athlete gracefully sliding into middle age, he loved field-work, even relishing all the gritty and physically demanding conditions that came along with studying animals in the wild. The one thing he detested was formality in any guise. Standing on the dock at Honest John's, Ehrhart could have been mistaken for a beach bum. He was dressed in his usual outfit of shorts and a ragged T-shirt, sunglasses, san-dals, and a bandanna headband. His boyishly handsome face bore a layer of stubble, with at least a few grains of sand mixed in. At this moment, there was something else on his face: a look of shock when the crew handed him the green turtle that had blundered into their gill net.

"I was stunned," Ehrhart recalls. "It just completely knocked me out."

His field notes for that day are written in the more banal prose of science. "Surprisingly they caught a small green turtle ... in the gill net," he wrote in a spidery, nearly illegible scrawl, and then added: "It had odd growths on its skin."

He had never seen anything like the tumors, a fact that was telling in itself. If anyone in the area should have seen growths like these before, it was Lew Ehrhart. He had seen hundreds of sea turtles since beginning to work with them, in a career that grew, improbably, out of the nation's space program. In 1972, when Ehrhart was teaching ecology as a junior faculty member at the University of Central Florida, the National Aeronautics and Space Administration (NASA) announced plans to build a new runway at the Kennedy Space Center. This would be a very special runway, to be used by the Space Shuttle, NASA's newest, most ambitious program since the moon shot program of the 1960s. The giant orbiter required an outsized runway. It would be the largest hard-surfaced runway in the world—nearly three miles long and a football field wide—surrounded by a dazzling array of sophisticated naviga-tional systems, signal lights, emergency buildings, and, of course, bleachers on which visiting dignitaries could be photographed welcom-ing the shuttle home.

The problem was that the area chosen for the new super-runway was located, like all of the Kennedy Space Center, in an environmentally sensitive area called the Merritt Island National Wildlife Refuge—220 square miles of salt marshes, brackish estuaries, hardwood hammocks, groves of native pine, and long, white-sand beaches. In spots, great blue herons are as thick as sparrows in a city. Come around a corner too quickly and a volley of egrets explodes into the sky. On the shore surrounding the marshes, cormorants jam themselves onto every sunny tree limb, resembling sleepy commuters waiting for the morning train. (The cormorants lack oil glands at the base of their feathers and so must wait for hours with their wings outstretched, drying.) And these are only a few of the permanent avian residents. The refuge is located on the Atlantic flyway, the primary migrating route for birds east of the Mississippi River. Before the runway could be built, NASA had to assess the impact such a huge project would have on the sensitive flora and fauna of Merritt Island. Since Ehrhart had written his doctoral dissertation on rodents of Florida, it was only logical that he was hired to be part of this team.

In the summer of 1973, Ehrhart was spending most of his time on Merritt Island catching spotted skunks for a population survey. Another biologist mentioned in passing that sea turtles nested on the nearby beaches.

"Really?" asked Ehrhart, intrigued. "How many?"

The scientist shrugged and gave him an incredulous look: "How the hell should I know?"

Back then, sea turtles were just another vertebrate to Ehrhart. One more animal to check out for the inventory. He knew that they were marine reptiles and that they nested at night during the summer, and that was about all he knew. But he was curious, so one night he managed to get his hands on a 1950s-era surplus military jeep that had been converted into a poor-man's dune buggy and went bouncing over the sand along Playalinda Beach, five miles east of the proposed shuttle runway. It was late into the night when he saw his first sea turtle crawling out of the surf.

"It was just incredible," Ehrhart says. "*They're* incredible. We take sea turtles for granted, but they're simply amazing creatures. If they were extinct and we knew them only from fossils, we'd be as fascinated by them as we are by T-Rex."

From that first sighting on Playalinda Beach, Ehrhart was hooked. He had been transformed into a full-fledged Turtlehead on the spot. Ehrhart would have preferred to spend every night monitoring and tagging sea turtles, but his other responsibilities limited his nighttime forays that first summer. Still, he managed to tag, measure, and weigh fifty-one turtles in 1973. In the summer of 1974, Ehrhart spent more time out counting nesting sites and found 111 turtles. In 1975 he recorded 120 loggerheads. By 1976 Ehrhart had convinced NASA to fund a full-fledged study of the local sea turtle population. It would turn out to be one small step for a man, but one giant leap for turtle kind. For the first two years of the study, a lack of reliable vehicles kept Ehrhart off the beaches on several occasions. The refuge provided two surplus jeeps, but neither of them was dependable. In 1977 NASA added a pickup truck to Ehrhart's ragtag fleet, but in July all three vehicles were broken down at the same time. The addition of a three-wheeled all-terrain vehicle (ATV) helped, but that conveyance didn't always work either. Finally, in 1978, Ehrhart managed to beg or borrow enough working vehicles, including three ATVs, so that the Turtleheads were able to conduct beach surveys six nights a week all summer long. From mid-May until late August, Ehrhart and his crew were on the beaches counting nesting turtles, from 9 P.M. until 3 or 4 A.M. The results were beyond anyone's expectations. All along Playalinda Beach, loggerhead turtles were nesting at the rate of up to 78 turtles per kilometer, depositing perhaps half a million eggs each summer. As Ehrhart concluded in his report to NASA, "from the point of view of nesting density, extent of nesting habitat, and potential for long-term conservation and management, no section of beach more important to the survival of western Atlantic loggerheads exists anywhere."

Another surprise was the number of green sea turtles nesting in the area. When Ehrhart had begun his study, one biologist had estimated the total number of adult females in Florida at just fifty. In the summer of 1978, the Turtleheads had counted fourteen nesting females on the one beach.

Ehrhart wasn't interested in just the turtles nesting on the Atlantic beaches, however. Those were easy enough to count. The turtles came out of the ocean. They dug nests in the sand. They deposited their eggs. Nothing to it, when the vehicles were working, other then staying awake all night. But Ehrhart suspected that a considerable number of turtles lived unseen in the lagoonal waters adjacent to the Kennedy Space Center. He had no proof of this, but he believed it was true because while working to establish historical baseline figures for turtle populations in the area, Ehrhart had stumbled upon government records from the last century. On the yellowing and brittle pages of reports sent to Congress by the United States Commission of Fish and Fisheries, Ehrhart read a description of a turtle fishery that thrived briefly in the Indian River Lagoon.

The fishery was centered some eighty miles south of the Kennedy Space Center, around the town of Sebastian. In the mid-1800s Sebastian was a small fishing village, similar to many others that clung to the banks of the Indian River Lagoon. Residents periodically skirmished with the Seminole Indians whom they had already largely displaced. They attempted to shelter themselves from the voracious salt-marsh mosquito that descended in great humming clouds several feet thick and hundreds of yards wide. But mostly, the citizens of Sebastian surrendered themselves to the torpor produced by the blinding sunlight and stifling humidity. One of the town's first white settlers was a German immigrant named August Park, who had arrived on the shores of the Indian River Lagoon in 1865. He made a modest fortune speculating in real estate and operating a trading boat that plied the waters along a ninety-mile stretch between Titusville in the north and Fort Pierce to the south. His granddaughter Mildred told a local historian in 1990 that August Park also "caught greenback turtles and shipped them to New York." She was almost certainly referring to green sea turtles, for the meat from logger-heads, which were also found in the Indian River Lagoon, was nobody's idea of good eating. Loggerhead meat was described in one nineteenth-century report as being "leathery and oily, and smells very strongly of musk; it is therefore, not generally eaten although some pretend that they have partaken of its flesh without nausea."

Other accounts from that era list several turtlers operating in the area, including one Mills Burnham, described as "a versatile individual ... [who] also became one of the area's first commercial fishermen." Using a schooner named *The Josephine*, Burnham caught turtles in the Indian River Lagoon and then sailed his catch up to Charleston, South Carolina, where he sold them to a middleman who, in turn, shipped the turtles to England.

August Park's family spent half the year living on the eastern side of the Indian River Lagoon, at a spot known as Blue Hole, near the in-let the turtles swam through to enter the lagoon. The other half of the year the Parks lived in town, presumably during the summer months when the turtle fishery closed down, due to the arrival into the lagoon of a large number of sharks. The German entrepreneur Park had five sons, one of whom was named Charles. This was probably the Charles "Pearke" interviewed by a government agent in the 1890s—who, it was said, "had followed the turtle business during the past ten years." According to that report, Charles caught turtles in mesh nets, 85 to 115 yards long. Some nets were staked down in the turtle's feeding grounds and checked for captures twice a day. Other nets were left to drift in the lagoon, watched over by two-man crews. When a turtle blundered into the net, the crew immediately pulled it into their boat.

Charles Park told the agent that he and his crews captured 2,500 tur-tles in 1886. In the winter of 1878, eight fishermen are recorded as hav-ing pulled only 1,600 turtles from the same waters. Even fewer turtles were caught the next year, although there were now sixteen fishermen working the lagoon. In 1895, Park reportedly caught a mere 60 turtles, a decline he blamed on the steamboats that by that time regularly traveled those waters. The more likely reason, however, was long-term overfishing by Park, Burnham, and others. The turtle fishery was, to use the official and evocative term, crashing. Another indication of this decline was the ever-shrinking size of the turtles pulled from the lagoon. The average weight of an Indian River turtle caught in 1890 was 50 pounds. In 1895 that average was down to just 36 pounds—a reduction of nearly 30 percent in just five years.

The last nail in the coffin was a natural disaster known in local lore as the "Great Freeze of 1894–95." Temperatures that winter plummeted to levels unheard of in the Deep South, killing acres of the orange trees that were already making the state famous and citrus growers rich. The freeze was also disastrous for sea turtles living in the lagoon. Sea turtles, like other reptiles, are poikilothermic, or cold-blooded. Unlike mammals, turtles are unable to use their metabolism to maintain their body temperature. They are pretty much at the mercy of their environment, which is why most sea turtles are restricted to warm tropical waters. (The only exception is the giant leatherback turtle, which is found in colder northern waters and may, to some degree, be warm-blooded.) Turtles have developed a number of strategies for dealing with extremes in temperature—the most common and useful is their ability to simply pick up and move when the water is too cold or too hot. Another escape from the cold is found in brumation, something like hibernation in mammals, for which turtles burrow headfirst into the muddy lagoon bottom and remain inactive until the water warms up. Although the phenomenon isn't well-understood, brumation is thought to be triggered when the water temperature drops below 60°F. But even this adaptation won't help if the water temperature drops below 46°F. Such chilly waters are usually lethal.

The lagoon around Sebastian is a particularly treacherous place for young sea turtles. The water there is shallow, with an average depth of only around five feet. When a cold wind blows from the north, the lagoon cools rapidly. The area offers only one outlet to the sea, making it nearly impossible for turtles to find their way out to warmer oceanic waters during a cold snap. It was this combination of shallow water and the lack of an escape route that doomed the turtle population near Sebastian during the Great Freeze. Hundreds, possibly thousands, of "cold-stunned" animals floated to the surface during that event, unable to move and easy prey for the turtlers, who simply rowed out into the lagoon and pulled the helpless creatures into their boats. Unlike the citrus growers, the turtlers must have supposed the event a blessing, for they had such an abundance of turtles that year that they shipped them by the crateload to northern cities as far away as New York's Fulton Fish Market. Any celebration in Sebastian would have been short lived, however. The turtle fishery was already on the verge of collapse, and it never recovered from that "bountiful" year. The government report concluded that "Since the cold spell turtles have been much scarcer than ever." In point of fact, the fishery had effectively vanished. Within a decade, the only evidence that Sebastian harbored a major fishery for *Chelonia mydas* was the name, found on navigational charts, "Turtle Pen Slough" where August Park's turtles awaited shipping to market.

From this tale of devastation, Ehrhart figured that there may still have been sea turtles living in the Indian River Lagoon, perhaps as far north as the Kennedy Space Center. After all, they did nest on the ocean-side beaches in that area. Ehrhart ran a small pilot study in 1975 and confirmed that some turtles did, indeed, live in Mosquito Lagoon, a section of the Indian River Lagoon just north of Merritt Island. Between July 1976 and September 1981, he and his students conducted the first investigation of sea turtles living in the Indian River Lagoon since the government reports of the 1890s. Using nets like the ones deployed by the fishermen at Sebastian, the budding Turtleheads set out to determine just how many turtles, and of what species, lived in the three interconnected bodies of water surrounding Merritt Island: Mosquito Lagoon, the Banana River, and the Indian River itself. As time went on, the initial enthusiasm for the project began to slip away. It was tough, grueling work, netting turtles in the heat and suffocating humidity. But that wasn't the real problem, not for aspiring Turtleheads. The trouble was that their efforts weren't productive. After nearly 300 hours spent netting on the Banana River, the team had failed to capture a single turtle. The results were only slightly more encouraging on the Indian River, where 1,637 hours on the nets produced a grand total of two turtles. Only in Mosquito Lagoon were turtles seen regularly—and even there captures were infrequent. Only two turtles were caught for every three days out. It was beginning to look as if Ehrhart's hunch were wrong. In a journal article about the investigation, Ehrhart admitted that four and a half years into the five-year study, "there was no evidence for the existence of significant populations of marine turtles" anywhere except in Mosquito Lagoon. But, he continued, "This conclusion was difficult to accept because of the occasional carcass strandings and [sightings] by fishermen that were reported."

But everything changed during the second week of January 1981.

Several miles up in the frigid atmosphere above the Canadian arctic, the polar jet stream, that enormous body of cold air racing at speeds in excess of 300 miles per hour, began to creep southward. In two days, the cold front generated by the southern loop in the jet stream had blanketed the eastern two-thirds of the United States with bitterly cold air. In upstate New York, the temperature plummeted to −18°F. All along the eastern seaboard the blast of chilled air created havoc. A commuter ferry off Nantucket Island was frozen solid in ice and had to be rescued by the Coast Guard. With the supply of natural gas dwindling, the governor of Massachusetts declared an "energy emergency," closed down all gas-heated schools, and warned of an imminent statewide "industrial shutdown" if a break in the cold weren't forthcoming. On 12 January the arctic winds roared into the Sunshine State, hitting Florida with some of the coldest temperatures on record. In the state capital, Tallahassee, the temperature dropped to an unheard-of eight degrees above zero. In Jacksonville, one man died of hypothermia when the mercury hit a low of 19°. Even in subtropical Key West, it was so cold that a group of tourists frantically called their travel agent "asking would I please get them out of there and to someplace warm."

Orange growers were hit hard by the freeze. Throughout the bitterly cold nights of 12 and 13 January, workers across Florida's central citrus belt labored, mostly in vain, to protect oranges from the freezing temperatures. They placed fuel-oil heaters called smudge pots throughout the orchards, sprayed millions of gallons of water on trees to coat oranges with a insulating layer of ice, and even pressed helicopters into service in an attempt to use the turbulence to mix cold and warm air. Despite these efforts, 20 percent of the state's orange crop failed to survive those two freezing nights.

The same arctic air that caused such damage in the citrus groves fell across the shallow waters of the upper Indian River Lagoon. Surface water temperature in the early morning hours of 13 January dropped to 38°F. Lew Ehrhart, remembering the massive cold-stunning event that followed the Great Freeze of 1894–95, knew that the anomaly would prove whether large numbers of turtles lived in the Indian River Lagoon. He stationed his students at strategic locations along the water and waited. They didn't have to wait long. One by one, turtles began to bob to the surface. In one week, the group had pulled 163 turtles from the water, most of which survived. Seventy-seven were found in Mosquito Lagoon, and 86 came from the Indian River, with the species nearly equally divided between green turtles and loggerheads. With his NASA contract set to expire in just a few months, Ehrhart had gotten the break he needed. It's not hard to get a sense of the pride, satisfaction, and outright relief behind the scientific prose in Ehrhart's journal article titled "Marine Turtles of the Indian River Lagoon System."

"This was the first evidence, then, of significant populations of green turtles and loggerheads in the Indian River," he wrote, concluding that the Indian River Lagoon was an important developmental habitat for sea turtles.

Now that he had the evidence he needed, Ehrhart was keen to extend his study farther down the Indian River Lagoon, especially toward Sebastian, the heart of the old sea turtle industry. The problem was, of course, money. NASA had no reason to fund sea turtle research so miles south of the Kennedy Space Center. So Ehrhart began beating the sparse bushes of wildlife research for a few dollars to spend on turtles. The biologist had already been warned by his former colleagues at Cornell that turtles were a dead end. Who ever heard of big bucks going toward anything in herpetology? they asked him. Their admonitions were like the famous scene from the movie *The Graduate*. A neighbor pulls young Dustin Hoffman's character aside and whispers a single word of advice in his ear: *"Plastics!"* Instead of *"plastics"* the word Ehrhart's fellow scientists whispered to him was *"Mammals!"*

If you want to advance in the field and get research funds, go after mammals, they urged. Preferably "charismatic megavertebrates," those superstars of the animal world, spectacular creatures that have a grip on the public's imagination: elephants, tigers, or, best of all, the adorable and rare panda. "Fangs or fur," as some put it. But, for heaven's sake, they advised him, don't go chasing after turtles!

Ehrhart thanked his friends for their advice. Then he ignored them. He was, after all—in the words of Paul Raymond—a Turtlehead through and through. But others in the scientific establishment were not. The simple truth was that turtles lacked cachet, and, as a result, the biologists who studied them lacked cash. Zeal and ingenuity, of the kind ably demonstrated by the Turtleheads, just wasn't enough.

It was by a combination of serendipity and necessity that Ehrhart turned his attention to the turtles to the south. In 1981 Paul Raymond was working on his University of Central Florida master's thesis, documenting the effect of beach renourishment on sea turtles. (Renourishment is the process of dredging sand from nearshore waters and pumping it onto beaches, an attempt to counteract erosion.) Through the Army Corps of Engineers, Raymond managed to get funding to research this question on a six-mile stretch of beach in south Brevard County, between the towns of Indiatlantic and Melbourne Beach. Loggerhead turtles were known to nest along the beach, but no one had solid evidence of just how many turtles actually came ashore there. While working at the beach, Raymond saw evidence of far more turtles crawls than he had seen up north. With the NASA money drying up, Ehrhart looked to the south. The number of nesting turtles was startling. From 14 May to 19 August, Ehrhart, Raymond, and a rotating cast of other Turtleheads spent every night on the beach. By summer's end, they had counted 1,304 nesting sites along the short stretch of beach—a density found at few other sites in the hemisphere. Even more tantalizing was the pattern they noticed when they started analyzing their data. Toward the northern edge of their study area, densities were relatively low. But the number of nests increased the farther south they went. Ehrhart had a hunch that the true center of activity was even farther south. But to find out, he needed funding. In addition to the money the Army Corps of Engineers was already providing for Raymond, Ehrhart managed to cobble together several small grants and donations from a variety of organizations and agencies. It was this funding pot that allowed the Turtleheads to set up camp at the Holiday Haven in the summer of 1982. They covered a larger area, extending the surveys another thirteen miles south, all the way down to Sebastian Inlet, just across the Indian River Lagoon from the town of Sebastian. By summer's end, the group had documented a phenomenal 10,000 nesting sites, proving that the region was by far the most important loggerhead nesting area in the hemisphere and one of the two largest such sites on the planet (the only place with more nesting females is on the island of Masirah, in the Indian Ocean, part of the Sultanate of Oman).

They also found green sea turtles nesting on the south Brevard beaches, although in much smaller numbers. Where the loggerheads had an average nesting density of up to 450 nests per kilometer a year, only an average of 1.5 green turtle nests were recorded on each kilometer of beach in the same time period. That number seems insignificant, but it isn't. Green sea turtles come ashore to lay their eggs later in the season than do loggerheads, and the researchers conducted beach surveys only through mid-August. The group likely missed more green sea turtle nesting sites than loggerhead nesting sites. Besides, the species had nearly been wiped out in Florida, and so every green sea turtle nesting on that coastline was tremendously important. Finally, green sea turtles show more site fidelity than their cousins, the loggerheads, returning year after year to nest at the beach on which they themselves hatched. The south Brevard beach was the ancestral home for green sea turtles. Despite the relatively smaller number of nesting green sea turtles (compared to loggerheads), Ehrhart had found the largest rookery for these endangered turtles anywhere in the continental United States.

As happy as he was with these scientific coups, Ehrhart still itched to find out how many turtles lived in the Indian River Lagoon, just west, over the sand dunes from the nesting beaches. The first netting operation on the Indian River Lagoon took place on 19 May 1982, only five days after the group began monitoring the beaches that year. The crews began dropping nets a few miles north of the Sebastian Inlet and started working their way south. As they had once discovered up in Mosquito Lagoon, finding turtles, even in a relatively small body of water, was as much an art as a science.

"Up in the northern part of the Indian River Lagoon we had gotten to know our spots pretty well by that time," says Paul Raymond. "We knew where the channels were. We knew the lay of the lagoon. Now, down in the south, we were starting over. We were probes, trying new areas and depths, hoping we'd get lucky."

Luck was slow in coming. They had caught precious few turtles by 1 July, when they reached Ballard Cove, a shallow, gracefully curving mile-long bay on the eastern side of the Indian River Lagoon.

And then, at 10:20 A.M., the little green turtle with tumors swam into their gill net.

After Becky Bolt handed Ehrhart the turtle on the dock at Honest John's Fish Camp, they all stood around for a while trying to figure out what was wrong with the creature. Ehrhart had no idea. Raymond was also stumped.

"If I had seen one before, you can bet I wouldn't have forgotten it," he says. "These were just hideous things."

They brought the turtle around the fish camp, showing it to many of the old-timers who hung out there. Nobody could recall seeing anything like it. One of Ehrhart's friends, a colleague from the University of Central Florida, was visiting that morning. Although not a biologist, he, too, was shocked by the growths.

"It was the first green turtle I had ever seen," recalls Harry Smith. "It was just an absolutely beautiful animal, but terribly disfigured by these things. The color and everything was beautiful. But there were these monstrously disfiguring eruptions on the underside and the flippers. It made me think of the movie *The Elephant Man*."

Ehrhart had to decide what to do with the turtle. The animal had been measured, weighed, and tagged (designated K1941). But it didn't seem right to just return something that unusual back to the wild without finding out more about the affliction. So Paul Raymond offered to drive the turtle up to Sea World the next day. Maybe the staff there would know what was wrong with it.

Early the next morning, after completing his beach monitoring, Raymond put K1941 into his car, covered it with a damp towel, and drove the sixty miles to Orlando. Before going to Sea World, he stopped off to show the turtle to his girlfriend, Barbara Schroeder. She took one look at the turtle and her jaw dropped.

Schroeder's memory of that first viewing sounds familiar: "I had never seen anything like it before." And, like Ehrhart and Raymond, the novelty of the growths is important in Schroeder's case, for she was a Turtlehead of the first order, part of the crew since the early days, doing nesting counts up at the Kennedy Space Center. She had received her bachelor's degree at the University of Central Florida in 1978, and continued to help out whenever possible. She took some graduate classes and put in time as a research assistant on Ehrhart's various turtle projects. She was working for the U.S. Fish and Wildlife Service on Merritt Island during the 1981 cold-stunning incident and helped save several cold-stunned turtles. Soon after that, she found work as an independent contractor, working primarily for NMFS, conducting aerial surveys for turtles from Cape Hatteras in the north, all the way down to

Key West. She had also seen hundreds of sea turtles. The tumors were a first for her, too.

A short, blond woman with an unflappable demeanor, Schroeder set the creature down on her lawn and meticulously photographed it from every possible angle: front, back, top, and bottom. In nearly every shot there is a hand-lettered cardboard sign Schroeder made. In black permanent marker it reads: "K1941. FL, Brevard Co., Indian River (near Sebastian) 1 July 1982. *Chelonia mydas.*"

When she had finished taking the photographs, Schroeder and Raymond put the turtle back into his car and drove over to Sea World.

Seventeen years after the fact, the pair can still vividly recall the spasm of fear set off by their arrival.

Schroeder remembers that "the guy in charge took one look at the tumors and said, 'Whoa, keep that thing away from me!'"

But it was the next remark that really frightened Raymond. "He stared at the turtle and then at me. And then he said, in this very, *very* concerned voice, 'You didn't touch this thing, did you?' And of course I'd touched it. I mean, I was a grad student at the time, and you're just not worried about things like that. We were far too nonchalant. We had no idea what we were dealing with. We just thought it was some sort of ... aberration."

Schroeder and Raymond left, shaken by the experience. The workers at Sea World's Aquarium Department were used to dealing with all sorts of marine diseases, from pneumonia to a variety of parasites. But even they had never seen anything like the lumps growing out of the sea turtle.

Still, the Turtleheads figured the tumors, although horrific, constituted a once-in-a-lifetime phenomenon: a strange disease (if it really *were* a disease) in a species of turtle rarely found in the Indian River Lagoon. Field biologists are always running across similar anomalies. Two-headed salamanders. Frogs with an extra leg. The aberrations may range from the mundane to the bizarre, but they are usually devoid of any larger biological significance. The strange creatures are measured

Clothahump, the first wild sea turtle that Ursula Keuper-Bennett and her husband Peter ever saw, in 1988, with Peter. Clothahump followed them around on nearly every dive with puppy-like curiosity, from 1988–1992.

A typical scene at the Turtle House, 1996. On the far right is Limu, (Seaweed), first sighted in 1995 and still a resident, but in 2000 showed large FP tumors. The swimmer, top left, is Hoahele (Fellow Traveler), arrived at the Turtle House in 1995, last seen covered with tumors in 1998 and presumed dead. The other two turtles are unidentified.

The last image of Clothahump, with tumors, 1993.

Pilikia *(Trouble) after taking a breath and preparing to head back down to the Turtle House. Seen only in 1995.*

Bandit, known since 1996.

Ursula Keuper-Bennett with Hoʻoulu *(Inspiration), known since 1992.*

Aikane, *Hawaiian for "Friendly," known since 1990.*

Amuʻala *(Coral Eater), known since 1995.*

Two images of the same turtle, Nui (Big), taken in 1994 and 1998 and known since 1990, showing identification based on the arrangement of facial scales. No two turtles have the same pattern.

A rapid flipper swipe across the turtle's face indicates displeasure—in this case warning a diver to back off.

Kaula *(Seer), the individual with the longest known residency at the Turtle House, known since 1989.*

Four-Spot, *known since 1992. This picture was taken in 1995, the last year this turtle was seen at the Turtle House. The fish biting at the tumors are likely eating parasites in the growths.*

George Balazs tagging a turtle on East Island, French Frigate Shoals, Hawaii, 1974.

Photograph provided courtesy of Black Hills Institute of Geological Research, Inc., Hill City, South Dakota. Photographer: Ed Gerken.

Archelon ischyros *lived 100 million years ago, now extinct. Archelon was fifteen feet long and weighed more than two tons.*

The Ofai Honu *(Turtle Stone)*, *a massive boulder with ancient petroglyphs of sea turtles in the jungles of Bora-Bora. According to legend, the* Ofai Honu *mated with a nearby cliff and gave birth to the island.*

Olive ridley sea turtle shells outside a former slaughterhouse in Mexico.

Dugald Stermer

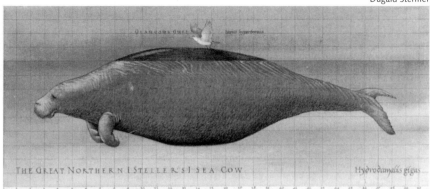

Steller's sea cow is the first known case of a marine animal going extinct because of human activity. The giant marine mammal was twenty-five feet long and weighed up to ten tons. It was discovered by a shipwrecked Russian expedition in the Bering Sea in 1741. By 1768, only twenty-seven years later, the giant sea cow had been hunted to extinction.

U.S. Geological Survey photographs by Page Valentine/Dann Blackwood

Trawler nets dragged along the sea floor destroy a huge amount of marine life. The photograph on the left shows the variety of creatures on the sea floor even at a depth of 275 feet. The photograph on the right was taken less than a third of a mile away after a scallop trawl had reduced the area to gravel.

The New York Aquarium, in Battery Park, Manhattan, where FP was first reported by scientists in 1936.

The first known photograph of an FP turtle in Hawaii. Taken 25 January 1958, Kaneohe Bay, Oahu.

Barbara Schroeder

The Turtleheads, 1978. Students at the University of Central Florida monitoring turtle nesting beaches under the direction of professor Lew Ehrhart. From left to right: Barbara Schroeder, Paul Raymond, Lew Ehrhart, Mary T. Mendonça.

Barbara Schroeder

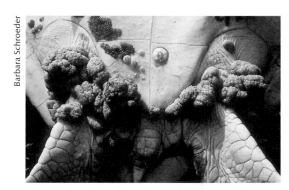

The first tumored turtle pulled from the Indian River Lagoon, Florida, 1982.

Osha Gray Davidson

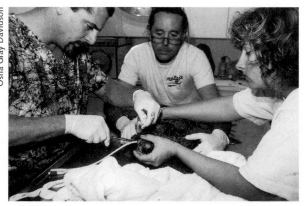

Richie Moretti (center) co-founder of the Turtle Hospital in the Florida Keys. Veterinary surgeon Doug Mader (left) and Sue Schaf, animal director of the hospital (right).

Tina Brown

Researcher Larry Herbst at the Turtle Hospital, Marathon Key, Florida, 1994.

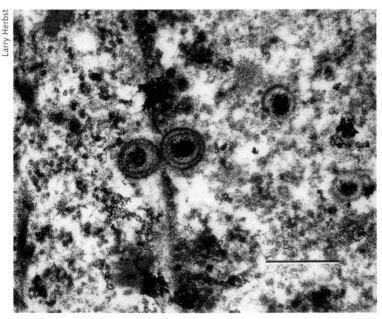

Larry Herbst

Electron micrograph of an experimentally-induced FP tumor showing two herpesvirus particles (the large round objects touching near the center of the photograph). The bar in the bottom right corner represents 200 nanometers.

A Mediterranean monk seal. Once common throughout the Mediterranean, by the early 1990s only 500 of these seals were left in the wild. In 1997 an epidemic killed at least 117 of the remaining seals.

A West Indian manatee, one of approximately 2,500 left in Florida's coastal waters.

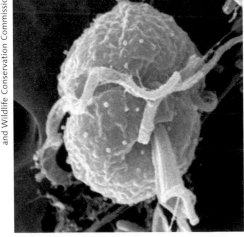

The dinoflagellate Prorocentrum.

Pfiesteria piscicida, *a toxic dinoflagellate associated with massive fish kills and human illness.*

Dr. Jan Landsberg, who discovered a link between FP and the dinoflagellate Prorocentrum.

George Balazs on Kaneohe Bay, Oahu, Hawaii.

George Balazs

A honu *(Hawaiian green sea turtle) hatchling.*

and weighed, their unusual characteristics are sometimes photographed. Then the information is filed away and forgotten.

That would almost certainly have been the fate of K1941, too, if Ehrhart's crew hadn't pulled another tumored green turtle out of the Indian River Lagoon in the following year. And then another and another and another. In the summer of 1983, out of a total of 19 green sea turtles netted by the group, 10 had tumors. What had seemed to be a monstrous anomaly had became the statistical norm. But perhaps the year was the anomaly. That can happen, too. In a given year, thousands of individuals of this or that species can inexplicably die—only to show a rebounding population in the following years. Again, what is of prime importance is the trend. But in this case the trend was just as alarming as the individual cases themselves. In 1984 Ehrhart's team caught 26 green turtles, and 13 of them had tumors. K1941 was no anomaly. Something was happening to the turtles in the Indian River Lagoon.

Meanwhile, Ehrhart had done a search of the scientific literature and found the 1938 Smith and Coates article in which the authors had described tumors identical to these. He found no mention anywhere in the literature of outbreaks of the disease on the scale that he was seeing in the Indian River Lagoon. Nothing even remotely close to it.

In the winter of 1985, another pocket of arctic air blew across the Mosquito River Lagoon, lowering the water temperature to 39°F. As in 1981, a large number of cold-stunned turtles floated to the surface—145 green turtles were collected in three days. It was, in nearly every detail, a duplication of the earlier cold-stunning incident. But this time there was one difference: close to a third of the hypothermic turtles had tumors. Many of the growths were much larger than the ones seen on K1941. They were draped over and grew out of the eyes of some turtles, blinding them so that they couldn't find food or escape from predators. The tumors ballooned out of the pockets below flippers, interfering with swimming. Many were necrotic, pus-filled, and crawling with leeches. Whatever was striking the turtles of the Indian River Lagoon, it was clear to Ehrhart that the condition could be lethal.

Something else alarmed him just as much, perhaps even more. As he surveyed the labyrinthine Indian River Lagoon system on a map, Ehrhart's eye traced the tangled braid of waterways and islands threading its way from Jupiter Inlet, 156 miles north to where Mosquito Lagoon opened to the Atlantic—covering a full third of the state's eastern shore. FP appeared to be spreading.

The professor realized it was time to share his findings with his colleagues. He mentioned the problem in letters and phone conversations with several biologists. But while Ehrhart was becoming more convinced that the tumors represented a major threat to green sea turtles in Florida, he was also growing increasingly frustrated by his lack of success in obtaining funds to research the problem.

"I can't seem to get anyone around here to pay much attention [to the disease]," he confided to one colleague and predicted that to conduct research into the disease he would "end up scrounging for small amounts of money from local and 'non-traditional' sources."

Ehrhart touched on the epidemic in a meeting held in the summer of 1985, a joint gathering of the Society for the Study of Amphibians and Reptiles, and the Herpetologists' League. But this wasn't the right forum in which to sound the alarm about the outbreak, and Ehrhart, together with one of his most dedicated Turtleheads, a young researcher named Blair Witherington, spoke primarily about the recent cold-stunning events in Mosquito Lagoon.

The proper venue to gain the maximum impact, Ehrhart realized, would be the 1986 Annual Workshop on Sea Turtle Biology and Conservation, the largest gathering of sea turtle scientists in the world. The workshop would take place in March that year at a rustic retreat in the extreme southeastern corner of Georgia, and Ehrhart wanted to prepare his paper meticulously, beginning with a report about K1941 and concluding with the increased prevalence since 1981 and the spread of the disease up into Mosquito Lagoon. The community of sea turtle scientists would likely be stunned by the data.

Ehrhart was in for a surprise himself, however.

As Lew Ehrhart worked on his paper over lunch in Florida, George Balazs was pulling his car into the parking lot behind a tan, two-story building at 2570 Dole Street in Honolulu, Hawaii. The sun had not risen yet, but the sky was glowing red over the Pacific as Balazs went inside. Especially in the early morning light, it was easy for people driving by to mistake the nondescript building for a part of the University of Hawaii, whose campus was next door. But the sign on the front lawn read: NATIONAL MARINE FISHERIES SERVICE, HONOLULU LABORATORY.

Balazs climbed the stairs to the second floor and made a pot of coffee in the tiny break room. When it was ready, he poured himself a cup (the first of several he would drink that day), spooned a clump of whitener into his mug, and headed down to his office in room 206. "Office" was a generous way of describing the space allotted to Balazs. It was a six-by twelve-foot section of a larger room, separated by cheap paneling. Balazs sat down at his desk, a clunky steel government issue, with a rubberized top that was cracked and curling. He took a swallow of his coffee, munched on a strawberry Pop-Tart®, and enjoyed the quiet. This was Balazs's favorite time of day. Soon the phone would begin ringing and it wouldn't stop until he left late that evening, long after the sun had set. Balazs had traded his "outsider" role as a sea turtle conservationist for the curse and the blessing of a federal job. The activist and former free spirit was now project leader of the Sea Turtle Program, a division of the Endangered Species Investigation at NMFS, a division of the National Oceanic and Atmospheric Administration, an arm of the Department of Commerce. Government bureaucracies are like Russian nesting dolls, the *matryoshka*, with each entity containing a smaller one. But if you could have opened the Sea Turtle Program in March 1986, inside you would have found nothing but George Balazs. There was no one for "leader" Balazs to lead. He had no employees and there was no budget beyond his salary. Balazs *was* the Sea Turtle Program.

Balazs removed a blue-lined pad and a pencil from a drawer and set them on his desk. For a few seconds he gazed at a poster hanging on the wall over his desk, a painting showing all seven species of sea turtles.

Then he set down his Pop-Tart®, picked up the pencil, and at the top of the page wrote "6th Annual Workshop on Sea Turtle Biology and Conservation." Balazs took another sip of coffee, set down his mug, and wrote the first sentence of the talk he would deliver at the Waverly, Georgia, workshop: "Neoplasms identified by the Registry of Tumors in Lower Animals (RTLA) as fibropapillomas are being commonly found on green turtles, *Chelonia mydas*, in the Hawaiian Islands."

Chapter 8

An Elusive Virus

THE NEWS that a bizarre new epidemic had two apparent epicenters, separated by a 2,500-mile-wide continent and then by a stretch of open ocean of approximately the same size, shocked the turtle scientists gathered at the 1986 meeting. No one was more surprised than the two biologists who had independently discovered the outbreaks and who delivered papers announcing their findings back-to-back.

At 2:30 P.M. Balazs walked to the podium and gave his presentation. He reported that in the previous year 35 percent of Hawaiian green turtles that had washed ashore or been found floating dead or debilitated had fibropapilloma tumors. In addition, 10 percent of nesting females had the same strange growths.

"Local divers and fishermen regularly report seeing afflicted turtles in coastal foraging pastures and underwater sleeping areas," Balazs told the crowd. "Such sightings are believed to have increased considerably over the past 20 years."

If members of the audience thought that these tumors might merely be unsightly blemishes, Balazs quickly dispelled such an innocuous interpretation.

The tumors "can result in reduced vision, disorientation, blindness, physical obstruction to normal swimming and feeding.... Observations in Hawaii also suggest that fibropapillomas can cause severe emaciation, increased predation by tiger sharks and humans, and probably a reduced ability to migrate and breed successfully. Entanglement in fishing line and other gear also appears to be more likely in afflicted turtles."

As Balazs concluded his talk, Lew Ehrhart took his place at the podium and presented essentially the same information. The primary difference was that whereas Balazs had been talking about the turtles in Hawaii, Ehrhart now spoke about diseased creatures in Florida.

The repetition was so strange—the interlude wasn't even long enough to produce a sense of déja vu—that one graduate student in the audience missed the significance of the event. "I was more surprised to see two papers on the same topic," she recalled later, "than to recognize the importance of the occurrence of the disease at two sites."

Ehrhart and Balazs were aware of each other's work on the tumor disease in a general way before the symposium. They had even corresponded briefly about the tumors. But until Waverly, the biologists had been too focused on their own work (and scrambling to fund it) to comprehend the extent of the problem anywhere else. Suddenly, at the symposium, everything came together. Ehrhart would look back on Waverly as a defining moment in his career. The effect was similar for Balazs. As he sat in the audience listening to Ehrhart's presentation, the Hawaiian biologist thought to himself, "We're on to something here. Somebody needs to get on to this."

By "somebody," of course, Balazs meant himself. Never one to do things by half measure, he returned from the 1986 meeting determined to make FP a priority, and not just for *his* office, but for turtle scientists worldwide. The question of *how* he would accomplish this ambitious goal was not at first evident to him. But just as in 1963, when he had decided to move to the tropics (without hesitation after watching a travelogue), and a decade later in 1972, when, as a junior biologist, he had resolved to determine the size of the *honu* breeding herd and then make sure the animals were protected, Balazs had determined his next goal. Now, all that remained was for him to find the means to achieve it. And he would do it with great skill. Inside Balazs's head, the intuitive and the rational coexisted in equilibrium. Some people are fairly straightforward. Others are a jumble of contradictions. Balazs fits neither category. True, he was filled with contradictions, but they were *integrated* contradictions, and if there was a secret to his success, that was it. Instead of favoring one part of himself over another, he embraced them all. Balazs was a pragmatic visionary.

The question now was how to make FP a priority.

"You don't just walk into the boss's office and say, 'We've got a problem and we need to get $100,000 so that we can start to pursue this properly,'" he recalls. "They'd laugh at you and walk you out the door. You need to build a scientific case that there truly is a problem." So that's what he set out to do: building an airtight case that FP was a problem, in Hawaii and elsewhere, and one that could possibly be managed. The NMFS is, after all, only interested in problems that have solutions. And among those problems, protecting endangered species ranked relatively low on the list of priorities, especially back in the mid-1980s. Powerful fisheries groups lobbied to keep the NMFS focused on helping them increase their bottom line. It was only under great pressure that the NMFS set up a Protected Species Program (as it was soon called) to begin with—and then it was allocated insufficient funds to do the job. In Hawaii, most of that money went to protect the Hawaiian monk seal, a marine mammal endemic to the archipelago, with a rapidly declining population. The Protected Species Program received crumbs of the overall NMFS budget. The monk seal program got crumbs of crumbs, and Balazs's turtle program got what was left. Working with the minuscule funds at his disposal, Balazs worked to set up a network to check on turtles stranded within the Hawaiian Islands. Each one would be examined for tumors, and, if afflicted with FP, rated for severity. He eventually got a half-time assistant on loan from the monk seal program, but, at least in the early days, Balazs was forced to look outside his agency for help. It was a lesson he learned well from his days fighting for legislation to protect the *honu*: coalition building. Balazs prefers the word "partners" to describe the many relationships he developed with people, in and outside of government.

"I had no resources, so I had to find some people who had some resources and who had some love for and interest in studying turtles," Balazs explains. He proved adept at forging links with anyone who could help achieve the goal of investigating FP—whether scientists at other government agencies or researchers at universities throughout the world or high school students willing to go out into the field and do research for school papers. While a few by-the-rules sorts grumbled about some of Balazs's partners ("These people aren't even qualified scientists for God's sake!"), Balazs was eager to work with anybody who might help him get a handle on the disease that afflicted the *honu*. And heaven help those who got in the way or who didn't, in Balazs's view, do enough.

Larry Ogren, with the NMFS's Southeast Region Office and one of Balazs's first mentors, recalls that Balazs once hounded him about what Balazs viewed as funding inequities.

"He wrote me letters, saying 'Larry, why are you getting most of the funding?' Ogren remembers. "I said, 'Jesus, George, I'm sorry. It's just that they're killing a lot of turtles down here and they're washing up on the beaches dead by the hundreds and it's in the public's eye.'"

The problem Ogren was talking about was trawler by-catch: turtles were being killed in tremendous numbers in the trawling nets of the shrimpers that plied the waters off the southeastern Atlantic and in the Gulf of Mexico. With commercial hunting of turtles banned, the number of turtles unintentionally caught and drowned in shrimp trawls had become the single largest source of sea turtle mortality in U.S. waters. A government study determined that as many as 55,000 sea turtles died annually in this way—mostly loggerheads and Kemp's ridley turtles. If left unchecked, such mortality rates spelt doom for the sea turtle populations of those areas—already devastated by centuries of hunting.

While by-catch was then, and remains today, the primary cause of human-caused sea turtle deaths, Balazs insisted that the tumor disease should not be ignored. It wasn't a case of either/or, he argued. *Both* threats needed to be evaluated and managed if sea turtles were to survive. Millions of dollars went into designing measures to mitigate by-catch, always with a careful eye on protecting the interests of commercial shrimpers. The result was the Turtle Excluder Device, or TED, a relatively simple gadget sewn into the shrimping nets, a trap door designed to allow turtles to escape while keeping shrimp in the nets.

It's understandable that sea turtle conservation measures focused on by-catch, and not simply because of the numbers involved. The emphasis on by-catch also owes much to our understanding of threats to biodiversity. The problems posed by trawler by-catch fall into either the first and second anthropogenic causes of extinction: hunting and habitat destruction. By-catch has a lot to do with hunting, since the turtles are killed by humans pursuing shrimp. And yet, since turtles aren't the target species, and since trawlers are best known for their destruction of habitat, some look at the problem in this context. However one looked at it, the point is that there were ways of seeing the problem, mind-sets for understanding it. Scientists, agency personnel, environmentalists, and commercial representatives could place by-catch into these existing structures and then argue about how best to remedy the situation. The arguments could be contentious—and TEDs remain controversial to this day—but at least a language existed for debating the seriousness of the problem and the funding for investigating it, and clear-cut bureaucratic lines existed for dealing with the problem.

None of this was true for fibropapillomatosis. Wildlife epidemics in general are poorly studied, unless they threaten commercial species. Funding devoted to examining marine mass mortalities was virtually nonexistent. George Balazs had to fight against a conceptual framework that simply didn't include disease. A sympathetic worker inside the NMFS Southeast Regional Office confided that efforts to generate interest in the disease at that facility were continually rebuffed. When he'd mentioned fibropapillomatosis, the typical reaction from his superiors was, "Oh, that's just another trendy term that is going around now."

The same funding problem frustrated Elliott Jacobson and Lew Ehrhart.

In October 1986 Jacobson wrote a member of the Sea Turtle Recovery Team that "We are only starting to appreciate the significance of this disease in individual turtles and there is no doubt in my mind that it potentially may have significant effects on dynamics of certain populations of green turtles. More money needs to be secured for more in-depth studies."

While supportive of Jacobson's work, the Sea Turtle Recovery Team had no money of its own to disburse. It served as an advisory panel to the regional NMFS office, and its members privately complained to each other about the agency's failure to recognize the implications of FP.

"This morning, Lew Ehrhart showed me a young green turtle so encrusted with fibrous papillomas as to be positively frightening," wrote one Sea Turtle Recovery Team member to another. "Moreover, it seems there has been a tendency to downplay this papilloma problem in some higher quarters. I believe the problem is a serious one."

In fact, the problem appeared to be getting worse. In the fall of 1986, Ehrhart wrote Balazs that what he was finding in the Indian River Lagoon was "scaring the hell out of me." While the percentage of tumored turtles caught remained roughly the same, Ehrhart wrote, the severity of the disease had grown. "We're beginning to see some real monsters," he told Balazs.

The key researchers (Balazs, Ehrhart, and Jacobson) used whatever means they had to further their work. For Balazs, it was largely a matter of perseverance. "He just never went away," says his friend Larry Ogren. "He never said, 'I'm sick and tired of all these hurdles and blocks put in front of me.' George was going to get to the bottom of it."

Ehrhart combined endless grant-writing with his ability to inspire the Turtleheads at his institution to work long hours. The two efforts came together when his former student, Paul Raymond, now working for NMFS in Miami, managed to garner agency funds for two small FP grants. One went to Ehrhart, to document the cases he was finding in the Indian River Lagoon. The other grant went to Elliott Jacobson to review existing literature on FP (a short task; there wasn't much) and to conduct the first in-depth study of the disease.

Since Jacobson's grant was for only $4,000, the term "in-depth" must be taken less than literally. Still, Jacobson examined one of the more important questions about the disease etiology. When Smith and Coates first described the disease in 1938, they observed tiny parasite eggs in many of the tumors. But establishing the role played by the eggs in the FP epidemic was difficult. The trematode eggs could have caused the growths, but, absent more information, it was just as likely that the eggs had just found in the tumors a hospitable environment. And yet another possibility: pure coincidence. Perhaps there was no relation whatsoever between the eggs and the tumors. Smith and Coates themselves looked into the question further and concluded in an article published in 1939 that the parasites were "probably not of primary importance" in the disease. John Hendrickson, however, had suspected that the tumors were caused by parasites when he first observed FP on turtles in Borneo in 1953. After reviewing the available literature, Jacobson believed that the jury was still out on this question. In fact, sometime soon after seeing his first FP cases at the Cayman Island Turtle Farm, the reptile expert had had a change of heart about what lay behind the tumor disease, and the evolution in his thinking is outlined in a correspondence he maintained with George Balazs. In mid-1981, one year after investigating the Cayman Island outbreak, Jacobson wrote Balazs, "As of yet there is not evidence for a viral etiology. The one thing we do see consistently with the papillomas is the presence of spirorchid trematodes eggs.... Currently it is my belief that these eggs may be the responsible agent for the papillomas." And two years later Jacobson wrote Balazs that "I still feel the disease is most likely a response to spirorchid trematode eggs and not of viral etiology."

But by 1986 Jacobson had done an about-face. He wrote Balazs, "I am back on the track of an elusive virus. At this point in time, this to me is the most logical cause of this disease."

What caused Jacobson's rekindled interest in the viral theory? The change was due in part to an unlikely source: elephants.

In 1984 Jacobson was called in to investigate a strange outbreak of growths in a herd of captive elephants. The animals were part of a herd of nearly 100 elephants on a sprawling estate in north-central Florida owned by Arthur Jones, best known as the inventor of Nautilus® exercise machines. A quirky man with varied interests, Jones produced and directed a television series called "Wild Cargo" back in the 1960s, featuring Jones, an avid pilot, capturing and transporting wild animals from around the world. In what some called a publicity stunt for his Nautilus® empire, Jones built on his Florida property one of the largest nonmilitary runways in the world to accommodate his fleet of three Boeing 707 jets. The jets were used to bring wild animals to his estate—crocodiles, a rhinoceros, a gorilla, and, of course, the herd of elephants. Two herds, actually. The first group of thirty-three came via a Texas importer. These were followed, eight months later, by sixty-three younger elephants flown directly from Zimbabwe. Several of the Texas elephants arrived at Jones's estate with growths already on their trunks, and Jacobson was hired to identify the problem. He examined samples of the growths under the microscope but was unable to find any evidence of a virus. Three months after the second group of elephants arrived, Jacobson got another phone call from the herd manager. The growths had shown up on some of the younger newly arrived animals. Biopsies were again taken, and Jacobson examined samples under the microscope.

"I wasn't even that excited about looking at them," he recalls, "because in the older elephants it wasn't very rewarding. And then, all of a sudden I put a slide on the scope—and it was loaded with these inclusions." An inclusion is a structure produced within a host cell by a virus at work replicating itself.

A few words about viruses are in order. First, a virus isn't alive, at least not in the normal sense of the word. The basic form of a virus is nothing more than a molecule of DNA or RNA (the organism's "blueprint"), surrounded by a protein coat. (The late Nobel laureate Peter Medawar once famously described the virus as "a bit of very bad news wrapped up in protein.") Lacking any mechanism for reproduction, the virus infects the cell of another organism and "plugs into" the ability of its host's cells to multiply. When that happens, the virus forms inclusion bodies, sometimes called "virus factories," where individual viral particles can sometimes be found. But finding inclusion bodies is tricky business. They're like transient auto "chop-shops," where stolen cars are stripped and sold for parts, the entire operation moving to a new location sometimes overnight. Inclusion bodies only exist while the virus is actually replicating, sometimes a matter of hours or days. That's why Jacobson didn't find the virus factories in the first group of elephants—the virus had already multiplied. With the newly infected younger elephants, Jacobson got lucky: the timing was just right to catch the virus in the act. He found inclusion bodies and viral particles and concluded that a virus was associated with the elephants' disease.

Jacobson began to reassess the role of a virus in FP. The similarities between the case of the infected elephants and the Cayman Island turtles were intriguing. Initial examination of turtle growths under an electron microscope had produced no evidence of inclusion bodies or viral particles. But what if Jacobson's timing had been off, as it had been initially with the elephants? "I really need to do a better job evaluating lesions at different stages of development," he wrote Balazs in November 1985. After recounting his recent experience with the north Florida elephants, Jacobson added, "I need to get the earliest recognizable papillomas in green turtles and concentrate on these lesions first."

But he also needed to investigate the role of the trematode eggs, and that's what he did in his NMFS study. For six months, the veterinarian followed the progress of six FP turtles, provided by Lew Ehrhart and kept in a special isolated tank at Sea World in Orlando. Jacobson performed twenty-eight biopsies on tumors from the six turtles used in the study. Looking at the tissue samples under the microscope, he didn't see a single egg. Jacobson also treated some of the turtles with a medicine that kills the parasites and determined that the treated turtles fared no better, or worse, than the turtles not receiving the medicine. None of this conclusively proved the matter—and others would continue to debate the issue—but Jacobson was now firmly convinced that (1) trematode eggs didn't cause FP, and (2) "a viral agent seems most likely" to be the infectious agent. The search for the elusive virus was on.

Chapter 9

Turtle Hospital

RICHIE MORETTI had all the trappings of success that marked his hard-driving entrepreneurial era. His highly profitable Volkswagen restoration business in Orlando, Florida, had made him a millionaire by the age of thirty and given him his second million by the age of thirty-five. In 1984, at the age of forty, Moretti acquired what was surely the ultimate marker of a type-A overachiever: chest pains. He wanted out of the rat race, and the sooner the better. Moretti sat down with his girlfriend, Tina Brown, and the couple discussed their options. Brown, a native of the Florida gulf coast, had grown up on boats, usually with a fishing pole in her hand. Whatever future they picked, Brown insisted that it had to include fishing. That sounded fine to Moretti, who had grown up on a lake in northern New Jersey and who had become an avid fisherman over the years in Orlando.

Moretti sold his auto business, Brown quit her job as a hairdresser, and the couple bought a ramshackle twenty-one-unit motel in the Florida Keys, next to a topless bar named "Fanny's," and settled into a laid-back life running the motel—and fishing.

One of the top sport fish in the area is the tarpon, a hundred pounds of sleek, silvery fighting power. On a whim, Brown put the first tarpon she caught into the saltwater pool at Hidden Harbor Motel. The guests liked the monster fish, which was named, appropriately, the Big Guy. The huge tarpon was such a hit that Brown decided to expand the motel's aquatic collection. Before long, grouper, stingrays, and a host of other local marine creatures shared the motel's 100,000 gallon seawater swimming pool. (The couple built a freshwater pool for humans.)

Then Brown had what at the time seemed like a simple idea. "Wouldn't it be nice to have cute little turtles in there, too?" she recalls thinking. That small addition would end up changing the couple's life. But first Brown hit a roadblock: sea turtles were already a protected species by then. It was against the law to keep them in captivity. The official in charge of protected species told Brown that there was one way that the couple could keep sea turtles: Hidden Harbor Hotel would have to become a licensed turtle-rehabilitation center, caring for sick and injured animals.

The idea appealed to both Brown and Moretti. They filled out the paperwork and learned about basic sea turtle rehabilitation, and in 1986 a pair of forty-pound green sea turtles, one male, one female, arrived from the Seaquarium in Miami. The Hidden Harbor Marine Environmental Project, Inc., was born. Fishermen and state and federal officials began bringing them injured turtles. The most common problems were all related to human activity. Some turtles had carapaces split by propeller blades, breaks that Brown and Moretti repaired with fiberglass. Other animals had gotten entangled in fishing line. They treated the resulting wounds with antibiotics and, if the line had worked itself too deep, amputated the flipper. Many loggerhead turtles mistook floating plastic bags or balloons for their favorite food, jellyfish, and ended up with blocked intestines. The treatment: a hefty dose of Metamucil® followed by a long, bouncing ride on a golf cart.

In 1986 a fisherman brought in something new. It was a young green turtle with a marble-sized growth on its left front flipper. A local veterinarian suggested an old-fashioned method of dealing with animal warts—tying a length of fishing line around it and gradually tightening the line until it cut its way through the growth. The process worked, and before long Toni the Turtle (as Brown had named it) seemed fine. No tumors returned, but Tony stayed in a "convalescent" pool at Hidden Harbor for another year before being released into Florida Bay, the large body of water between the Keys and mainland Florida. During that year and in the one that followed, more and more of the turtles brought to Hidden Harbor had these growths—and frequently the tumors were far more debilitating than Toni's: larger, often growing on the eyes, blinding the turtles and leading to starvation and death.

Brown and Moretti had learned a fair amount about rehabilitating injured turtles, but whatever was wrong with these turtles was beyond their means to help. In 1987 they asked state officials for help and were told to contact a professor at the University of Florida in Gainesville, Elliott Jacobson. Jacobson agreed to come down to the Keys to surgically remove the tumors on the hotel's latest FP turtle. After the operation, Jacobson determined that the animal was too sick to remain at Hidden Harbor. He took it back to Gainesville with him, but the turtle soon died. When Jacobson necropsied the animal, he made an alarming discovery. The turtle's kidneys were full of tumors. The external tumors were bad enough, but the fact that FP caused growths in vital organs meant that the disease was even deadlier than Jacobson and other researchers had previously believed.

Alarmed by both the increase in the number of FP turtles they were seeing and by new evidence of internal tumors, Moretti and Brown started asking around, talking with other fishermen and wildlife officials to determine the extent of the problem in the Keys. They contacted Pat Wells, the park manager at nearby Lignumvitae State Park. Wells told the couple that he, too, had noticed an increase in the number of tumored turtles over the past couple of years, with nearly all of them coming from the poorly flushed waters of Florida Bay. Wells saw few FP turtles out at the reef. In 1980, he informed them, the federal government had started keeping track of the number of dead or injured turtles washed up on Florida's shores. Officials found an increase both in the number of stranded turtles and in the percentage of tumored turtles in Florida Bay. By 1987 more than half the turtles stranded there had FP. Florida Bay had joined Indian River Lagoon and Hawaii as a hot spot in the FP epidemic.

Moretti's early retirement plans had suddenly changed. An easygoing life of fishing and admiring the sunsets was now out of the question. Brown recalls that "we decided that this disease had been dropped in our lap. We had to do something about it." Moretti phoned Elliott Jacobson and said he wanted to help fight the disease. Jacobson explained that the first order of business was to run a series of experiments to determine what caused the disease. For that, a research center was required.

"Okay," responded Moretti. "Tell me what you need."

In short order, the Hidden Harbor Motel had on its grounds five 800-gallon tanks to hold FP turtles and additional staff and volunteers to help take care of the equipment and the turtles. Next, Moretti bought Fanny's, the topless lounge next door, and spent a quarter of a million dollars converting it into a modern veterinary clinic—devoted exclusively to sea turtles, of course. While local doctors and hospitals donated much equipment, the $100,000 annual operating costs for running the facility came out of the hotel profits. By 1991 the Turtle Hospital was ready for business. All that was needed was a full-time researcher ready to investigate the cause of FP.

Up until 1991, Larry Herbst's curriculum vitae seems to be a portrait of a biological researcher in search of himself. In the mid-1980s, when he was in his late 20s, Herbst published papers on the colonization mechanisms of a neotropical pioneer tree, the nutritional needs of fruit bats, the relation between body size and proboscis length in honeybees, genetic variation in lions, and several studies of the armadillo. Actually, says Herbst, "I did all those things because I couldn't figure out a way to do what I *wanted* to do." Which was to become a marine biologist.

Like many of his generation, Herbst's interest in the ocean world owed a lot to the television series *The Undersea World of Jacques Cousteau* (and, to a lesser extent, the Lloyd Bridges show *Sea Hunt*). But Herbst was equally influenced by the real world that lay just outside his home in Rockaway Beach, New York, on the south shore of Long Island. "It's on a peninsula, just a quarter-mile wide," he explains. "So I had Jamaica Bay on one side and the Atlantic Ocean on the other. I was immersed in that environment."

After earning his veterinary degree at the University of Florida in 1991, Herbst began a residency in laboratory animal medicine at the University of Florida to earn a Ph.D. in biomedical research. The director of the program gave Herbst wide latitude in defining his research, which would be funded in part by the National Institutes of Health. "Basically," Herbst recalls, "he told me to find a neat project and do whatever I wanted." Herbst turned to Elliott Jacobson. "I told him: 'I'm interested in wildlife and I have this funding; can you help me develop a Ph.D. project that involves biomedical research but also is relevant to wildlife and conservation? Because if I can do something like that I'll be really happy.'"

It was a particularly fortuitous set of circumstances. Moretti had just finished setting up the research lab on Marathon Key. Jacobson has been waiting for the right graduate student to come along to investigate FP. And Herbst wanted—at long last—to study a marine creature from a biomedical standpoint. Very quickly it was determined that Herbst would write his dissertation on the cause (etiology) and course (pathogenesis) of fibropapillomatosis.

The first and most important question for Herbst to answer was: is FP transmissible? More narrowly, Herbst wanted to know whether FP was caused by an infectious agent. This was the same fifty-year-old question that neither Smith and Coates in 1938 nor any researcher since had managed to investigate fully.

If anything, the need for transmission studies was even more pressing in the 1990s as advances in medicine over the decades had opened up new possible avenues to explain epidemics like FP: environmental factors (particularly pollutants), genetic predisposition, stress, and immunosuppression to name just a few. The germ theory of Louis Pasteur had given way to a new and far more complicated view of disease.

That complexity was mirrored in a workshop organized by George Balazs and a colleague and held in Honolulu, coincidentally, just before Larry Herbst began to work on FP. The idea of a workshop for the leading researchers in the field came from Balazs's immediate superior at the NMFS, Bill Gilmartin, head of the Protected Species Program in Hawaii. After listening to Balazs's reports about FP for several years (not to mention his continuing requests for more funding for research into the disease), Gilmartin suggested that Balazs convene a gathering of experts to share information and devise a research plan. The workshop would rationalize the agency's response to FP and provide a science-driven nuts-and-bolts justification for steering more money toward fighting the disease. Balazs was thrilled with the idea and immediately set to work turning it into a reality. He identified and invited the top people in the field ("Hell," Balazs recalls, "they were the *only* people!"), including Elliott Jacobson, Lew Ehrhart, John Harshbarger (from the tumor registry), Wendy Teas (who was in charge of the NMFS sea turtle stranding and salvage program in Florida), a parasitologist, a veterinary pathologist, and a few others. All involved remember the three-day meeting as an exciting time. The resulting document, "Research Plan for Marine Turtle Fibropapilloma," which contained virtually everything that was known about FP at that time (and most of what was hypothesized), quickly became the standard reference work for the disease. The list of possible causes of the tumor disease was daunting, including a virus (or viruses), parasites, pollutants, environmental factors such as a change in water temperature, weakened immune systems, genetics, contamination of the turtles' food chain, nonviral transmissible tumors, and others. But the research plan to investigate those questions was also impressive, with highly focused objectives that were clearly articulated.

As compelling as the document was, Balazs believes its real success lay in getting it into the right hands. "You can always produce documents," he says. "And they sit on shelves in your offices. But the *moving* of that document in large quantities to whomever and wherever anyone would look at it—that was the thing that made the agency sit up and take note."

Before the workshop, Balazs ran the NMFS FP activities in Hawaii "on shoestring and baling wire." And afterward, the floodgates of funding weren't exactly opened wide, but at least Balazs could afford better quality shoestrings and a significant increase of baling wire.

WAS—that's the acronym Larry Herbst uses to characterize the list of possible FP causes when he began his research. It stands for Wild-Assed Speculation. "Any possibility you can think of," says Herbst, "you could come up with a rational hypothesis for." The antidote for WAS, said Herbst, was a series of strictly controlled transmission studies. "There were so many possibilities," he recalls, "that until somebody could sit down and do some work to either rule some things in or out, it was just a wide open field."

In December 1991 Herbst began narrowing the field with the simplest of experiments. He injected two captive-reared green turtles with a mixture prepared from ground-up FP tumors. Herbst also injected three other turtles with the eggs of parasites associated with the tumors. (Although Elliott Jacobson was already convinced that the parasites were opportunists, not the cause of the growths, he knew that the question hadn't been definitively answered and urged Herbst to run this experiment). Six months later, the turtles with injected parasites showed no signs of tumors. The two turtles that had received the tumor extract began to develop small swellings at the site of the shots. As the summer wore on and the water temperature increased, the tumors grew more quickly. The growths became so large that Herbst had to surgically remove portions of them. At first the tumors formed only at the inoculation sites. But a year and a half after the experiment began, the disease had evidently spread through the body of one turtle. Tumors began sprouting from its neck, front flipper, tail, and plastron. Less than two years after the injections, both turtles were dead. All three of the turtles that had received the injections of parasites eggs remained tumor-free.

While Herbst was encouraged that he was on the right track in hunting down the elusive virus, he also knew that there were limits to what could be concluded by his first experiment. There are some types of tumors that are transplantable, that is, they don't arise from infectious disease. Herbst would address that possibility in the next experiment. In 1992 he injected three turtles with a mixture of tumor extract, but this time he passed the liquid through a series of very fine filters. Anything larger than 0.2 microns in diameter was trapped by the filter—neither cells, fungi, nor bacteria would pass through. The only material that could be left in the saline extract and was capable of causing tumors was a virus.

Herbst injected each turtle at three sites: the right eyelid, a forelimb, and a rear limb. The turtles were returned to their tanks at Hidden Harbor, and Herbst waited for tumors to develop. Based on his previous experiment, he didn't expect to see any growths for several months. And, true to form, the turtles showed nothing for the first five months. But as the six-month mark passed, Herbst anticipated the tumors sprouting at any time. But they didn't. Nor was there any evidence of tumors at seven months. Or eight. Or a year. Fifteen months after the injections, the three turtles still appeared normal in every way. One possible explanation was that the original tumor from which the extract was obtained didn't contain any viable pathogens. But Herbst had simultaneously run another experiment to check that possibility. He had injected three other turtles using the same extract, but unfiltered. Two of them had developed tumors.

Doubts grew instead of tumors. Perhaps FP really wasn't caused by a virus at all. Maybe the tumors really were noninfectious, just transplantable. But, then again, maybe there *was* a virus—only a very large one. Or perhaps the agent, whatever it was, was small enough to pass through the filter on its own but for some reason didn't. Maybe it was stuck to the cellular debris and never made it through the filter. Or maybe—No, this wouldn't do. "Maybe" and "perhaps" belonged in the despised realm of WAS. Herbst would run a third series of transmission experiments—this time using more subjects (both tumor donors and recipients) and a larger filter, although still small enough to allow virtually nothing but a virus through.

In early July 1993 Herbst began the third study. This time he used tumor extract from two different turtles. Half the resulting material was put through a 0.45 micron filter. This cell-free extract was then injected under the skin of two groups of captive-reared turtle hatchlings. Injections were administered on the right side of the turtles' body, with either unfiltered extract or "sham" injections (containing only saltwater) injected on the left side. In September, Herbst repeated an identical procedure with two more groups of turtles.

Then, once again, he waited.

The world, of course, hadn't stood still while Herbst was carrying out his experiments. The most significant development in FP was contained in a paper published by Elliott Jacobson and three colleagues in late 1991. The group, with Jacobson as lead author, looked at tumors from two FP turtles using an electron microscope. No evidence of viral activity was found in tumors from the first turtle. Fourteen tumors from the second turtle were also scanned, and in one small area of one of the tumors Jacobson found the first evidence a virus: immature and mature viral particles. The mature particles were between 110 and 120 nanometers in diameter. In shape, location, and size, the particles were consistent with those in the herpesvirus family.

The study raised many intriguing issues for Jacobson. True, the particles were found only in one small area of one tumor, but no herpesvirus had previously been observed in a green turtle, outside of animals suffering from gray patch disease at the Cayman Turtle Farm. Furthermore, herpesvirus was known to cause tumors in other animals and had been linked by Jacobson to the papillomas that struck the elephant herd in northern Florida just a few years earlier. The primary drawback to linking herpesvirus to FP was the fact that herpesvirus was notorious for acting as a secondary infection. Still, Jacobson's finding was an exciting one and surely bolstered Larry Herbst's confidence as his third transmission study continued.

Fifteen weeks after the September group of turtles had been inoculated, two of them showed a very slight swelling at the injection site. Turtle skin is by its nature bumpy, and Herbst was at first uncertain about what he was seeing. But very quickly the swellings grew larger. They were, indeed, tumors. Soon other turtles started showing the same growths: It was clearly FP. But most important, the tumors were showing up on both sides of the turtles' bodies, produced by filtered as well as unfiltered extract.

Within a few months the evidence was clear: Herbst had successfully transmitted FP using a solution containing nothing larger than a virus.

Despite Jacobson's belief that a herpesvirus was the agent responsible for FP, Herbst had his own theory. He recalls, "Once I showed it was an infectious agent, I thought, 'Okay, I'm going to go ahead and prove it's a papillomavirus.'"

Herbst certainly wasn't alone in this bias—even Elliott Jacobson himself had suspected papillomavirus when he first saw the disease at the Cayman Island Turtle Farm in 1980, a reasonable theory given the fact that papillomaviruses were known or suspected to cause tumors in dozens of animals. In 1994 he prepared a filtered tumor extract similar to the ones he had used previously, with one exception: this time he exposed the material to chloroform. This is important because there are two broad classes of viruses: those that are covered with a protein envelope and those that are not. The enveloped viruses are very sensitive to organic solvents such as chloroform. Viruses without envelopes are hardier—they'll continue to infect a host even after a chloroform bath. Papillomaviruses don't have envelopes; herpesviruses do. So Herbst expected the turtles inoculated with the chloroform-treated material to sprout tumors. But they didn't. Not a single tumor developed at any site that received the chloroform extract.

"That ruled out papillomavirus pretty completely," says Herbst.

Through his series of experiments at the Turtle Hospital, Herbst had made a number of critically important advances in understanding FP. But the question of how the disease was actually transmitted in the wild nagged at him. After all, there are no scientists in the field giving wild turtles injections of tumor extracts. Could the disease be transmitted horizontally, that is, from turtle to turtle? Unlike the previous advances, the answer to this question didn't come from a well-planned experiment. It was, more or less, a lucky break.

In each experiment Herbst had at least one control turtle, an animal kept with the others but that received no injections of tumor extract. This was standard experimental procedure and was done for two reasons. First, to see whether the disease was horizontally transmitted and, second, to make sure that some other factor, such as a chemical or another agent in the water, wasn't really causing the tumors. If the control animals also developed growths, that would indicate that something other than the injections was involved in FP. But none of the control animals ever developed FP at Hidden Harbor. While that strongly suggested that the injections were causing the tumor growth, there was a downside as well. Why *didn't* the control turtles, which shared tanks with tumored turtles, ever get the disease? It was a question that, despite his other successes, concerned Herbst. "I was really beginning to wonder: How *do* animals catch this thing?" he recalls.

Herbst used three control turtles in his 1994 chloroform experiment, putting them into the tanks with the two groups of turtles in August and December of that year. The animals were monitored for a year, and, as we already know, only those that received injections that hadn't been treated with chloroform developed tumors. In most cases, when pathology experiments are concluded, all the animals are killed. But in experiments involving protected species like sea turtles, that can't be done. Nor did Larry Herbst or anyone at the Turtle Hospital want to kill any animals. They were there to save turtles, after all. So Herbst surgically removed tumors from affected animals, and if they showed no signs of regrowth after a year, they were assumed to be tumor-free (and virus-free) and released into the wild. The 1994 experiment was completed and the manuscript was submitted to the journal *Diseases of Aquatic Organisms* in September 1995. It was accepted in October of that year. Herbst had already operated on the turtles with tumors, between six and nine months after they had received inoculations. But tumors regrew on some of the animals, and new tumors continued to appear on others. A year after the experiment had begun, none of the three control turtles showed signs of tumors, however, and they could have been released. But they weren't.

"I can't say that there was any deliberate decision [to keep them]," recalls Herbst. "That was the time that I moved to New York, so there were gaps in efficiency."

Thank heavens for inefficiency. In January of 1996, fresh from completing his doctorate at the University of Florida, Herbst had been hired as a clinical laboratory animal veterinarian at the Albert Einstein College of Medicine, in New York City. That same month he received a call from an excited Richie Moretti. One of the control animals had developed tumors.

Herbst's first thought was that there had to be a mistake. "We rechecked all the identities," he says. "I checked all my notes to make sure we didn't have them misidentified and that I hadn't actually treated all these animals." But it wasn't a mistake. And a year later, in March 1997, a second control turtle from that same experiment sprouted growths.

It was the first record of horizontal transmission, despite the fact that nontumored turtles had been sharing tanks with tumored turtles for years at the Turtle Hospital. "What that tells me," says Herbst, "is that it's relatively hard to transmit, but that it occurs."

There's no denying the significance of Herbst's research at Hidden Harbor. Researchers now knew that FP was associated with a virus, probably a herpesvirus, and that the infection could be transmitted, at least in the lab, from one turtle to another. But the largest question of all remained unanswered.

Perhaps a herpesvirus caused the disease, but what caused the *epidemic* was a different question altogether.

For decades, at the very least, the disease had remained extremely rare. When Smith and Coates first investigated FP in 1937, they found just three tumored animals among the 200 examined in the Florida Keys. In 1886, Charles Park captured 2,500 green turtles in the Indian River Lagoon—but there's no record of his ever finding any turtles with tumors. And yet, netting in those same waters nearly a century later, Lew Ehrhart found FP in more than half the green turtles he caught. In the years following, the rate climbed over 72 percent. In Hawaii the sighting of a turtle with a tumor was unusual enough to warrant a photograph in 1958. By 1983, George Balazs recorded a tumor prevalence rate of 31 percent among stranded turtles, and 53 percent by 1990. In Florida Bay, stranded turtles showed tumors in 40 percent of cases in 1980, 53 percent in 1987, and 70 percent in 1990.

And there were more reports of the disease all the time. Researchers reported cases of FP in the Bahamas, Nicaragua, Panama, Puerto Rico, Barbados, Brazil, the Virgin Islands, Venezuela, Colombia, Costa Rica, Belize, Sri Lanka, Japan, Bonaire, the Dominican Republic, Taiwan, and Indonesia.

In some of these cases, the new reports of FP were likely due to increased awareness of the disease. But there was clearly more at work in places such as Grand Cayman Island—once the nesting grounds for the vast green turtle population of the Caribbean. No mention of turtle tumors in this area has been found in any of the writings from Columbus's time forward. But when Jim Wood, the manager of the Cayman Turtle Farm, and his wife, Fern, did a 1993 study of captive-reared turtles released from the farm and recaptured in nearby waters, they found that 66 percent had FP.

Australia also presented evidence of a growing problem. Two sites in eastern Australia showed an increase in incidence of the disease, with the rate in a third site going as high as 80 percent by the late 1990s. In 1996 the disease was confirmed for the first time in western Australia.

There was no doubting that the disease had spread geographically and increased dramatically in incidence in a relatively short time.

Just as alarming was the fact that the disease had jumped species. For years, the disease was called Green Turtle Fibropapilloma (GTFP) because it had been seen only in that one species of sea turtle. But in 1986 Lew Ehrhart and his assistant Blair Witherington found the first confirmed case of the disease in a loggerhead turtle, while netting in the Indian River Lagoon. Witherington remembers the discovery as "a disturbing milestone." Other individual cases of FP in loggerheads trickled in, but the disease still appeared extremely rare, until a team of researchers, led by Barbara Schroeder—another of Ehrhart's original Turtleheads—began studying the loggerheads in Florida Bay in 1990. Between 1990 and 1996, 11 percent of the loggerhead turtles they captured had the disease; "a rate," they reported, "that is apparently unprecedented in this species."

Biologists soon found that FP affected other species of sea turtles as well. In 1987 an FP-like tumor was reported for the first time on a nesting olive ridley turtle in Costa Rica. A decade later, the growths were observed on 10 percent of nesting turtles at the site, with one tumor measuring more than five inches in diameter.

A probable case of FP was reported on a nesting Kemp's ridley, the most endangered sea turtle in the world, in Mexico in 1993. Another tumored Kemp's ridley was found dead off the Florida Keys in December 1996, and a tissue sample identified the growths as FP.

The once rare disease, confined to a single species of sea turtle, was now found in every ocean basin, had increased to epidemic proportions at several discrete locations, and had jumped species—all within the space of a decade or two. Something had caused FP to change from an anomaly to a global pandemic involving several species. Nor was FP the only marine epidemic to explode during this period. Something was happening in the oceans.

Chapter 10

A Marine Metademic

DISEASE is as much a part of the natural order as is health, although most of us would rather not dwell on that fact. It's true that some diseases are the result of behavior. Drink too much alcohol and after a few decades you're likely to end up with a cirrhotic liver clotted with scar tissue. Smoke a couple of packs of cigarettes a day and—as even tobacco companies now admit—you may develop lung cancer, emphysema, heart disease, or other chronic illnesses. These diseases are called abiotic—that is, caused by nonliving agents. Infectious diseases, biotic ones, don't always require specific behaviors like drinking or smoking to work their mischief. Pathogens are generally mere actors in the grand and pitiless drama of natural selection.

Epidemics such as FP are something else again.

Most human epidemics are rooted in human behavior. Take, for example, the disease whose name is synonymous with epidemics: plague. First recorded in ancient times, plague is best known for a fourteen-century outbreak in Europe that killed a third of the population. The infectious agent of the disease is a bacterium (*Yersinia pestis*) that resembles a microscopic safety pin; it is spread by fleas living on rodents; but it is more to the point to say that the epidemic that burned through Europe was a result of overcrowding, poor sanitation, and living cheek-to-furry-jowl with a large population of rats. It's almost inconceivable that the *disease* plague would have become the *epidemic* plague without these other factors. That's why the great nineteenth-century German pathologist Rudolf Virchow observed that "epidemics are like sign-posts from which the statesman of stature can read that a disturbance has occurred in the development of his nation."

Deciphering the words on those signposts—understanding the exact nature of the disturbance—is a difficult task, and one made doubly difficult when the "nations" involved aren't human. There are precious few wildlife epidemiologists, and most of them have cobbled their training together with great difficulty, perseverance, and a healthy dollop of luck, since there are no formal programs in wildlife epidemiology. If our knowledge of wildlife epidemics in general is therefore sketchy (to put it generously), we terrestrials know next to nothing about the mass mortalities that occur in the ocean. And even among marine epidemics, the ones we know most about involve economically important species of fish. It's no accident, after all, that NOAA, the U.S. government agency responsible for our oceans, is housed in the Department of Commerce.

One important thing we do know about marine epidemics is that beginning in the early 1980s, just as FP hot spots were erupting simultaneously in Florida, Hawaii, and Grand Cayman Island, researchers around the world began seeing mass mortalities in a wide variety of oceanic life. Teams of marine biologists didn't wake up one day and decide to go out looking for diseases in the oceans. The epidemics were just so numerous, so widespread, with mortality rates so high, that scientists had to pay attention. Still, it took years for researchers to discern and investigate the patterns emerging from these incidents.

It wasn't until the fall of 1999 that the first article on the subject appeared in a scientific journal. The article, by Cornell University marine ecologist Drew Harvell and a dozen coauthors, includes a table listing selected marine epidemics between 1931 and 1997. Of the 34 mass mortalities cited, 27 of them (nearly 80% of the total) occurred between 1980 and 1997. The authors warned that in addition to the recorded outbreaks "epidemics must also be affecting less apparent species, many of which may be disappearing without notice."

What we're witnessing could be described as an epidemic of epidemics—call it a "metademic"—in the ocean realm. This metademic is particularly worrisome because it cuts across all taxonomic groups. Marine epidemics are burning through a host of life forms from plants to invertebrates to marine mammals, threatening oceanic biodiversity on a scale unprecedented in modern times. If there is a signpost on this marine metademic, the words of Sylvia Earle, former chief scientist of NOAA, are written on it:

"The oceans," Earle declared simply in 1998, "are in trouble."

Manifestations of that trouble are found along coastal waters throughout the world, wherever humans have influenced the environment. In 1988 dead and dying harbor seals began washing ashore on beaches from Sweden to Ireland. Nearly 20,000 seals—60 percent of the entire population—died. When researchers isolated the virus responsible, they realized they were looking at a pathogen that was new to science. The virus was a member of the morbillivirus family, and researchers named it phocine distemper virus, or PDV (*Phoca* is the name of the genus that includes these seals). The seals showed no immunological defenses to PDV, suggesting that the virus was as new to the animals as it was to the scientists studying it.

While researchers in Europe were still chasing down the agent responsible for the seal deaths there, American scientists were documenting a dramatic rise in strandings (the technical name for beachings) among bottlenose dolphins along the Atlantic coast. In a twelve-month period, dolphins stranded along their annual migration route between New Jersey and Florida at ten times the normal rate. By one estimate more than half the total near-shore population in this area died. Scientists later discovered that the dead dolphins were infected with two more new morbilliviruses—dolphin morbillivirus (DMV) and porpoise morbillivirus (PMV).

Soon, scientists were finding more mass die-offs of dolphins, whales, and porpoises in Ireland, the western Atlantic, the Caribbean, and the Gulf of Mexico. In the western Mediterranean, a sudden epidemic wiped out more than 20 percent of the dolphin population.

It's easy to focus on the problems of large and charismatic creatures like porpoises, seals, and, yes, sea turtles. But that understandable tendency obscures the scale and importance of the rise in marine epidemics. Creatures, large and small, have been dying en masse. The first widespread marine epidemic of this modern era was also the worst mass die-off in modern times, with a mortality in the billions, its victim driven to the edge of extinction. Outside of marine biologists, few people have heard about this epidemic. The reason is that the stricken animal lacks the large and expressive eyes of more charismatic animals. In fact, it lacks eyes altogether. The animal's most notable characteristic is its long, razor-sharp black spines—a feature better suited for puncturing the soles of human feet than for tugging at heartstrings. The creature is a sea urchin, *Diadema antillarum*, a ubiquitous resident of coral reefs and seashores of the Caribbean. At least it *was* ubiquitous until 1983. In January of that year, *D. antillarum* near the Panama canal literally began falling apart. The progression of the disease went like this: First the sea urchins lost their ability to clean fine particles of dirt and sand from their shells. Then the skin covering their spines sloughed off. Next, the spines themselves began to break and fall off. The urchins seemed disoriented, leaving their hiding places in seagrass beds and between rocks and roaming out onto open sand flats in broad daylight, where predators gobbled up many of them. Finally, the urchins' shells simply crumbled. One scientist summed up the process as "what you would expect had someone poured a powerful, concentrated acid on the urchins." The course of the disease was swift: from first symptoms to full disintegration took anywhere from a couple of days to slightly less than a week. The epidemic spread quickly, too, mostly following the currents that flow through the Caribbean. A year after the outbreak began in Panama, the epidemic ended—possibly because there were so few victims left to transmit the disease. Like a fire that has consumed all combustible materials, the disease may have simply gone out. A staggering 95 percent of all *D. antillarum* in the Caribbean had died, with the sea urchin going extinct in several locations.

The pathogen responsible for this calamity has never been identified, but scientists suspect the culprit was a water-borne bacterium, new to the *D. antillarum*, and that was introduced into the Caribbean through the Panama canal. Water-borne, because the swath cut by the epidemic seems to have followed ocean currents; a bacterium, because bacterial remains were found in some dead sea urchins and because sea urchins are plagued by other bacterial diseases; a non-native pathogen, which can in large part be inferred from the extreme mortality rate and from the site of the epidemic's origin: the opening to the Panama canal, where ships entering the Caribbean from the Pacific typically dump their ballast water, along with any stowaway microbes.

If this theory is correct, then the *D. antillarum* epidemic is the deadliest known marine example of "pathogen pollution"—the introduction by humans of disease-causing agents into new environments. Although the principle has been understood for some time, scientists are now attempting to assess the magnitude of the problem. Peter Daszak, a leading expert on emerging infectious disease among terrestrial wildlife, and the man who coined the phrase "pathogen pollution," warns that the incidence of wildlife epidemics caused by this process is "grossly underestimated." As humans continue to introduce species into new areas, the problem of pathogen pollution, which Daszak believes is already endangering terrestrial global biodiversity, will likely grow.

If the disastrous case of *D. antillarum* is any indication, we should be just as concerned over pathogen pollution in the oceans.

It is impossible to rule out the possibility that pathogen pollution may, in some cases, have played a role in spreading FP. While the University of Florida's Elliott Jacobson doesn't see a problem in returning treated turtles into populations already rife with the disease, he is highly critical of programs in which captive-reared turtles are released into the wild. The close quarters in which captive turtles are raised can promote the spread of viruses from one animal to another. And if they're released into the wild, these highly migratory creatures can carry the disease hundreds of miles, infecting new populations. Writing in 1996 specifically about the Cayman Island Turtle Farm's practice of annually releasing a large number of farm-reared turtles, Jacobson opined: "I expect that no one has a clue as to the potential risk to wild populations of marine turtles due to this action." The practice, he warned, carries the potential for "ecological disasters."

Marine biologists are particularly concerned about diseases of corals, partly because coral reefs are the heart of global marine biodiversity, but also because corals are very sensitive to environmental conditions, and so they are excellent indicators of overall marine health—an early-warning system of trouble to come. The proliferation and spread of coral diseases and mass mortalities in recent years is another sign that the home of sea turtles, the oceans themselves, are in trouble.

Some scientists consider a condition called "coral bleaching," in which unusually high sea surface temperatures (SSTs) leads to mass coral mortalities, one of the earliest and most convincing pieces of evidence that global warming poses a serious threat to life on the planet. They point out that 1998 was both the warmest year on record (going back 150 years), and the year that saw the worst known episode of coral bleaching, with unprecedented mortality rates of a number of coral species on reefs in thirty-two countries, located in every tropical ocean basin, from the Pacific to the Indian Ocean, and from the Caribbean to the Mediterranean Sea. A staggering 16 percent of the world's coral reefs died from the bleaching in just a nine-month period.

One of the areas hardest hit by the 1998 bleaching episode was a reef off the Caribbean coast of Belize in Central America. Although the first recorded episode of bleaching had come from the Caribbean in 1964, the condition had not been seen on Belizean reefs until September of

1995 when researchers reported "massive coral bleaching" following the warmest sea surface temperatures in that area since reliable data were first obtained using satellite readings in 1984. The bleached corals survived the 1995 episode. But 1998 was far worse, with temperatures remaining higher for several weeks. The result was the complete collapse of the dominant coral population, *Agaricia tenuifolia*, a type of lettuce coral, over an area encompassing 145 square miles. It was the first recorded mass mortality of a coral population due to bleaching in the Caribbean. The die-off made news reports even in the popular press.

But the prologue to this event received less attention, despite the fact that it is potentially more important than the story that was widely circulated. Even before the water temperatures began rising in 1998, the population of *Ag. tenuifolia* had only a tenuous foothold on the reef. As the dominant coral, it was a newcomer. A dozen years earlier, in 1986, some 70 percent of the coral cover in the area was composed of staghorn coral (*Acropora cervicornis*), one of the primary reef-building corals in the Caribbean. But then disaster struck—not bleaching this time, but a blight called white-band disease (WBD). The pathogen responsible for the disease has never been identified, but WBD is thought to be caused by bacteria. The disease leaves a characteristic and gruesome "signature" on its victims. Starting at the base of the coral, the disease moved upward at a rate of a few millimeters a day, causing strips of living coral tissue to curl into small balls and slough off, leaving behind a sharply defined white band of exposed skeleton, followed by a darker area below, where clumps of algae have quickly colonized the dead zone. Over a period of years, WBD wiped out the intricately branching colonies of staghorn corals that dominated the Belizean lagoon. By 1993, there were virtually no staghorn colonies left. They had been reduced to piles of broken coral rubble—and replaced by what had previously been a minor player on that reef: the relatively slow-growing lettuce coral *Ag. tenuifolia*.

Richard Aronson and William Precht are the marine community ecologists who had first alerted other scientists and the public to the

1998 bleaching die-off in Belize. They are also the authors of several important studies of WBD and its effect on reefs throughout the Caribbean. They determined that the mass mortality of *Acropora* in Belize due to WBD was far from unique. After scrutinizing hundreds of reports chronicling die-offs of the two most important acroporids found in the Caribbean (staghorn and elkhorn corals), Aronson and Precht concluded that "white-band disease has probably been the most significant factor on a regional scale in reducing populations of these primary [reef] framework builders."

According to Aronson and Precht, WBD is "changing [the] face of Caribbean coral reefs," replacing major reef-building corals with colonies of slower-growing species (which may not be able to keep up with rising sea levels), or, in many cases, with algae.

Ecologists frequently refer to this type of change as "restructuring"—a benign way of spelling cataclysm. Restructuring a coral reef into an algal reef is the marine equivalent of chopping down a tropical rain forest and replacing it with a typical suburban lawn. In the restructured rain forest, what's missing is the five-tiered understory containing 90,000 species of plants, the riot of insect life (with species numbering in the tens of millions), the many shy and elusive birds with their showy plumage and trilling calls, the blizzards of multihued butterflies, the troops of jabbering monkeys living in the high reaches of the canopy—and all the other countless, and thus-far-uncounted, creatures that make up a rain forest community. In place of all this, imagine an unbroken expanse of Kentucky bluegrass. You may find lots of ants—but only a few species of them. There will be the occasional ladybug, perhaps some sparrows, robins, and cardinals. And that's about it. The restructuring taking place today on many coral reefs is of the same magnitude.

Aronson and Precht are also paleoecologists, scientists who attempt to understand conditions on ancient coral reefs by examining the fossil record. By analyzing core samples of the Belizean reef, the pair discovered that nothing similar to the *Acropora-to-Agaricia* transition had occurred at the site for at least 3,800 years. The event was simply without precedent in the modern era.

Scientists aren't sure why coral diseases are proliferating and spreading. But human-caused changes in the ocean appear to be involved. In 1981 (just as the metademic of marine diseases was taking off) Anfried Antonius, the researcher who wrote the very first scientific description of a coral disease, wrote that "Besides direct reef-destruction by man . . . there can be no doubt that the gravest danger threatening coral reefs in modern times is the synergistic effects of man-made stresses and natural diseases."

There's good reason to believe that Antonius's observation can be extended to the metademic of marine diseases, to the long and growing list of mass die-offs that include seagrasses, fishes, mollusks, seals, whales, and—most relevant to our tale—sea turtles.

Even surrounded by the evidence, the very idea of a human-disease nexus seems implausible. We've always considered microbes to be our mortal enemy—as, indeed, they often are. And yet, things must look very different to Thalassa, goddess of the sea. To her, it must appear that humans and pathogens have forged a grand and fatal alliance. Together, people and germs have become a scourge of the ocean—threatening the ancient sea turtle with extinction.

Nowhere is this alliance so evident as in that body of water out of which Lew Ehrhart's Turtleheads plucked the small tumored turtle on 1 July 1982: Florida's Indian River Lagoon.

Chapter 11

Cells from Hell

FOR SEVERAL WEEKS the Jepsons had looked forward to their Thanksgiving vacation by the sea, especially the twelve-year-old twins, Vanessa and Gloria, who were so enthusiastic about the four promised days of camping by the ocean you might have thought they lived a thousand miles inland. But the Jepsons (not their real name) lived just a couple of miles from the Atlantic shore in central Florida and the girls could visit the beach nearly every day if they wanted to, and they usually did. In between their house and the sea was the Indian River Lagoon—nearly a mile wide at that point, separating the Florida land mass from a narrow barrier island. Water molded the twin's lives the way the sky shapes people living in, say, the Dakotas.

Not everyone who lives by the sea is formed by it. The trinity of television, air-conditioning, and shopping malls allows most Americans to insulate themselves from the environment to a degree never before possible. But the Jepson girls took to the water so completely in large part because their father, Bill, a thirty-seven-year-old policeman had spent nearly *his* whole life by the sea and the Indian River Lagoon. Whatever the activity, if it were done on water, Bill Jepson had excelled at it. Water skiing, swimming, boating, fishing. Especially fishing. Like most Floridians, Bill had grown up using light spin-tackle. Recently, however, he had been drawn to fly-fishing after seeing the movie *A River Runs Through it*, with its elegiac shots of men with delicate poles flicking parabolas of line back and forth through the shimmering mountain air, until the line settled upon the water and trout rose to their fate. The camping trip resembled the rest of Bill Jepson's life: It revolved around family and fishing.

They checked into their campsite at Long Point Park, a popular spot just a mile and a half north of Sebastian inlet, on Thanksgiving Day, 1998. At daybreak on Friday morning Bill and a friend were already out on the water casting for flounder from Bill's boat. But the fish weren't biting, and at 10 A.M. the pair weighed anchor and headed to a line of spoil islands just off the west side of the Indian River Lagoon. These islands were man-made mounds of dirt, sand and muck pulled from the bottom when the Army Corps of Engineers dredged the Intracoastal Waterway (a highway for boats, stretching from Maine to Florida) beginning in the early 1900s. Despite these origins, and the environmental damage done by their creation, many of the more than 200 spoil islands in the Indian River Lagoon were quickly colonized by mangroves and other native plants and are now safe havens for many species of flora and fauna. The islands Bill and his friend Doug fished were particularly nice, surrounded by a shallow sand bottom and beds of seagrass. Bill pulled on his rubber waders (a sort of waterproof bib overall), put on his rubber boots, and stepped into the water. It was freezing! The chill November water made Bill think about the neoprene waders he'd had his eyes on for several months. Not only were the waders made from the same insulating material used in SCUBA wetsuits—but they came with neoprene socks already attached to the bottoms. Warm *and* dry from top to bottom. Maybe Bill's wife Brenda would get him a pair for Christmas. He'd have to start dropping some hints.

The fishing around the spoil islands was excellent. Two and half hours after they had first slipped into the cold water, Bill and Doug had several decent-sized trout to show for their efforts. With their catch packed on ice, they pointed the boat back toward the campground. Bill glanced at his watch. It was only 12:30. He asked Doug whether he wanted to make one last stop, off Long Point Flats, west of the campground. "Why not? That's what we're here for," Doug said.

After crossing the Indian River Lagoon, Bill killed the engine and let the boat drift into shallow water before dropping anchor off Scout Island, a beautiful area, crisscrossed with nature paths and connected by a wooden bridge to Long Point Park. There were a few primitive campsites on the island, but it retained a wild feel that allowed visitors to imagine what it was like on the Indian River Lagoon a century earlier, when only the slow, silent rowboats of turtlers worked the brackish coves around the inlet. White wood storks, with wingspans of six feet or more, still roosted in the trees on Scout Island, and even a few bobcats remained in the undergrowth. If you were quiet and patient, you might spot otters and manatees in the waters around the island. Bill loved the area for its wild beauty. The place had another distinction, one Bill didn't know about: Only a couple of miles north was where the first FP turtle in the Indian River Lagoon had been found sixteen years earlier. Bill and his friend once again hitched up their waders, pulled on their boots, and climbed quietly out of the boat.

Bill immediately sank into several inches of muck. Large sections of the Indian River Lagoon were choked with the stuff, a combination of soil and decomposed vegetation washed into the lagoon by runoff. Its consistency and color had led some locals to call it "black mayonnaise."

Grunting from the effort, Bill took a couple of steps, hoping to make it to a firmer sandy bottom. But it remained muddy underfoot and the going was difficult. He'd fish in one spot for a while and, when he went to move to another, he was once again pulling against a muddy bottom that sucked his boots down. With every slow and awkward step the top of the boot rubbed against his bare shin, just below where his waders ended. He wondered aloud to Doug what they must have looked like to someone on shore. It was as if they were dragging invisible weights behind them, each step taking several seconds as they fought the muck. Pulling against the muck, Bill lost his footing and fell over backward into the water. He got up, but not before flooding his waders with chilly water. They had been at it for a half-hour, slogging through this mud— and they hadn't even caught a fish. Bill shouted to Doug: "This is nuts. Let's head back." His friend agreed.

After a hot shower, the men spent the rest of the day relaxing with their families. As Bill climbed into the tent that night he remembered the neoprene waders he wanted. "Look at this," he told Brenda, pointing at the irritated red line on his shin from where his boots had rubbed his skin raw. "Think maybe I should get one of those neoprene suits?" he asked.

The next morning was beautiful: another great day for fishing. Bill and Doug headed back out, this time fishing only from the boat. Doug's family was leaving early that afternoon, so after a few hours, the two men returned to camp. When Brenda saw that the red line on Bill's leg had grown more inflamed, she ordered her husband to sit down so that she could take a closer look. She worked as a dental assistant in an oral surgery practice, where she had ample opportunity to see a wide range of infections. A couple of tiny pus-filled spots had popped up along the line. She got out some antibiotic cream and put it on the wound. "That should take care of it," she told Bill.

When Brenda awoke on Sunday morning, she realized that Bill wasn't in the tent. She sat up and called his name, softly, so that she wouldn't wake the girls. Surely, he wouldn't have gone out fishing by himself. Bill's voice suddenly came from outside the tent, "Hey, come out here and look at my leg." Brenda unzipped the tent flap and crawled out into the morning sunlight. Another hot day. Bill was standing just a few feet away. "Look at this," he said with a studied casualness that put Brenda on the alert. Shielding her eyes from the still-rising sun, she saw that his left leg was swollen to twice its normal size and the entire limb was red. The small lesions that had broken out at the site of the original abrasion now spread down his leg and had grown in size, too.

"What do you think?" Bill asked.

The only thought in Brenda's head was that they needed to get Bill to a doctor as soon as possible. She awakened the twins and told them as calmly as she could that they needed to put things into the car and go home because dad wasn't feeling so good. The girls were scared when they saw his leg. Bill tried to reassure them, saying that it was no big deal, just some weird infection. Not mollified, the girls still did their best to hurry and help pack up the camp. On the drive home they all watched the lesions on Bill's leg grow almost before their eyes. Each sore began as a red spot the size of a pinhead. Within an hour it was as big as a dime. In another hour it turned gray with pus, and then it burst open and drained. Bill had started sweating profusely and was racked by chills, a sign of fever. By the time they arrived home, his leg was a splotchy crimson, and the skin was so tight it was shiny. "His leg felt hot, like it was burning up," recalls Brenda. She wanted to take him to the hospital, but Bill said no. He'd just see their family doctor in the morning. Machismo was an essential part of Bill Jepson's personality, just as it was for most cops. He boasted of having a high pain threshold, and over the years he'd had ample opportunities to test it. He'd broken both wrists and had had both knees kicked out—one had been so badly damaged that it had needed to be replaced with a plastic kneecap. Pain was nothing new to Bill. He believed in toughing it out.

"Bill, this is serious," Brenda insisted. "Whatever's going on with your leg is a really bad infection if you're getting a fever."

At Brenda's continued insistence, Bill finally agreed to drive over to the walk-in clinic, just three blocks from their house. The doctor on duty looked at Bill's leg and told him he had better get over to the hospital emergency room right away.

Out in the car, Bill refused again, saying that he just wanted to go home. Brenda wasn't sure what to do, but she agreed to take him back to the house. After depositing her husband on their living room couch, Brenda ran next door to a neighbor who worked as a nurse at a local hospital. The woman came over, took one look at Bill's leg and said to

Brenda, in an imperious voice she usually reserved for the emergency room, "Don't listen to him. Just take him to the hospital. Now."

Fifteen minutes later, Brenda was helping her still-reluctant husband into the emergency room. By now Bill had started to become disoriented. Brenda asked him to describe the pain, so that she could tell the doctor if Bill became unable to talk. "It feels like my whole bone is on fire inside my leg," he told her. He added, "It's like someone took your curling iron and put it inside the bone in my leg and turned it on high."

The emergency room was busy that night, not unusual for a holiday weekend. The Jepsons were told they were looking at a four-hour wait to see a doctor. The triage nurse asked what was wrong. Brenda had earlier wrapped Bill's leg in gauze, in case whatever was causing the problem was infectious. Now, as Brenda unwound the gauze, she watched the horrified reaction on the nurse's face. Not only was the leg swollen and discolored, but the lesions that had started out at the site of the abrasion now covered the entire surface, dripping pus from Bill's toes up to his thigh.

"Oh, my God," said the startled nurse. She clamped a hand over her mouth and hurried off to get a wheelchair.

"This is not good," Bill whispered to his wife. "This is not even a little bit good."

The nurse returned and whisked Bill off in the wheelchair.

The doctor's reaction was almost identical to the nurse's. He stared, open-mouthed, at the leg, oozing from lesions. He started Bill on an intravenous antibiotic. Word of Bill's problem must have spread through the hospital because for the next four hours, as the medicine dripped into a vein in Bill's arm, a steady stream of doctors and nurses came through to take a look. When they left the room, each one wore the same puzzled and worried look. The lesions now covered Bill's groin and were marching rapidly down his right leg.

Brenda was growing frantic. Since no one could tell her what was wrong with her husband, she had little confidence in the treatment they prescribed. And if it *didn't* help, well, she didn't want to think about that. All she knew was that the situation was extremely serious.

Although the hospital staff wanted to admit Bill, he refused, still insisting that he preferred to see his own doctor on the following day. The doctors at the hospital finally agreed to release him, *if* he'd fill a prescription for an oral antibiotic, start taking the pills that night, and go see his doctor as soon as possible the next day. Bill agreed.

Brenda also agreed, shoving her misgivings to one side. She still wasn't convinced that the hospital doctors could help her husband, and, more important, their family doctor happened to be an expert on toxic and poisonous bites.

After a night of fitful sleep, Brenda drove Bill to their doctor's office on Monday. Her husband's legs were now both equally swollen and the pus-filled lesions extended all the way down the right leg as well as the left. Even their doctor couldn't say exactly what was going on. But Brenda recalled him mentioning something—it was a strange word, a long, technical-sounding one she hadn't heard before and that sounded like a kind of dinosaur. She meant to ask him more about it later but forgot to.

The doctor kept Bill on the oral antibiotic prescribed at the hospital and started him on high doses of Trovan, a broad-spectrum antibiotic, released less than a year earlier. Trovan is a powerful drug, used for treating a variety of infections, including the bacteria *E. coli* and *Streptococcus* and pathogens that are resistant to other antibiotics. After the U.S. Food and Drug Administration expressed concern in 1999 over the drug's potential to cause liver damage in certain patients, the manufacturer issued a warning that Trovan should be reserved for use in patients with serious life- or limb-threatening infections. Bill clearly fit this category. He had his first dose of Trovan that day in his doctor's office and then he and Brenda went home.

They held their breath and waited to see what would happen.

Two days later, the pustules started drying up. The pain that had been nearly constant since Sunday morning slowly ebbed away. Within a week, Bill's fever had broken and the sores that had covered his legs had begun healing.

"After the first few days, I knew that I was going to make it," Bill recalls. "And I hadn't been so sure that Sunday night at the hospital. I didn't want to say anything to Brenda, but I thought I was going to lose my leg .... or worse."

No one ever told Bill for sure what had caused his life-threatening problem. He remembers his doctor later saying that a skin culture taken when the lesions were active came back indicating the presence of *Listeria*, a pathogenic bacterium. But there are several reasons to doubt that *Listeria* was the problem, according to Dr. Stephen Gregory, a microbiologist at the Rhode Island Hospital and the Brown University School of Medicine who has spent a dozen years studying *Listeria*. Listeriosis is almost always contracted orally, by eating contaminated food. Its primary symptoms are gastrointestinal distress—one of the few problems Bill Jepson did not suffer from during his illness. And although the bacterium is extremely common, fewer than 2,000 cases of the disease are diagnosed annually. "It's really a pathogen of immunocompromised people," says Gregory. "If they found antibodies for *Listeria* in his tissue culture, that's not surprising. We all ingest *Listeria* very frequently and carry antibodies to it. But a healthy guy falling into water doesn't come down with this." And Gregory adds that he's also never heard of the bacterium causing skin lesions—the primary presenting symptom in Bill Jepson's case.

"If it was *Listeria*," Gregory concludes, "it's the only case of its kind I've ever heard of."

Several months later, Bill had still not been back fishing in the Indian River Lagoon, and he had no plans to do so any time soon. When his girls were supposed to take a school field trip onto the Indian River Lagoon, a trip in which they had enthusiastically taken part for the past five years, they refused to go.

"I asked them why not," says Bill, "and they told me, 'Because we don't want our legs to look like yours.'"

Two months later, Brenda was reading the newspaper when an article caught her attention. The Florida Department of Health was studying the cases of thirteen individuals who had developed a series of ailments that included skin lesions, memory loss, and neurological problems. Bill had recently complained to Brenda of difficulty in finding the right word—even for common ones. He had chalked it up to the aging process.

Brenda could feel the hair on the back of her neck rise as she continued reading. The victims shared one common attribute: their symptoms had developed soon after they had come into contact with water in the Indian River Lagoon or other nearby estuaries. Investigators had named the ailment "Estuary Associated Syndrome." The cause remained a mystery, but, according to the article, some scientists believed that the organism implicated was a kind of microscopic creature called a dinoflagellate. Then it struck her. *Dinoflagellate.* That was the strange word their family doctor had used after seeing Bill's leg.

Dinoflagellates have been around for at least 200 million years, but other than a handful of aquatic specialists, few people had heard of them until the 1990s. That's when a newly discovered dinoflagellate, christened *Pfiesteria piscicida*, was blamed for massive fish kills first in North Carolina estuaries and then in Maryland. Millions of fish were found floating on the surface, dead or dying, their bodies sometimes covered with bloody lesions. JoAnn Burkholder, a professor of aquatic botany at North Carolina State University, first identified the dinoflagellate. She and her colleagues at NC State, including Edward Noga, documented *Pfiesteria's* bizarre and extremely complex life cycle. Using a scanning electron microscope, they photographed the dinoflagellate assuming 24 vastly different forms. *Pfiesteria piscicida* has never been found in the wild in Florida, but several dinoflagellates similar to *P. piscicida*—dubbed PLS for "*Pfiesteria*-like species"—have been.

Dinoflagellates have always been hard to classify. Many photosynthesize like plants, but, like animals, they eat other organisms, primarily algae and bacteria. (In fact, dinoflagellates belong to an entirely separate kingdom, called Protista.) Burkholder discovered that *Pfiesteria* does something that no other dinoflagellates had been known to do: it engages in "ambush-predator" behavior. Most of the time *Pfiesteria* acts like most other dinoflagellates, feeding on algae and other tiny organisms. But when a critical mass of fish swim by, the placid *Pfiesteria* instantly changes both form and function. The tiny creatures use their two tails to swarm toward the fish. Then, according to Burkholder, the *Pfiesteria* produces a potent neurotoxin that stuns the fish. Dazed and lethargic, the fish simply stop swimming. Next, the microorganism secretes a second compound that dissolves animal tissue, thought to be the cause of the lesions. Disoriented and now hemorrhaging blood, sloughing scales, with their deeper tissues exposed, the fish are helpless. The dinoflagellates assume yet another form, become carnivorous, and gorge on their victims. When the feast is through, the satiated *Pfiesteria* morph back to their harmless algae-munching state, or they become cysts, tiny inert balls, and settle to the bottom in a state akin to suspended animation until the next attack. The gory process is over in just a few hours. It's easy to see how *Pfiesteria piscicida* got its nickname, "the cell from hell."

Public concern over the massive fish kills turned into something just short of panic when Burkholder announced that *Pfiesteria* was linked to severe health problems in humans, some of whom simply breathed the air surrounding a dinoflagellate outbreak. Symptoms of *Pfiesteria* exposure were said to include skin lesions, lapses of short-term memory, immune suppression, and mood disorders. Burkholder herself was among the victims. After accidentally breathing fumes from a tank of *Pfiesteria*-killed fish in her laboratory, the scientist became nauseated, her eyes burned, and she had trouble breathing. Later she developed problems recalling the simplest things—phone numbers, people's names, familiar words that should have rolled off her tongue. The sense of alarm and foreboding sparked by Burkholder's reports is captured in the title of a best-selling popular book about the scientist's discoveries: *And the Waters Turned to Blood.*

Concern that the bad publicity would cause North Carolinians to suffer monetary losses from declines in tourism and in the seafood industry (which it did), led to an inevitable backlash, with some charging that Burkholder had caused "*Pfiesteria* hysteria" without proof to back up her claims. Naysayers also blamed the media for sensationalizing the story. "Pfiesteria, the Latest, Damaging Media Bug," was the title of one such report which averred that "There is no conclusive evidence that there are human health effects" from *Pfiesteria*.

The author couldn't be called wrong, but that's only because in the disputatious realm of science there is nothing so rare as "conclusive evidence." There are, instead, levels of probability. Consider, for example, the case of AIDS, the most devastating new disease to emerge in the last few decades. Although AIDS was first discovered in 1981, and despite the expenditure of millions of dollars and countless hours of research, it wasn't until April 1984—with deaths from the disease surpassing 2,000 in the U.S. alone—that there was anything approaching "conclusive evidence" that AIDS is caused by the HIV virus. (And even that is still debated in some circles today, with the worldwide death toll nearing 19 million by the end of 1999.)

Scientists have rightly been called "practitioners of a discipline that seeks, but never finds, absolute truth." The only thing absolute about truth, scientists know, is its relativity. Still, for science to have meaning in everyday life, especially the branch that deals with health issues, practitioners must help the public place theories on a continuum, one that begins in the gossamer fantasy of "absolute truth" and ends in the fragmented chaos of "wild-assed speculation."

In other words, one goal of scientists should be to help the rest of us distinguish the probable from the barely plausible.

Although no one has found "conclusive evidence" that *Pfiesteria* causes human ailments—at least not with the same level of certainty that links HIV to AIDS—the Environmental Protection Agency has confirmed that "Preliminary evidence suggests that exposure to waters where toxic forms of *Pfiesteria* are active may cause memory loss, confusion, and a variety of other symptoms including respiratory, skin, and gastro-intestinal problems."

Since that warning was first issued, two major studies have solidified the link between human disease and *Pfiesteria*. The first, published in a top medical journal, *The Lancet*, determined that people who had been exposed to *Pfiesteria* toxins in the wild (as opposed to a laboratory setting) were significantly more likely to suffer from neuropsychological symptoms including problems with learning and higher levels of thinking, than were people who hadn't been exposed. The thirteen authors also found that as the degree of exposure increased, so did the risk of illness. The problems were most striking in a learning test in which individuals were read a list of fifteen unrelated words and then asked to recall them. The individuals who had been most heavily exposed to *Pfiesteria* toxins scored lower in this test than 95 percent of the general population. But there was some good news from *The Lancet* study as well. The symptoms appeared to be reversible. Between three and six months after their reported exposure to *Pfiesteria* toxins, the test scores for all the individuals in the study had returned to normal.

The second study was produced in the fall of 1998 by EPA neurotoxicologist Kenneth Hudnell, who found significant vision problems in fishermen who had been exposed to water where there had been large scale fish kills thought to be caused by *Pfiesteria*. Unlike *The Lancet* study, however, Hudnell's work indicated possible long-term physical degeneration.

With the accumulation of clinical and experimental evidence that *Pfiesteria* caused human health, critics of Burkholder's work focused on her second and even more controversial charge: that the rash of *Pfiesteria* fish kills was sparked by human activity. The North Carolina researcher pointed the finger specifically at nutrients coming from sewage and from agricultural runoff, including, and especially, manure from giant hog farms.

"Seventy-five percent of the kills that we've observed have occurred in nutrient-overenriched areas," Burkholder told a journalist in 1997.

The process is complex, but it can be simplified without misleading too much: Nutrients stimulate algae growth. *Pfiesteria* (in its benign form) eats algae. So if you increase nutrients, you increase algae. And if you increase algae, you increase the dinoflagellate population.

"Increasing pollution from ever-increasing pressures of more people, their sewage and urban runoff, and more animals and other kinds of farm runoff, is the biggest problem facing our estuaries," wrote Burkholder in 1996. "All the evidence we have suggests that this dinoflagellate began to be highly active in toxic outbreaks just within the past ten to fifteen years as pollution has continued to increase in many of our waters, and as wetland areas to filter the pollutants have been eliminated."

Of course, this was the last thing powerful corporate agricultural interests in North Carolina wanted people to hear. The warnings came at the worst possible time for the industry: just as giant hog farms were coming under intense public scrutiny, prompted largely by a five-part Pulitzer-Prize winning series in the *Raleigh News & Observer* (19–26 February 1995) documenting the growth and problems of what the paper called the state's "pork revolution."

The first article in the series began:

> Imagine a city as big as New York suddenly grafted onto North Carolina's Coastal Plain. Double it. Now imagine that this city has no sewage treatment plants. All the wastes from 15 million inhabitants are simply flushed into open pits and sprayed onto fields. Turn those humans into hogs, and you don't have to imagine it at all. It's already here.

The series documented how, in a single decade—between 1983 and 1993—North Carolina had moved from the traditional pattern of medium-sized family farms raising perhaps 250 hogs at a time to a factory-type system where giant corporations contracted farmers to produce 20,000 hogs in a single confined operation. The number of hogs on North Carolina soil more than tripled in that decade, from just over 2 million to about 7 million. By 1997, for the first time, hogs outnumbered people in the state (9.7 million hogs to 7.5 million people). And nearly all the hogs were concentrated in the eastern third of the state—on watersheds draining into coastal areas and estuaries.

The pork revolution made North Carolina the number two hog producer in the nation (after number one, Iowa), with revenues exceeding $2.5 billion, more than was earned by any other North Carolina agricultural product, including poultry and the old North Carolina staple, tobacco. And while agribusiness leaders assured the public that their state-of-the-art techniques in hog rearing would prevent any environmental problems, some activists warned of disaster. Even generally cautious scientists went public with their concerns about the effect of so much raw sewage. "There are now 2 million hogs in the Cape Fear River basin alone," Lawrence Cahoon, a water-quality expert at the University of North Carolina, Wilmington, told the *News & Observer*. "Is hog waste treatment up to the same standard as human sewage treatment? Certainly not. And if it's nowhere close, then you've got a mammoth potential problem on your hands."

The problem isn't limited to North Carolina and Maryland nor is *Pfiesteria* the only toxic marine microorganism of concern. Harmful algal blooms occur around the globe and involve dozens of organisms. Harmful algal blooms aren't new—on the contrary, in the fossil record going back several million years there is evidence of giant blooms of algae species that are often responsible for today's massive fish kills. While they may not be new, like FP and so many other marine diseases, reports of harmful algal blooms are on the rise. Wading through the vast literature on the phenomenon that has accumulated over the past two decades, the word used more and more frequently to describe harmful algal blooms is "epidemic."

Harmful algal blooms in places as distant from one another as Scandinavia and North Carolina "need to be viewed ... as possible local manifestations of, and further evidence for, an apparent global epidemic of novel phytoplankton blooms," wrote Theodore Smayda, one of the world's leading experts on the subject, in 1990.

"The health of large marine ecosystems—their diversity, productivity, and resilience—is threatened by a 'global epidemic' of coastal algal blooms," concurred Harvard epidemiologist Paul Epstein in 1993.

Even when the word "epidemic" isn't used, it hovers in the background, as in the 1992 statement issued by a panel of U.S. scientists, stating that "The nature of the [harmful algal bloom] problem has changed considerably over the last two decades in the U.S. Where formerly a few regions were affected in scattered locations, now virtually every coastal state is threatened, in many cases over large geographic areas and by more than one harmful or toxic algal species. There is a growing consensus in the scientific community that the number of harmful events in U.S. waters .... have increased dramatically over the last several decades."

Of approximately 5,000 species of microalgae known to exist, fewer than 100 are considered toxic. The best known are those, mostly dinoflagellates (which are not, strictly speaking, algae), responsible for "red tides," enormous blooms of billions of cells, coloring several square miles of surface water with colors that, despite their name, actually range from red to orange to brown. Red tides are a relatively common historical phenomenon in Florida, where they were first mentioned by the Spanish explorers Álvar Núñez Cabeza de Vaca along the Gulf Coast in 1530. The culprit wasn't discovered for another four centuries: the dinoflagellate *Gymnodinium breve*, which produces a brevetoxin that kills fish (a half billion died in a single outbreak) by disrupting their breathing. *G. breve* has also been known to cause asthma-like respiratory problems in humans and in 1995–96 a persistent red tide of *G. breve* killed 150 Florida manatees. The mass mortality of this giant marine mammal, a relative of the extinct Steller's sea cow, caused widespread grief among Florida's nature lovers, where state-issued manatee license plates are an indication of the animals' popularity. Only approximately 2,300 Florida manatees remained, and that number had been reduced by 6 percent in a single year.

G. breve is also suspected in a record number of sea turtle strandings along the Florida Gulf Coast in 1995–96. Some 106 dead or dying turtles washed up on shore (nearly three times the previous recorded high), many of them exhibiting signs of brevetoxin poisoning: respiratory problems, disorientation, and lethargy. *G. breve* cell counts in the waters where the turtles stranded were high enough to cause fish kills.

The infamous Florida red tide is a naturally occurring phenomenon that begins in waters far offshore. Still, humans may be influencing some of the myriad factors that cause the dinoflagellate to grow and multiply rapidly, prolonging the blooms and increasing their lethal capacity when currents carry them into coastal waters.

The problem will likely grow worse as the population grows in the nation's coastal fringe, the fastest-growing section of the country. Although coastal counties comprise just 17 percent of the land area of the lower 48 states, they already contain more than half the nation's population. The rush to the coast began in the 1960s when the coastal population jumped a phenomenal 16 percent in a single decade. The growth continues at a slower but steady pace, with 165 million Americans predicted to be living on the coasts by the year 2015—up from 61 million in 1960.

Even among crowded coastal areas nationwide, Florida's coastal counties stand out. For the nation as a whole, the five counties predicted to have the greatest percentage population increase between 1994 and 2015 are all in Florida. Each week, the state's population adds another 4,400 people.

The Indian River Lagoon may appear pristine in some spots, but, as a whole, the waterway is among the most altered in the nation. Having never seen the Indian River Lagoon in its pristine state, it's all too easy for visitors to simply marvel at the richness of life found there today. The Florida population boom that got underway in the 1960s began a decade earlier on the northern reaches of the Indian River Lagoon, fueled by the nation's space program centered in Cape Canaveral. There were just 45,000 souls living in the five-county Indian River Lagoon region back in 1950. By 1960, the population has increased more than fourfold, to 200,000 people. At the end of the century there were approximately 1 million people living in the Indian River Lagoon region. The exploding population has radically altered the Indian River Lagoon in a host of ways. For example, there are currently 120,000 septic tanks in the Indian River Lagoon drainage area and effluent from more than 84,000 of them may be finding its way into the lagoon, contaminating the water with bacteria and flooding it with nutrients. Although the Florida legislature banned the practice in 1990, for decades dozens of municipal wastewater treatment plants discharged effluent directly into the Indian River Lagoon or into rivers that fed into the lagoon, adding tons of nutrients over the years.

Factors other than human waste are changing the Indian River Lagoon as well. The region is home to one of the largest citrus-growing areas in the country, producing 38 percent of Florida's huge citrus crop. Fertilizers, pesticides, and herbicides all wash into the Indian River Lagoon. Years ago, runoff from citrus groves would have had a chance to filter through wetlands and mangrove forests before entering the lagoon. But once development was put into high gear, those areas were considered unproductive wastelands. They were torn up and paved over or changed beyond recognition. Three quarters of the area's saltwater marshes were altered to control mosquitoes, and most mangrove forests are gone. The changes serve to funnel runoff directly into the Indian River Lagoon. In one county alone, 120 million pounds of soil enters the Indian River Lagoon annually—enough nutrient-rich dirt, as one newspaper article put it, "to fill 2,222 dump trucks." Where some creeks enter the Indian River Lagoon, the muck is now twelve feet deep and the rotten-egg stench that is the trademark of oxygen-starved areas fouls the air. An estimated 80,000 pounds of pesticides flow into the Indian River Lagoon annually. At high enough concentrations, pesticides are known to kill marine animals, and in a laboratory setting, lower, sublethal doses of pesticides have been shown to retard growth rates of some creatures. But we still know very little about the effects on marine organisms of chronic exposure to low levels of pesticides and herbicides.

Humans have hit the Indian River Lagoon with a triple whammy. Not only have the natural filters along the waterway been virtually eradicated, but inland communities and agribusinesses have constructed a maze of canals and drainage ditches that more than double the size of the watershed draining into the Indian River Lagoon—from 572,000 acres in 1916 to more than 1.4 million acres today. Even if the additional water pouring into the Indian River Lagoon weren't filled with chemical-laden sediment, the vast amounts of freshwater this artificial system adds to the brackish lagoon is enough to radically alter conditions in the Indian River Lagoon. In addition, floodwaters pent up in the highly polluted Lake Okeechobee are released into a canal that eventually ends up in the Indian River Lagoon. A massive release of freshwater from Lake Okeechobee into the St. Lucie River in March 1998 has been linked to a major outbreak of fish lesions there.

Even if dinoflagellates weren't the cause of Bill Jepson's problems (and that remains an open question), his life-threatening illness was still likely the result of the many changes humans have made to the Indian River Lagoon. By altering the water flow, flooding it with nutrients, agricultural chemicals and sediments, and changing its floor through dredging, we may well have created an environment in which a host of pathogens can thrive. When one considers these tremendous changes it doesn't seem terribly surprising that, as Lew Ehrhart put it in 1999, "Almost every turtle we pull out of the water has FP."

The Indian River Lagoon bears the same name as when August Park cast his turtle nets into those waters a century and a half ago, but it is today a different place altogether.

Chapter 12

The Environmental Key

WHEN A DOG-EARED report crossed Jan Landsberg's desk in early 1994, the marine biologist was so busy investigating a mysterious epidemic then killing reef fish in South Florida that she barely registered the title: "Research Plan for Marine Turtle Fibropapilloma."

Taking a break from examining sick fish, Landsberg quickly flipped through the proceedings. It was a result of the 1990 Honolulu workshop that George Balazs had organized, the publication that he had printed up by the hundreds and then shipped out to every agency and research institution he could think of—including the Florida Marine Research Institute in St. Petersburg, where Landsberg worked. It may have looked like any other technical memorandum issued by the NMFS, but to Balazs it was also something quite different: The report was a net Balazs had cast upon the waters of science and into which he hoped to gather minds with new ways of looking at the blight killing his beloved *honu.*

It was the maps that got to Landsberg—the stark black silhouettes of the Hawaiian Islands with white arrows indicating disease sites. The maps, and accompanying charts, showed that in Oahu's Kaneohe Bay, between 49 and 92 percent of the 121 turtles captured at four separate habitats in 1989–90 had the disease—some of them with numerous huge tumors. But over on the east coast of the Big Island of Hawaii, at a site known as Kiholo Bay, 140 turtles had been caught at 11 locations between 1987 and 1990, with many recaptures. Not a single Kiholo turtle showed signs of FP.

"I looked at that and just thought, 'Gee, someone should look at this environmentally,'" Landsberg recalls. That someone turned out to be Jan Landsberg, of course.

Her background made her the ideal person for the job. Her area of expertise gave Landsberg a fresh perspective on a possible explanation for why some *honu* populations remained completely healthy, while others quickly succumbed to the tumor disease.

Landsberg was earning a reputation for her innovative work in the little-explored area of algal biotoxins, poisons created by single-celled organisms for protection and predation. Landsberg's interest was even more finely tuned: She studied the effect that these biotoxins had at sublethal doses.

The field was ripe for investigation. Usually the biotoxins produced by harmful algal blooms kill quickly, and the results are dramatic and highly visible. Hundreds or thousands of dead fish are left floating on the ocean surface. Or, in the case of shellfish poisoning, diners are rushed to the hospital suffering from severe gastrointestinal cramps or bizarre neurological symptoms: tingling lips, paralysis, memory impairment, and, in extreme cases, coma or death.

Landsberg wanted to slow things down, conceptually speaking, while simultaneously opening them up. She was engaged in a scientific struggle to see the bigger picture.

"The old view of harmful algal blooms," Landsberg explains, "is that they come, they bloom, they go away. I'm more interested in the question, What is their effect over time?"

She had been pursing this environmental goal for most of her professional career. Landsberg had grown up in grim and sooty postwar London, where, in 1956 alone, when Landsberg was two, "killer smog" was blamed for 1,000 deaths, the product of the large amount of low-quality coal that was burned in homes and factories. The only wildlife she had known were the budgerigars—parakeets—her parents had kept. She loved her "budgies," and her childhood diaries were filled with information and stories about animals. Landsberg knew, even then, that she wanted to work with animals when she grew up, only not, she stresses, as a veterinarian.

"Because we lived in London," she explains, "I thought that all veterinarians did was give shots to cats and dogs. Well, I wanted something a bit more varied."

So when she was earning her doctorate at London University, Landsberg decided on an area that seemed a bit exotic. She studied fish diseases. If this doesn't appear to have the cachet of, say, studying gorillas in the mountains of central Africa, it is, at any rate, a good deal more exciting than administering vaccinations to Mrs. Dalloway's pampered grave terrier in a second-story flat off Cavendish Square. And it did turn out to be fascinating for Landsberg. With no jobs available for ichthyologists in the UK, she was forced to look for work abroad—and ended up on a kibbutz in northeastern Israel. She loved the work on aquaculture, the people, learning Hebrew and virtually everything else about life on Kibbutz Nir-David, except the fact that she lived in a tiny shed under extremely primitive conditions. After six years she took a research position in Tel Aviv, commuting to work from Jerusalem. But the housing gods once again were not smiling upon Jan Landsberg. For four years she lived in a cramped, dark, damp, and bug-infested basement apartment.

"One day I was sitting in my apartment and the five thousandth cockroach walked through for the twelve thousandth time and I thought, 'That's it.'" She had been in Jerusalem for four years and had begun to make a name for herself in fish parasitology, especially with her work on a parasitic protozoan called *Cryptosporidium*. It wasn't long before Landsberg was offered a full-time, if temporary, position at a laboratory in the United States.

The job was at the North Carolina State University and her boss was Ed Noga, the veterinary researcher who codiscovered *Pfiesteria piscicida*, and, by chance, the discovery occurred around the time Landsberg arrived at the lab.

"For the first time in my life," she says, "I was in the right spot at the right time."

It was a fascinating period for Landsberg, but when her position expired she once again had to look for work. This time she found a permanent home at the Florida Marine Research Institute, then an arm of the Florida Department of Environmental Protection.

It was there, in November 1993, that Landsberg was tapped to study an epidemic killing tropical fish—an incident that would give her special insight into the FP epidemic.

The first reports came from a tropical reef fish collector working the waters off Boynton Beach, Florida. The man told officials that he had seen hundreds of fish—angelfish, parrotfish, rock beauties, and more—with bloody sores on their heads, rotting fins, their entire bodies covered by white slime. The fish also behaved oddly, twitching madly. News of more diseased reef fish came almost immediately, all from the greater Palm Beach area of southeastern Florida. These were followed by reports from Islamorada in the upper Florida Keys. Same strange symptoms, same varieties of fish. The epidemic lasted for three months, until February 1994, with thousands of fish dead and a greater number sick.

Landsberg was thrilled. Not that she bore the fish of southern Florida any ill will. It was just that when she was called on to study a fish kill there was usually nothing there to study. Most fish die-offs are rapid, transient, now-you-see-it-now-you-don't events. Usually by the time anyone thought to call Landsberg, the victims usually had been devoured by predators or carried off by tides or currents. And even if there were fish remains at the scene, they were usually so decomposed that lab analysis was impossible.

So a slow-moving disease outbreak represented a rare opportunity for study. By mid-December Landsberg was out at Briney Breezes Reef off Boynton Beach collecting samples of diseased fish and bringing them back to her laboratory in St. Petersburg for examination.

In January, Landsberg had observed to a reporter from the *Miami Herald* that the outbreak was similar to an even larger 1980 episode that struck tens of thousands of reef fish from the Dry Tortugas, some 70 miles west of Key West, all the way up to Jupiter, Florida—a distance of more than 250 miles.

In both cases, the affected fish were found to be suffering from a variety of parasites: bacterial infections, amoebae, protists. But Landsberg believed these were all secondary infections.

"These fish become stressed from reasons we don't understand yet," she told the reporter. "Then they become weakened and attacked by everything that's out there."

Although she wasn't yet prepared to tell the reporter, Landsberg already suspected what that original stressor was.

What had caught Landsberg's attention immediately was the fact that some families of fish were getting sick, while others remained healthy. She had pored over lists of the fish affected by the two outbreaks, looking for similarities. And then she had seen it: diet. The fish that showed symptoms were from families that ate mostly algae or seaweed. The fish that didn't get sick were almost entirely species that ate plankton—minute drifting organisms—or fed upon the many small creatures on the reef bottom, coral polyps, mollusks, polychaete worms. Landsberg eventually published her findings in a journal article in which she speculated that the two mass mortalities were likely caused by dietary biological toxins that immunosuppressed the victims, leaving them open to infection by a range of pathogens.

Balazs's report came just when she was formulating this theory, and it ignited a spark. But Landsberg was overwhelmed studying the fish kills, and the workshop report got filed away. She might never have gotten back to the subject if the Eighteenth Annual Sea Turtle Symposium in 1997 hadn't been held almost in Landsberg's backyard—in Orlando, Florida. When she first heard about the symposium, Landsberg called her friend, Barbara Schroeder, the former Ehrhart student and forever-Turtlehead whom Landsberg had gotten to know when Schroeder had worked for the Florida State Department of Natural Resources some years earlier.

"I've got these little ideas," Landsberg explained to her friend. "Do you think anybody in the turtle world will listen to what I'm saying?" And she added, a little apologetically, "I mean, my ideas are pretty off the wall."

Schroeder encouraged her to go to the Orlando symposium and at least talk with George Balazs.

So in early March of 1997, Landsberg drove over to Orlando—it was a straight shot of 100 miles on Interstate 4—to talk with George Balazs about her theory. She had nothing to lose, really. She figured that the worst Balazs could do was to blow her off as a fish-disease expert who had strayed a bit too far from her field. She had no way of knowing that Balazs's motto was "Collaborate or Die!"

When they met at the symposium, Balazs listened intently to Landsberg's idea about a possible dietary factor in the FP epidemic. Landsberg describes the Hawaii researcher as being both "very gung-ho" and at the same time oddly cautious. That is to say that Balazs thought the idea represented an exciting avenue for investigation and he encouraged Landsberg to pursue it. But his pragmatic side, the one that had to come up with funding for research, held back. "Let's think about *how* to do this," he told her.

That's where things stood until a couple of months later when Landsberg contacted Balazs and asked if he could send her samples of algae from the different turtles' habitats. "No problem" he told her and started organizing the effort that same day.

Why go looking for other factors, such as dietary biotoxins, when FP had already been induced in the laboratory, simply by injecting a cell-free, chloroform-treated tumor extract? After all, the laboratory turtles had been raised since they were hatchlings on a diet of commercial turtle chow, so it was unlikely that they were somehow ingesting biotoxins. Didn't this show that the introduction of an enveloped virus (probably a unique herpesvirus) was both necessary and sufficient to cause FP?

Not surprisingly, that is the opinion of Larry Herbst, the researcher who conducted the transmission studies at the Turtle Hospital. He attributes the hunt for additional environmental cofactors at least in part to a widespread misunderstanding about the nature of herpesviruses.

"People have a preconception that herpesvirus is this ubiquitous latent infection that comes out under stressful conditions," he says.

Where would they have gotten that idea? Probably from their own experience with herpes simplex virus (HSV-1), which causes cold sores on the lips or mouth, or with HSV-2, the cause of genital herpes. The lesions caused by both these viruses frequently show up when the individual is under stress.

Many researchers *had* raised this issue in reference to FP, arguing that even if a herpesvirus were the etiologic agent, the turtles might never develop tumors, or symptoms of any kind, unless they were immunosuppressed—quite possibly as a result of what humans were doing to the turtles' environment. Peter Lutz, a leading marine turtle physiologist and coeditor of the widely respected book *The Biology of Sea Turtles*, brought up this very point in 1999. "The picture is very cloudy now," he said, talking about FP in general, and added, "a key area [for research] is immunosuppression."

Many studies have found that certain pollutants—heavy metals, pesticides, estrogenic compounds, to name a few—suppress the immune system in mammals, including humans. The recent massive die-off of North Sea seals, very possibly a consequence of immunosuppression caused by pollution, served as an example to FP researchers. This line of thinking was given a boost by a study of turtles with FP that found that the animals showed immune dysfunction.

But ever since he conducted his transmission studies, Larry Herbst hasn't given the immunosuppression angle much weight. Again, he bases that opinion mostly on the Turtle Hospital studies.

"They were clinically healthy animals," he insists. "They had good antibody responses. They appeared very healthy—in fact healthier than some of the wild turtles. Now, I can infect apparently healthy turtles and they get sick, they get tumors. That tells me that I don't have to give them immunosuppressive doses of some chemical. I don't have to stress them out."

Herbst does allow that stress (which can cause immunosuppression) is always a factor—in both captive *and* wild animals. There's no such thing as a stress-free existence. But were the turtles in his studies stressed enough to become immunosuppressed? "No way," he answers confidently. "These were healthy animals."

Herbst's view on immunosuppression was, however, speculative. Hard data, particularly from wild turtles, were needed.

The data to answer this question finally came from another researcher whom Balazs had gathered into his net, Thierry Work, a wildlife disease specialist heading the Honolulu Field Station of the National Wildlife Health Center. With funding supplied in part by Balazs's organization, Work set out to determine whether immunosuppression played a primary role in the FP epidemic. From April 1998 to February 1999, Work captured several turtles from two very different locations. From Kaneohe Bay on the island of Oahu, where FP was rampant, Work caught several turtles, both with and without tumors. He also caught turtles from the Kona Coast of the Big Island of Hawaii, where FP had not been found. Work drew blood samples from the turtles and released the animals back into the ocean. Back in the lab, Work tested the blood for immunological response.

"We found that there was no significant difference in immune response between nontumored turtles from Kanehoe Bay and those from Kona," Work says. He did find, however, that the most heavily tumored turtles from Kaneohe Bay were immunosuppressed, while those with light cases of the disease, those with fewer, smaller tumors, maintained a healthy immune system. These results strongly suggested that immunosuppression was a *result* of the disease, and not the *cause* of it.

That finding may at first appear to have ended Jan Landsberg's investigation of biotoxins and FP even before it started. After all, the premise of her earlier paper on the Florida reef fish kills was that biotoxins in the diet of the affected fish led to immunosuppression which, in turn, led to a variety of opportunistic infections. But there are dozens of algae, cyanobacteria, and dinoflagellates that are known to produce biotoxins, and each one can have a different effect on the creature unlucky enough to encounter it.

Very early on, Landsberg had focused on a specific biotoxin called okadaic acid. Among its attributes was an unusual one. Okadaic acid promotes tumors.

By the late 1970s, pharmaceutical companies were already beginning to see the potential of rain forests to supply new compounds useful in treating disease. Given the difficulties in gathering samples under water, the hunt for such medicinally useful biological agents in the oceans was a few steps behind. In the island nation of Japan, however, researchers were already actively searching for such compounds in the sea. The Fujisawa Pharmaceutical Company in particular was aggressively looking for anticancer agents, and they had found something intriguing from a common black sponge found on the Pacific coast of Japan, *Halichondria okadai*. They named the compound okadaic acid, after the sponge in which it was first found, and were encouraged to discover that okadaic acid killed cancer cells. Unfortunately, okadaic acid also killed normal cells, and the company dropped its research into the compound.

At the University of Hawaii, a doctoral candidate named Kazuo Tachibana continued working on okadaic acid, elucidating the exact structure of the compound. His findings were published in the *Journal of the American Chemical Society* in 1981. In the very last paragraph, Tachibana added what was to be a crucial caveat about okadaic acid. It was likely, he wrote, that the compound wasn't produced by the sponge itself, but by some other microorganism growing on the sponge. That was likely because sponges are filter feeders, catching all sorts of tiny organisms in their latticelike structure. What was perhaps the most

important revelation of the entire piece is found in the final footnote—
added at the last minute after the article was in final proof form.

"Professor T. Yasumoto has informed [us]," read the note, "that he
has isolated okadaic acid from the dinoflagellate *Prorocentrum lima. P.
lima* therefore is a likely progenitor of okadaic acid."

Professor Takeshi Yasumoto of Tohoku University in Japan had
been searching for years for the cause of ciguatera, the most common
form of seafood poisoning in humans. It was already well known by
then that surface blooms of algae caused illness and disease in people
who ate contaminated shellfish, but Yasumoto and his colleagues were
trying a different approach. They believed that ciguatera was caused by
a benthic microorganism—one living on the ocean bottom rather than
the surface (a hypothesis first published by another researcher in
1958)—and that this organism produced a toxin that bioaccumulated up
through the food chain, from herbivorous fish to carnivores such as
barracuda, until reaching humans. In 1977 Yasumoto was the lead
researcher in a small group that identified a dinoflagellate they called a
"likely culprit" in the disease: *Gambierdiscus toxicus*. The biotoxins
involved are some of the most potent on earth. Eating fish containing as
little as one-tenth of a microgram of ciguatoxin is enough to cause illness in a human. (To put this in perspective: a typical grain of salt
weighs about 600 times as much.)

In their search for the cause of ciguatera, Yasumoto and his colleagues found several other toxic dinoflagellates. One was *Prorocentrum lima*. Other investigators later linked *P. lima* to outbreaks of
another, less common, type of seafood poisoning called diarrhetic shellfish poisoning. But what interested Jan Landsberg most was another
property of *Prorocentrum* and its toxin okadaic acid. In 1988
researchers at Japan's National Cancer Center Research Institute found
that okadaic acid was a potent tumor promoter.

In some cases, a single event—exposure to high levels of radiation,
for example—is enough to cause cells to mutate and proliferate into
tumors. In other situations, however, the process involves two stages,

initiation and promotion. The chemical compound 7,12-dimethylbenz (a)anthracene (DMBA) is well known for its ability to initiate the formation of cancer cells. But unless applications of DMBA are followed by applications of another substance, a tumor promoter, growths rarely result. Similarly, the second substance alone is also unlikely to cause tumors. Put the two together, however, and look out. The Japanese researchers in 1988 found that mice treated with DMBA followed by an application of okadaic acid were seven times as likely to develop tumors as mice treated with either substance alone.

A two-stage process of tumor development is also known to occur in interactions between some viruses and chemicals. One of the earliest experimental examples of such a process involved the cottontail rabbit papillomavirus (CRPV). When rabbits were injected with CRPV, they commonly developed cancers within a year. When a tar extract was spread on patches of their skin, in the absence of CRPV, cancers rarely developed—and then only after a period of up to two years. But when viral injections were combined with tar, numerous tumors followed within just two months.

Some disease processes occur only in laboratories, where factors that never coexist in the "real world" are artificially brought together by scientists. Wild rabbits infected with CRPV, for example, are unlikely to fall into a puddle of carcinogenic tar in the course of the day. But viruses and tumor-promoting substances in the environment do sometimes come together, resulting in tumors. In the 1980s researchers in Scotland found that cattle infected with a papillomavirus that isn't generally associated with cancer developed bladder cancer after eating bracken fern, a plant that contains some very potent biotoxins, but which, by itself, doesn't cause bladder cancer.

Viewed through a scanning electron microscope, the dinoflagellate *P. lima* is quite beautiful. A simple but elegant oval seen from above, perfect in its symmetry (except for a slight variation at its base, where the whiplike flagella insert), *P. lima* has a sleekness to its architecture, a precision that suggests a mathematical formula given corporeality. Its silhouette is, ironically, a microscopic version of a *honu* hatchling's shapely carapace. Some forms of *Prorocentrum* are planktonic: They drift through the water, riding ocean currents. These are generally non-toxic species. *P. lima* and several of its okadaic acid–producing sister species, however, grow on seaweeds and macroalgae, where they could easily be consumed by turtles.

There were two question Landsberg wanted to answer: (1) Did toxic *Prorocentrum* species grow on the kinds of algae that turtles ate? (2) Was there any association between the presence of the dinoflagellates and FP?

Shortly after receiving Landsberg's request in April 1998, Balazs had gone to work collecting samples of the algae species that *honu* commonly ate in Hawaii and tapping into his island network to get others to help in the job. Balazs's drive to know everything about the *honu*, a characteristic that some less-focused researchers disparaged as "obsessive," was critical to the effort. A decade earlier, Balazs had been lead author of a 107-page investigation for NMFS on the habitat and diet of Hawaiian turtles at various sites throughout the archipelago. The report was based on meticulous field observations noting what turtles were eating when Balazs encountered them, recording what grew in known turtle foraging grounds, and analyzing turtles' stomach contents. (Balazs pioneered a technique for obtaining these samples by inserting a plastic tube into the stomach through a turtle's esophagus and gently flushing with water.) Always updating his work, in 1994 Balazs was coauthor of the first published report on how the *honu* were eating nonnative algae, species that had come to the Hawaiian Islands either accidentally, packed in shipments of shellfish, or as introduced commercial species. If anyone knew what the *honu* were eating, it was Balazs.

For Landsberg's study, Balazs and his helpers carefully gathered samples of the turtles' favorite foods at eight turtle foraging areas on five islands. (Balazs already had years of data on the incidence of FP at each site.) The samples were then analyzed to determine whether toxic species of *Prorocentrum* were present—and also in what quantity.

Finally, Landsberg placed the two data sets side by side, comparing the presence and amount of *Prorocentrum* at each site with their FP rates. A startling picture emerged.

At the three sites with the greatest prevalence of FP, not only was *Prorocentrum* found, but it was also found in the greatest abundance. And the three sites with the lowest FP rates had little or no *Prorocentrum*. The actual numbers are quite startling; the differences aren't just apparent, they're overwhelming.

For example, at a feeding ground off the island of Molokai, where tumor prevalence was rated high, the mean number of toxic *Prorocentrum* cells found per gram of algae was 280. But at Punalu'u on the Big Island, with an extremely low prevalence rate, Landsberg found no *Prorocentrum* whatsoever. In Kaneohe Bay, Oahu, again with high FP prevalence, 239 *Prorocentrum* cells were found in each gram of material analyzed. And at Kahaluu on Hawaii, low prevalence was correlated with just 2.3 cells of *Prorocentrum* per gram.

The study also examined actual turtle tissue for evidence of okadaic acid. A total of eighteen stranded and dying turtles were euthanatized and their kidneys analyzed to determine how much okadaic acid they contained. (To be precise, it wasn't okadaic acid that they looked for but a derivative of okadaic acid that was unlikely to have come from any other source. The researchers use the phrase "presumptive okadaic acid" when discussing this metabolite.) To correlate levels of presumptive okadaic acid and FP, the researchers used a scale Balazs had devised to assess tumor severity. He had argued for some time that researchers too often looked merely at FP *rates* without taking into account the *severity* of the disease in each instance—and so Balazs worked with a handful of other researchers to refine his system, based on the size and number of tumors. The scores ranged from zero (no tumors) to four (extreme affliction). The most severely afflicted turtles, with tumor scores of three and four, had significantly higher levels of presumptive okadaic acid than did turtles with only moderate cases (a score of 2).

Probably the most significant finding of the work with the stranded turtles is that nontumored animals were smaller than the ones with tumors. While the importance of this isn't immediately apparent, the study calls this finding "critical."

Landsberg explains that from this fact one can infer that some level of exposure period is at work. Turtle size is mostly a function of age. The larger the turtle, the older it likely is. And the older it is, the longer it's likely to have been exposed to *Prorocentrum* and the dinoflagellate's tumor-promoting toxin.

One nagging question in all this is a major difference in the diets of the Hawaiian *honu* and Florida's green turtles. The *honu*'s primary food source is algae, whereas their cousins in Florida have always been partial to the lush meadows of *Thalassia testudinum*—or, as it's commonly known, turtle grass. If a toxic dinoflagellate growing on algae is involved in the pandemic, how is one to account for this difference in diet between different populations of sea turtles? The short answer is that we can't, at least not yet, not with certainty. But there are reasonable hypotheses. One is based on the fact that seagrass beds around the world have been drastically reduced or wiped out altogether in the last fifty years. Algae, stimulated by nutrients, outcompete seagrasses. Deforestation, agriculture, and coastal development, as well as the mining of sand and coral, all put sediments into the water column, blocking the sunlight that photosynthesizing seagrasses need to survive. Scientists can only guess at the total reduction in seagrass meadows in the world's coastal waters, but where surveys have been done, the damage has been astonishing. Over the last half-century, the Philippines has lost an estimated 50 percent of its seagrass meadows with the Indonesian archipelago suffering only slightly lower losses.

Losses have been particularly heavy in the Caribbean, where spectacular beds of *Thalassia testudinum* once supported the huge population of green turtles that numbered in the scores of millions, if not in the hundreds of millions. By the early 1980s, when the FP epidemic exploded, large sections of the Caribbean had been entirely denuded of seagrass.

In the Indian River Lagoon itself, where Doc Ehrhart's Turtleheads first documented the FP epidemic, an estimated 30 to 50 percent of seagrass beds have been eliminated by stormwater runoff, with that figure running as high as 90 percent in some areas.

Florida Bay, the other primary FP hot spot on the mainland, has seen similar devastation of its once luxuriant seagrass meadows, which used to cover an estimated 95 percent of the bottom. Located at the southern tip of Florida, between the Everglades and the Florida Keys, the bay is the primary drainage area for the Everglades and much of the agricultural lands to the north. Freshwater flowing into the bay has been reduced to a trickle because of diversion for sugarcane fields, urban development, and flood control. Beginning in 1948, the Army Corps of Engineers built a system of canals that now siphons off 1.7 billion gallons of water each day—water that would have naturally ended up in Florida Bay. This diversion has tripled the salinity of water in the bay. Salinity coincided with other environmental events—an increase in nutrients from agricultural sources (feeding algae blooms) and higher than normal temperatures—to trigger yet another marine epidemic. This time it was a slime mold that attacked seagrass in the bay. Eventually, one hundred square miles of seagrass died from the blight.

It wouldn't be at all surprising if green turtles changed their diet from seagrass to algae, given the decimation of turtle grass around the world. And living on that algae could be toxic dinoflagellates such as *Prorocentrum*. Jan Landsberg even proposed such a scenario back in her 1995 study on the reef fish die-off.

"The absence or decline of preferred foods such as *Thalassia*, which recently occurred as a result of the seagrass die-off in Florida Bay," she wrote, "may cause turtles to switch to a different and perhaps potentially toxic diet."

Landsberg and Balazs have already begun the next step in their investigation, expanding the study area in Hawaii and surveying turtle foraging sites in Florida to determine the presence of toxic *Prorocentrum*. Already, preliminary findings in the Florida Keys suggest that, as in Hawaii, the areas with the highest prevalence of FP also have extremely high levels of the suspect dinoflagellate.

To see whether biotoxins play a key role in the FP pandemic, it's important to compare conditions in disease hot spots such as Grand Cayman Island, Indonesia, and Australia.

Jim Wood, the former manager of the Cayman Island Turtle Farm where Elliott Jacobson first saw the disease in 1980, found that 66 percent of the turtles released from the Turtle Farm and later recaptured had FP.

"When we did our releases," Wood says, "we picked a certain number out of the tank and let them go around the island. Subsequently, several of these turtles would develop these papillomas. Yet their cohorts—the ones kept at the Turtle Farm—didn't. We never had, to my knowledge, a single case of a young turtle at the Turtle Farm ever developing papillomas. Yet they're the *same* group of turtles. You let them go in the wild, they get it. Keep them at the turtle farm, they don't."

But merely releasing the turtles didn't doom them to FP. Wood found a significant association between *where* the turtles went and incidence of the disease.

"If we let turtles go on the west side of Grand Cayman, which is open ocean," he recalls, "we never recorded a case of a turtle having papillomas." But turtles released at a different site met a very different fate. Grand Cayman is long and narrow, running nearly fifty miles east to west. On a map, it looks as if some giant animal took a bite out of Grand Cayman near the western edge. The result of that bite is a large bay, known as North Sound, a body of water six miles north to south and nearly four miles wide at its mouth. A long coral reef blocks the sound's entrance, resulting in water that is slow to mix with oceanic waters. Wood found that the turtles recaptured in North Sound were far more likely to develop tumors than their cohorts released into the open ocean.

"To me it was just very much an environmental thing," he says. "And no one will ever convince me that it's not. It just seems to me that there's something different in those two environments."

Fred Burton agrees with Wood. Burton is the Environmental Programs Director of the National Trust for the Cayman Islands. Asked to describe the area in which FP rates are extremely high, Burton responds: "The North Sound is actually in trouble." He cites in particular the increased sediments, the result of decades of dredging in the area.

Wood adds that while the North Sound might not be as polluted as, for example, "the Houston [Texas] ship channel," development along its shores in the 1970s and 1980s led to an increase in the number of septic tanks. "In a coral type environment it just leeches directly into the water system," says Wood. "I'm sure it has a higher level of nutrients than it had 20 years before. The clarity was really quite good, but you did have areas where you got excessive algae growth and probably eutrophication [the rapid increase in the level of nutrients entering a body of water]."

The Indonesian experience with FP reveals a similar pattern. Rather than being raised in captivity as on Grand Cayman, green turtles are still commonly caught in the wild, slaughtered, and sold for meat in Indonesia. A trio of scientists from James Cook University in Australia did a year-long study of turtles brought to a slaughterhouse on the southern tip of the island of Bali, from January to December 1994. Of the 4,407 green turtles examined, 21.5 percent were afflicted with FP. Once again, the environment in which the turtles were found had a lot to do with whether they were diseased. The turtles were divided into two groups. One included animals caught near the industrialized urban centers of Jakarta and Surabaya. The FP rate for this group was 26.3 percent. The second group consisted of turtles captured mostly in waters surrounding the sparsely inhabited islands on the eastern end of the Indonesian archipelago—some 1,300 miles from Jakarta—and had an FP rate of 17.7 percent. The difference in the FP prevalence rates between the two areas is statistically significant.

It would be helpful to fine-tune these figures, to know just how many of the turtles in group 1 were caught in or close to Jakarta Bay itself, and what proportion of FP turtles were from there. What makes this more than a little interesting is the fact that unlike North Sound in the Cayman Islands, Jakarta Bay isn't just somewhat polluted—it is massively polluted, with nutrient levels nearly off the scale. Jakarta Bay has rightly been called an example *"par excellence* of the terminal stage of coral reef eutrophication." It's hard to know exactly where to begin when cataloging all the insults humans have inflicted on this once-paradisiacal ecosystem, where nearly 100 species of hard corals were cataloged in the 1930s (the entire Caribbean has about 50) and where only 16 species are counted today—and the remaining colonies are fragmented, sickly and shrinking.

More than 10 million people live in Jakarta, one of the most densely packed cities in the world, with 130,000 people jammed into each square mile in some neighborhoods. Untreated sewage pours into Jakarta Bay at a rate of 7 million cubic feet per day, feeding huge algae blooms. Then there's the more than 2,000 tons of solid waste that are dumped or washed into Jakarta Bay daily; the fumes spewing from the millions of vehicles choking Jakarta's streets; the enormous quantities of sediments and nutrients flowing into the bay from rivers due to agriculture, logging, and mining upstream, unfiltered by the mangrove forests that once surrounded the bay but which have long since been destroyed—well, you get the idea. Jakarta Bay is one of the most polluted bodies of water in the world and the fact that turtles living in or near it have higher rates of FP than those caught in relatively clean water again suggests a human role in the pandemic. Unfortunately, the turtles in group 1 weren't limited to Jakarta Bay, and so we can only wonder what the incidence of the disease is in animals actually living in those polluted waters.

Australia's experience with FP is analogous, but with an interesting new wrinkle. The disease has *never* been seen in green turtles nesting at Heron Island, the primary nesting grounds for the species on the southern end of the Great Barrier Reef. Of all the major coral islands in that magnificent 1,200-mile-long chain, Heron Island is one of the furthest from land—and so the least affected by human influences. But FP has been found in turtles at other locations. The disease went from zero incidence at Repulse Bay (in sparsely settled northern Queensland) in 1988, to 3 percent the following year, and up to 12 percent in 1999.

But the Australian epidemic has been greatest in Moreton Bay, affecting anywhere from 8 percent all the way up to 80 percent of turtles depending on the section of the bay. According to Mark Read, a senior conservation officer for the Queensland government, in Moreton Bay as a whole, the FP incidence fluctuates between 10 and 20 percent from year to year. A large portion of the bay is open to the ocean and is well flushed. But as you head south, the bay is separated from the sea by a series of sand islands and narrows at the same time. "If we move down into this constricted area," states Read, "the incidence of [FP] increases up to 80 percent of animals captured, which is damn high!"

It is, in fact, one of the highest rates in the world.

Moreton Bay shares some important characteristics with the other FP hot spots. The bay is the drainage area for Brisbane and surrounding communities, with a total population of more than 2 million people—the largest population center, and the fastest-growing one, in the territory of Queensland. Water carrying sediments and nutrients from an area covering 5.4 million acres ends up in the Moreton Bay. Population growth and erosion from nonurban areas are critical factors in water-quality problems here as in the other FP hot spots. A 1989 symposium titled "Moreton Bay in the Balance" concluded that "the major potential water quality problem in Moreton Bay is the continuing increase in nutrient loading and resultant increased aquatic plant production. ...Increased phytoplankton biomass and relatively infrequent 'red tide' events have already been detected in this area. Additional nutrient loading could be expected to exacerbate both effects with consequent increased damage to the aquatic ecosystem."

That warning appears to have been borne out starting in 1996, when health officials noticed a microorganism called *Lyngbya majuscula* blooming in ever larger quantities in Moreton Bay. In April and May 1997, *Lyngbya* covered nearly three square miles in the northern section of the bay. In the following year, long strands of the stuff, some up to a foot long, once again covered the sea-floor, growing on seagrass and rocks. It returned with a vengeance in 1999 and then exploded in 2000, covering a record 11 square miles in the region.

Bulletins on the enormous bloom were featured on Australian newscasts, in part because of the amazing speed with which *Lyngbya* spreads—up to 2,000 square feet per minute at the edge of the bloom. What this means is that if you were standing in water twenty-five feet from the edge of a *Lyngbya* bloom, a minute later you'd have *Lyngbya* washing around your ankles—not a happy scenario, because *Lyngbya* toxins cause skin rashes resembling second-degree burns.

"It gets in your eyes, and your lips swell up and crack," complained one Brisbane-area fisherman. "People walk along the beach and the skin on their feet starts to peel."

Researchers suspect increased nutrient levels coming from disturbed upstream soils may be causing the spectacular *Lynbgya* blooms.

Despite the frequent media references to Fire Weed (as *Lyngbya* is commonly known in Australia) as an algae, it is, in fact, a type of bacterium. It's a cyanobacterium, to be precise, one of the oldest living organisms on earth, found in the fossil record going back at least 3.3 billion years. And it's a producer of many forms of biotoxins.

An Australian, George Francis, was the first scientist to write about cyanobacteria's poisonous qualities, back in 1878, after he witnessed a thick build-up of "pond scum" that was, he recorded, "like green oil paint, some two to six inches thick, and as thick and pasty as porridge." His observations of animals that drank this contaminated water are vivid and chilling:

> Symptoms—stupor and unconsciousness, falling and remaining quiet, as if asleep, unless touched, when convulsions come on, with head and neck drawn back by rigid spasm, which subsides before death. Time—sheep, from one to six or eight hours; horses, eight to twenty-four hours; dogs, four to six hours; pigs, three or four hours.

In addition to causing burning skin rashes, the cyanobacterium that's causing problems in Moreton Bay, *Lyngbya majuscula*, produces two biotoxins with a common trait. Lyngbyatoxin A and aplysiatoxin are both potent tumor promoters.

Colin Limpus is to Australia's sea turtles what George Balazs is to the *honu*. They each serve as a sort of turtle ambassador in their respective waters. Limpus is currently investigating to see whether there is a connection between the *Lyngbya* outbreaks and the high incidence of FP in Moreton Bay. Takeshi Yasumoto, the researcher who first isolated okadaic acid from *Prorocentrum*, believes that such a link is likely, going so far as to call the biotoxins produced by *Lyngbya* as "the most probable cause" of FP.

In the early 1990s Yasumoto investigated a case in Madagascar in which a person died after eating a green sea turtle. Laboratory analysis found lyngbyatoxin A in the turtle's tissues. The victim's symptoms were consistent with lyngbyatoxin A poisoning, and Yasumoto found *Lyngbya*—but not *Prorocentrum*—growing on the seagrasses and algae preferred by the turtles in the region. And as a final suggestive factor, says Yasumoto, "I was told by the local people that the turtle showed tumor-like abnormalities in the neck and limbs."

Jan Landsberg and George Balazs recognize the possibility that biotoxins produced by *Lyngbya* blooms may be involved in FP. "The potential role of marine cyanobacteria and their chronic effect should certainly be considered," they wrote in their FP/dinoflagellate paper.

But their experience in Hawaii doesn't support the linkage. *Lyngbya* rarely turned up in samples from turtle foraging grounds taken during their study, and the cyanobacteria are known to grow along the FP-free Kona Coast just as it is in areas associated with high levels of FP.

Still, different tumor promoters could play the same role in the FP pandemic at different locations. After all, human alteration of the marine environment affects the growth and toxicity of both dinoflagellates and cyanobacteria. And that's precisely the one characteristic shared by all FP hot spots: humans have radically changed the marine environment in which the diseased turtles live.

Chapter 13

Children of the Sea

IT'S A BIT OF A HIKE from the highway down to Kiholo Bay, over a rough, poorly marked trail that winds first through sparse vegetation typical of this desertlike section of Hawaii's Kona Coast, then under a stand of magnificent coconut palms that shade burbling fish ponds carved into rock by ancient Hawaiians, and opening finally to our destination: a lagoon of such pale turquoise that the water appears to float, untethered and dreamlike, above the ground. The effect is heightened by the pond's contrast with its shoreline of jet-black lava, where sensual coils and undulations still seem elastic, as if they could begin flowing again at any moment (although they cooled to rock more than a century ago).

"There they are!" says an excited George Balazs, pointing to a group of turtles basking on the shore of Wainanali'i Pond. I follow his pointing finger to where five immature turtles lie motionless in the midday heat. Balazs and his colleague Marc Rice of the Hawaii Preparatory Academy (another of the countless Balazs collaborators) dubbed them Obake Turtles, the Japanese word for ghost. That's exactly what they look like: apparitions glowing a hallucinatory white in the blinding sun.

The same fine chalky silt that gives the pond its extraordinary color is responsible for the Obake Turtles' ghostly appearance. The silt settles on their carapaces and then bakes to a powder as they bask in the brilliant sunlight for up to eleven hours at a time.

Although the pond at Kiholo Bay is worth seeing for its surreal beauty alone, I had another reason for asking Balazs to take me here—it is FP-free. Of the more than 400 individual turtles Balazs has examined here regularly since 1987 (many of them checked several times), not one has ever shown signs of the tumor disease that is epidemic in other parts of Hawaii.

As we clamber over lava boulders to get a better look, Balazs explains that the Kiholo turtles make a convincing case for *honu* site fidelity. Only a few of the hundreds of turtles tagged here have been recaptured anywhere else.

"At night, they rest on submerged ledges or on the bottom of the pond," he says. "Just before dawn, they leave the lagoon and swim into the bay to munch on algae." After that, they may haul out onto the shore and go into a trancelike state that approaches catatonia. That might seem like a rather boring existence to us mammals, but their "homebody" nature may also keep the Obake Turtles free of the tumor disease.

For years, researchers have cited "genetic variability" to explain why FP isn't found in certain turtle populations while others are decimated by it. The theory is sound. Genetic factors have been linked to dozens of human illnesses from breast cancer to Parkinson's disease. So Balazs had the DNA from Obake Turtles sequenced and compared the results to the DNA from *honu* populations in which FP is rampant. The result: The tests showed that the Kiholo turtles belong to the same breeding stock as other *honu* populations in the Hawaiian Islands, suggesting that the absence of FP among the Obake population is likely the result of factors other than genetic variability.

A strong piece of evidence for an environmental link came in 1999 when Ursula Keuper-Bennett spotted a young turtle at the Turtle

House bearing a tag from Kiholo Bay. It was a rare Kiholo immigrant that had somehow, for whatever reason, ended up 100 miles to the northwest. Later that summer, Ursula though "Kiholo" (as they named it) showed early signs of FP, white spots on its neck and a thickening at the corner of the left eye. By the summer of 2000, Kiholo's spots and slight thickening had become tumors. In the dozen times Kiholo had been checked for FP between March 1989, when it was first tagged, and October 1996, the turtle had never shown a sign of the disease. A year at Honokowai and Kiholo had developed a full-blown case of FP.

The other news from the Turtle House isn't good. In a single year, the FP infection rate hovers around 70 percent. That's bad enough, but the trend over the long term is even worse.

After a dozen summers spent monitoring the *honu* off Honokowai, Ursula reported to Balazs in the summer of 2000 that "Every single turtle we've gotten close enough to either has or has had FP." (Researchers have documented cases of spontaneous regression, but they don't yet know whether the animals can still spread the disease or, indeed, whether the growths can return.)

She continued, "One *honu* from 1991 and two *honu* both from 1992 who've hung tough against the disease have developed FP this summer! It now means every single *honu* from the Old Times [early 1990s] that is still around today has or had FP. One-hundred percent infection."

Years ago, when Ursula was first diving in Hawaii, the arrival of a juvenile *honu* at the Turtle House was an occasion for joy, something to be celebrated. "Now," she says, "when a kiddie comes to the Turtle House I want to yell at it to swim away."

Reports of new outbreaks in the marine metademic continue, appearing mostly in scientific journals. Although human connections are often suspected, they are usually difficult to prove. But even Larry Herbst, the first researcher to transmit FP in a laboratory and one of the most consistently skeptical voices challenging those who look beyond a viral etiology for FP, believes humans may play an important role in the FP pandemic.

For Herbst, the issue has never been about biotoxins or immunosuppression, though he concedes that the former may be a factor in whether an already infected turtle dies from the disease. "There are any number of factors affecting the course of a disease," he says. "Biotoxins may be one." But Herbst insists that, to his way of thinking, a virus, probably a herpesvirus, is both necessary and sufficient to cause FP in healthy animals. But, he allows, there is more to the story.

Where wildlife ecologists often go wrong, says Herbst, is in focusing exclusively on the environment's effect on the victim.

"[Wildlife ecologists] tend to look at disease," Herbst explains, "as an epiphenomenon," meaning, of secondary importance. "They believe that something else had to have affected the animals first. When something else affects that animal, it then becomes unable to protect itself, and these things come out in a stressful situation."

And, in fact, that often *is* the case. Herbst explains: "When food runs out and the animals are starving, you do see a lot of disease outbreaks in those animals. And you could argue that the disease is just a secondary effect. The *real* thing that's killing the animals is lack of food."

But sometimes the situation is more complex. According to Herbst, some wildlife ecologists forget that the environment also affects the pathogen itself. Instead of concentrating exclusively on how a human-altered environment may hurt turtles directly, Herbst believes that more attention should be paid to how that same environment may *help* viruses.

He cites a multitude of factors that can make an environment pathogen-friendly: nutrient and sediment loading, altering the physical makeup of the coastal bottom, changing the temperature of the ocean. An interesting list: humans do all these things.

"Something as simple as dumping a bunch of organic material into the water can actually allow some of these viruses to hang out longer," Herbst says. "And some viruses don't survive very well on sand. But if you put them in a muddy sediment they can persist for a long time."

Global warming may also play a role in the FP pandemic. Warmer water appears to accelerate the course of the disease in turtles with FP, leading to faster tumor growth and increased mortality.

Then there's the effect of overcrowding. Every time a square acre of seagrass is lost, whether it's the result of dredging, sedimentation from runoff, or disease, sea turtles are forced to crowd together that much more. It's a simple formula, really, says Herbst: habitat destruction leads to overcrowding, which leads to an epidemic. All it takes is a single infected animal entering an overcrowded environment.

But I ask Herbst whether turtle density has increased enough to account for the pandemic of FP. Even given widespread habitat destruction, surely the number of sea turtles per square mile is just a fraction of what it was a couple of hundred years ago. Herbst laughs. "No one has the measurements to substantiate any of this," he readily admits. "This is just me speculating like crazy."

Once again, we return to the fallback position: "More study is needed."

Which makes me think of what Sam Ka'ai had to say about scientific research when I paid him a visit at his home in Hawaii.

Sam Ka'ai is a *kahuna*, a traditional Hawaiian spiritual leader. In addition, the *honu* is his *'amakua*, or familial deity. Even in the old days, before the Endangered Species Act prohibited catching and eating turtles, his ancestors didn't eat *honu*. In return, the turtles protected the Ka'ais from danger when they were at sea, delivering them from sharks and storms.

Turtles were everywhere in Sam Ka'ai's world. Painted and woven images of *honu* hung on the walls of his home, which was perched, birdlike, on the western slopes of Maui's sacred Mount Haleakala. A huge bleached-white turtle skull sat on a shelf. Beside it was a hawksbill shell, yellow and cream-colored streaks against a light brown background—shooting stars plummeting from a tropical sky. Ka'ai had a turtle tattooed on his left calf, just inches above tattooed waves encircling his ankle.

"No, no, no, no," Ka'ai was saying into his cordless phone, as he paced his living room floor. "You thank the *honu* first, *then* you pass the bowl counterclockwise."

A *kahuna* has certain areas of expertise. Ka'ai is a storyteller and a master carver of sacred wooden objects. But by necessity, he spent much of his time on the phone helping young Hawaiians learn the old rituals.

Ka'ai finished his phone conversation and dropped into a chair opposite mine. He was short and stout and his once-black beard was beginning to turn gray. But what you noticed immediately were his arms. They were massive. Wood carvers often have strong arms, but not like these. From the shoulders down to his fingers, everything was muscle.

Ka'ai owed these arms to his years spent paddling and sailing across the Pacific Ocean in a traditional Polynesian canoe, a 62-foot-long double-hulled craft named the *Hokule'a*. The voyages of the *Hokule'a*, which was the first traditional craft to recreate the ancient Polynesian voyages, helped to rekindle ethnic pride, not just in Hawaii, but throughout Polynesia. The undertaking was difficult and dangerous. Ka'ai had been one of a sixteen-member crew aboard the *Hokule'a* that left Hawaii for Tahiti in March 1978. Five hours out to sea, the boat encountered huge swells and high winds. It capsized. Ka'ai and the other crew members spent the night in shark-filled waters, clinging to the hulls and waiting for morning, when they hoped a plane would spot them. On the next afternoon, with the men weakening under the effects of a blazing tropical sun, and with chances for rescue dwindling as the *Hokule'a* drifted out of flight corridors, a crew member named Eddie Aikau decided to go for help, paddling a surfboard. He disappeared without a trace. Finally, Ka'ai and the rest were rescued.

Two years later, Sam Ka'ai and several others from the original crew once again attempted the voyage. This time they were successful, sailing the 3,000 miles from Hawaii to Tahiti in just over a month, an achievement that was celebrated throughout Polynesia.

Ka'ai was now sitting in his chair, massive forearms resting on his knees. I imagined those arms clinging through the night to the

Hokuleʻa, and I wanted to ask Kaʻai whether he had called on his *ʻamakua* then, and whether he had received a reply, but I knew that such a question would have been improper. There is, inevitably, a distance between traditional Hawaiians and whites, or *haole.* Conversations between the two are freighted by several centuries' accumulation of ill will. It is a history of imperialism, betrayal, and attempts at cultural, if not actual, genocide on the part of whites. This past doesn't vanish just because a particular *haole* smiles and acts politely. Before I had spoken a single word, Kaʻai was already regarding me warily. Still, he had agreed to talk with me about the cultural significance of the *honu* to his people, and in our conversation, though he remained formal and even grave, he opened the door a crack, just enough to glimpse the sacred link between Hawaiians and the *honu.*

"Turtle is seen as a benevolent character who inhabits the spiritual world and the physical world at the same time," he said, looking straight ahead as he talked. "It is the link between the two. Turtle is the foundation."

For millennia, sea turtles had been to many Pacific islanders what the buffalo was to the Plains Indians of North America, a source of physical, spiritual, and cultural nourishment. The buffalo provided Plains people with food and vital goods. In part because of the many gifts given by the buffalo, the animal was venerated by Plains cultures as the embodiment of generosity, strength, and wisdom. Similarly, throughout the Pacific, sea turtles have been a traditional source of food (both meat and eggs) and of important everyday items. Shells were made into fish hooks, jewelry, and ceremonial items. This heavy dependence in daily life was reflected in the spiritual relationship that links Pacific islanders to turtles. Like the *honu* in Sam Kaʻai's house, sea turtles are everywhere in the creation myths, sacred carvings, and rich ceremonial life of the Pacific.

When Kaʻai finished, I brought up the subject of the disease called FP. I didn't mean to go into such detail, but once started I found myself unable to stop. The words poured out. I quoted journal articles and unpublished studies. I had read dozens of these and bits of information were whizzing around inside my head like the shiny metal spheres in a pinball game, setting off flashing lights of possible connections and vague significances wherever they struck. Remembering that day, I think that I was simply trying to make sense out of the jumble of data.

Through it all, Ka'ai remained silent—as if I gave him much of a choice, short of slapping a piece of duct tape over my mouth.

When at last I realized that I had been jabbering on far too long, I stopped and sat there, my face aflame with embarrassment. Ka'ai allowed silence to reclaim his room before speaking. And when he did speak, there was anger in his voice.

"Studies are like the tide," he said, spitting out the words. "It flows in and out. But nothing is done."

Based on what we already know, there *is* much that we could do to end the marine metademic that burns through the sea, claiming those ancient mariners, green turtles, and the countless and uncounted species that are likely winking out every day. We could stop treating the ocean as if it were the world's largest garbage dump and start treating it like the sacred source of all life that it is. We could end our mindless plundering of the sea, a process that plays havoc with complex marine ecology, unweaving millennia of evolutionary relationships. We could balance growth and development with habitat preservation. We could, finally, get serious about stopping global warming.

We could, we could, we could—but will we?

Through it all, the man who knows most about the *honu* and about its tumor disease remains optimistic—it's a hopefulness that comes from his near-daily interactions with the turtles themselves. As we watch the ghostly Obake Turtles basking languorously on the shore of Wainanali'i Pond, Balazs smiles.

"I look at these animals," he says. "I handle them. I swim with them. And it's a constant reminder of just how precious they are. My wife is a medical social worker—she works on a stroke unit. Every day of the week, she deals with people who have had strokes. She deals with the families, with the devastation, with some successes. When you're that close to a situation you say, we've got to do the very best we can. We can't just throw up our hands. Maybe the answer will need tremendous amounts of resources and time to solve. But, what do you do? Throw up your hands and say, 'Just let it happen'?"

He shakes his head forcefully.

"Sorry, that's just not my philosophy. That's not the way I was put together. You stay close to the animals, and it keeps you motivated to keep going and to say there *have* to be gates that can be opened that can lead to a solution, gates that we can't even dream about right now. And if we don't keep trying, how will we ever learn to open the dang things?"

Lew Ehrhart, the founding father of the Florida Turtleheads, told me much the same thing as we stood on the shore of a different ocean, the Atlantic, looking out at the most important nesting beaches for green turtles in the Western Hemisphere, in the Archie Carr National Wildlife Refuge on the central Florida coast, where Ehrhart has been doing surveys for two decades.

"We just have to keep at it," he said. "An answer isn't going to come easily, and I doubt it'll come soon. But I always think in terms of the long view. What's this"— and he indicated the glistening beach stretching into the distance—"going to look like in twenty or thirty years?"

For Ehrhart, as for Balazs, it's the mystical joy that comes from working with individual turtles that keeps him going, a passion he tries to impart to his students. "I tell them that they won't make much money and they'll sweat a lot, and get dirty and wet and uncomfortable. But they might just look back on these nights monitoring nesting turtles as some of the best times of their lives."

As he said this, a flock of five brown pelicans came gliding out of the north, following the waterline and riding an ocean breeze in perfect formation, passing directly over us and disappearing to the south—without once flapping their wings.

We looked up and remained silent for the full minute it took for the pelicans to sail majestically by. And when they had finally dwindled into the distance, Lew Ehrhart, the eminent, Cornell-trained biologist, and I, someone who earns his keep by using words, smiled at each other and both said: "Wow!"

At twilight on my last evening in Maui, Ursula, her husband Peter, and I went down to the shore where they handed me a yard-long stalk of red ginger flowers and told me to throw it into the ocean as far as I could.

"It's a promise to return to the Turtle House," explained Ursula, who could be described as devoutly nonreligious, a veritable born-again atheist. Like many people in that category, she is profoundly spiritual. She creates her own rituals for nearly everything. I gripped the flower stalk like a javelin, took a step forward, and tossed the staff of flowers into the air. It arced up into the night sky—a flash of brilliant red against the gathering darkness—and fell back into the sea.

I haven't exactly returned to the Turtle House. I have stood on the shore at Honokowai in March, when Ursula and Peter were back in snow-cloaked Toronto, and watched the blue-green waves riding up from Pailolo Channel, covering the Turtle House and its slowly dying inhabitants. But return takes many forms, and while it may be just a rationalization, I hope I've fulfilled the pledge I made that evening on the beach by telling the story of the Turtle House in these pages.

Besides, and far more important, wherever I go—wherever any one of us goes—we are always in the Turtle House. Sam Ka'ai got it right and maybe the best I can do is to repeat what he told me when I left his house the day of our talk.

I thanked him for meeting with me, we shook hands, and I headed toward my rental car, which wore a patina of fine Maui red dirt. His voice startled me.

"Hey," he called. I stopped and turned. Ka'ai was leaning against the doorway. Those huge arms of his were folded across his chest, arms that, I remember, had clung through that terrible night to an overturned canoe in the middle of the vast Pacific. But now the tropical sunshine was splashing over his face, and in that dazzling light I suddenly realized that beneath his thick beard he was, for the first time, smiling. A small smile, to be sure. But a smile.

"Remind them," he called out in a voice that was at once both grave and hopeful. "Remind them: We are *all* children of the sea."

Bibliography

Adnyana, W., P. W. Ladds, and D. Blair. "Observations of fibropapillomatosis in green turtles (*Chelonia mydas*) in Indonesia." *Australian
Veterinary Journal*, Vol. 75, No. 10, 1997, pp. 737–42.

Aguirre, Alonso, et al. "Adrenal and hematological responses to stress in
juvenile green turtles (*Chelonia mydas*) with and without fibropapillomas." *Physiological Zoology*, Vol. 68, No. 5, 1995, pp. 831–54.

Aguirre, Alonso, et al. "Evaluation of Hawaiian green turtles (*Chelonia
mydas*) for potential pathogens associated with fibropapillomas." *Journal of Wildlife Diseases*, Vol. 30, No. 1, 1994, pp. 8–15.

Amerson, A. B., Jr. "The natural history of French Frigate Shoals, North-
western Hawaiian Islands." *Atoll Research Bulletin*, No. 150, 1971, pp.
1–303.

Anderson, Donald. "Turning back the harmful red tide." *Nature*, Vol. 388,
7 August 1997, pp. 513–14.

Antonius, Anfried. "Coral reef pathology: a review." *Proceedings of the
Fourth International Coral Reef Symposium*, Vol 2 (Quezon City,
Philippines, 1981), pp. 3–6.

Aronson, Richard, and William Precht. "Stasis, biological disturbance, and community structure of a Holocene coral reef." *Paleobiology*, Vol. 23, No. 3, 1997, pp. 326–46.

————. "White-band disease and the changing face of Caribbean coral reefs." *Hydrobiologia*. In press.

Aronson, Richard, et al. "Coral bleach-out in Belize." *Nature*, Vol. 405, 4 May 2000, p. 36.

Audubon, John James. *Birds of America*, Vol. 5 (New York: George R. Lockwood and Son, 1870).

Balazs, George. "Fibropapillomas in Hawaiian green turtles." *Marine Turtle Newsletter*, No. 39, December 1986.

————. "Green turtle's uncertain future." *Defenders*, December 1975, pp. 521–23.

————. "Preliminary assessment of habitat utilization by Hawaiian green turtles in their resident foraging pastures." Technical Memorandum, NOAA-TM-NMFS-SWFSC–71 (Honolulu: Southwest Fisheries Science Center, National Marine Fisheries Service, NOAA, March 1987).

Balazs, George, and Ernest Ross. "Observations on the preemergence behavior of the green turtle." *Copeia*, No. 4, 1974, pp. 986–88.

Balazs, George, and Samuel Pooley. "Research plan for marine turtle fibropapilloma." Technical Memorandum, NOAA-TM-NMFS-SWFSC–156 (Honolulu: Southwest Fisheries Science Center, National Marine Fisheries Service, NOAA, March 1991).

Balazs, George, et al. "Interim recovery plan for Hawaiian sea turtles." Administrative Report, H–92–01 (Honolulu: Southwest Fisheries Science Center, National Marine Fisheries Service, NOAA, February 1992).

Barilotti, Steve. "Our mother ocean." *Surfer*, September 1996.

Barker, Rodney. *And the waters turned to blood* (New York: Simon & Schuster, 1997).

Barragan, Ana, and Laura Sarti. "A possible case of fibropapilloma in Kemp's ridley turtle (*Lepidochelys kempii*)." *Marine Turtle Newsletter*, No. 67, 1994, p. 27.

Birkeland, Charles. *Life and death of coral reefs* (New York: Chapman & Hall, 1997).

Bishop, Richard, and Arnold van der Valk. "Wetlands." In *Iowa's natural heritage* (Des Moines: Iowa Natural Heritage Foundation and the Iowa Academy of Science, 1982).

Borel, Joan. "Turtling in the Keys." In *The Monroe County environmental story*, Jeannette Gato, ed. (Big Pine Key, FL: Monroe County Environmental Education Task Force, 1991).

Bossart, Gregory. "The Florida manatee: On the verge of extinction?" *Journal of the American Veterinary Medical Association*, Vol. 214, No. 8, 15 April 1999, pp. 1178–83.

Bruckner, Andrew, and Bruckner, Robin. "Emerging infections on reefs." *Natural History*, Vol. 106, December 1997–January 1998, p. 48.

Burkholder, JoAnn, et al. "Distribution and environmental conditions for fish kills linked to a toxic ambush-predator dinoflagellate." *Marine Ecology Progress Series*, Vol. 124, 1995, pp. 43–61.

Carlton, James. "Apostrophe to the ocean." *Conservation Biology*, December 1998, pp. 1165–67.

Carmichael, Wayne. "The toxins of cyanobacteria." *Scientific American*, January 1994, pp. 78–86.

Cesar, Herman. *Economic analysis of Indonesian coral reefs* (Washington, DC: World Bank, December 1996).

Chaves, Anny Quiros, et al. "Fibropapilloma in the ostional olive ridley (Lepidochelys olivacea) population." *Proceedings of the Eighteenth Annual Symposium on Sea Turtle Biology and Conservation* (3–7 March 1998, Mazatlan, Mexico). U.S. Department of Commerce NOAA Tech. Memo NMFS-SEFSC-436, 2000.

Clinton, William. "Remarks by the president to the National Ocean's Conference," 12 June 1998, Monterey, California.

Colón, Fernando. *The life of the admiral Christopher Columbus by his son, Ferdinand* (New Brunswick, NJ: Rutgers University Press, 1959).

Cooperative Research Centre. "Brisbane River." In *Brisbane River catchment study* (Indooroopilly, Queensland, Australia: CRC for Coastal

Zone Estuary and Waterway Management, 2000). http://www.coastal. crc.org.au/html/body_brisbane_river_moreton_bay.html

Culliton, Thomas. "Population: Distribution, density and growth." National Oceanic and Atmospheric Administration, on-line, 1998. http://state-of-coast.noaa.gov/bulletins/html/pap_01/pop.html.

Curry, Robert. "Coupling marine and terrestrial watershed processes." Presentation at Sanctuary Currents '96, sponsored by the Monterey Bay National Marine Sanctuary, 9 March 1996.

Curry, Sadie, et al. "Persistent infectivity of a disease-associated herpesvirus in green turtles after exposure to seawater." *Journal of Wildlife Diseases*, October 2000, pp. 292–97.

Dall, William. Letter to the editor, *Nautilus*, August 1892, p. 48.

Daszak, Peter, et al. "Emerging infectious diseases of wildlife—Threats to biodiversity and human health." *Science*, Vol. 287, 21 January 2000, pp. 443–49.

Davidson, Osha. *The enchanted braid: Coming to terms with nature on the coral reef* (New York: John Wiley & Sons, 1998).

De Swart, Rik. "Impaired immunity in seals exposed to bioaccumulated environmental contaminants." Ph.D. diss., Erasmus University, The Netherlands, 1995.

De Swart, Rik, et al. "Morbilliviruses and morbillivirus diseases of marine mammals." *Infectious Agents and Disease*, Vol. 4, 1995, pp. 125–30.

Dennison, William, et al. "Proliferation of the cyanobacterium *Lyngbya majuscula* in Moreton Bay, Australia." In Charpy and Larkum, eds., *Marine cyanobacteria*, Special issue of *Bulletin de l'Institut Océanographique*, 1999, pp. 501–6.

Devine, Robert. *Alien invasion* (Washington, DC: National Geographic Society, 1998).

Dodge, John. "Dinoflagellate taxonomy." In *Dinoflagellates*, David Spector, ed. (Orlando, FL: Academic Press, 1984).

Domning, Daryl. "Sea cow family reunion." *Natural History*, April 1987, pp. 64–71.

Dozier, Craig. *Nicaragua's Mosquito shore* (Tuscaloosa: University of Alabama Press, 1985).

Dustan, Phillip. "Vitality of reef coral populations off Key Largo, Florida: Recruitment and mortality." *Environmental Geology*, Vol. 2, 1977, pp. 51–58.

Ehrhart, Llewellyn. "Habitat protection revisited: Debunking the Noah solution." *Proceedings of the Seventeenth Annual Symposium on Sea Turtle Biology and Conservation* (4–8 March 1997, Orlando, Florida). U.S. Department of Commerce NOAA Tech. Memo NMFS-SEFSC-415, 1998, pp. 48–51.

———. "Marine turtles of the Indian River Lagoon." *Florida Scientist*, Vol. 46, Nos. 3/4, 1983, pp. 337–46.

———. "Threatened and endangered species of Kennedy Space Center, marine turtle studies," Vol. 4, Part 1. Report to the National Aeronautics and Space Administration, Contract No. NAS10–8986, KSC TR 51–2. Kennedy Space Center, Florida, 21 August 1979.

Ehrhart, Llewellyn, and Paul Raymond. "Loggerhead turtle, *Caretta caretta*, and green turtle, *Chelonia mydas*, nesting densities in south Brevard County, Florida, 1981–1984." In *Ecology of East Florida sea turtles*, NOAA Technical Report, NMFS 53, May 1987, pp. 21–25.

Ehrhart, Llewellyn, and R. G. Yoder. "Marine Turtles of Merritt Island National Wildlife Refuge, Kennedy Space Center, Florida." *Proceedings of the Florida and Interregional Conference on Sea Turtles* (St. Petersburg, FL: Florida Department of National Resources, Marine Research Laboratory, 1978), pp. 25–30.

Ehrlich, Paul, and Anne Ehrlich. *Extinction: The causes and consequences of the disappearance of species* (New York: Random House, 1981).

Environmental Protection Agency. "What you should know about *Pfiesteria piscicida.*" Fact sheet #EPA 842-F-98-011 2000.http://www.epa.gov/owow/estuaries/pfiesteria/fact.html. (Created 13 October 1998.)

Epstein, Paul. "Climate, ecology, and human health." *Consequences*, Vol. 3, No. 1, 1997, pp. 3–19.

————. *Marine ecosystems: Emerging diseases as indicators of change* (Washington, DC: Health Ecological and Economic Dimensions, Global Change Program, 1998).

Epstein, Paul, et al. "Marine ecosystems." *The Lancet*, Vol. 13, November 1993, pp. 1216–19.

Fisher, Raymond. *Bering's voyages* (Seattle: University of Washington Press, 1977).

Fisher, James, et al. *The red book: Wildlife in danger* (London: Collins, 1969).

Food and Agriculture Organization. "Forest resources assessment 1990: Global synthesis." FOA forestry report #124 (Rome, Italy: FOA, 1995).

Foote, Jerris, et al. "An increase in marine turtle deaths along the west central coast of Florida (1995–1996): Is red tide the culprit?" *Proceedings of the Seventeenth Annual Symposium on Sea Turtle Biology and Conservation* (4–8 March 1997, Orlando, Florida). U.S. Department of Commerce NOAA Tech. Memo NMFS-SEFSC-415, 1998, pp. 180–82.

Ford, Corey. *Where the sea breaks its back* (Boston: Little, Brown, 1966).

Fosdick, Sam, and Peggy Fosdick. *Last chance lost?* (York, PA: Irvin S. Naylor, 1994).

Fujiki, H., et al. "Indole alkaloids: Dihydroteleocidin B, teleocidin and lyngbyatoxin A as members of a new class of tumor promoters." *Proceedings of the National Academy of Sciences of the United States of America*, Vol. 78, No. 6, 1981, pp. 3872–76.

Fujiki, H., et al. "The 3rd class of new tumor promoters, polyacetates (debromoaplysiatoxin and aplysiatoxin) can differentiate biological actions relevant to tumor promoters." *Japanese Journal of Cancer Research*, Vol. 73, No. 3, 1982, pp. 495–97.

Garman, S. "The reptiles of Bermuda." *Bulletin of the United States National Museum*, Vol. 25, 1884, pp. 287–99.

Garrett, Laurie. *The coming plague* (New York: Farrar, Straus and Giroux, 1994).

Geiser, David, et al. "Cause of sea fan death in the West Indies." *Nature*, Vol. 394, 9 July 1998, pp. 137–38.

Ginsburg, Robert, comp. *Proceedings of the Colloquium on Global Aspects of Coral Reefs: Health, hazards and history.* Miami: Rosenstiel School of Marine and Atmospheric Science, University of Miami, 1994.

Gladfelter, W. "White-band disease in *Acropora palmata*: Implications for the structure and growth of shallow reefs." *Bulletin of Marine Science,* Vol. 32, No. 2, 1982, pp. 639–43.

Glynn, Peter. "Coral reef bleaching: Ecological perspectives." *Coral Reefs,* Vol. 12, 1993, pp. 1–17.

Golder, F. A. *Bering's Voyages,* Vol 2 (New York: Octagon Books, 1968).

Goolsby, D., et al., "Flux and sources of nutrients in the Mississippi-Atchafalaya River Basin." In *Gulf of Mexico hypoxia assessment,* NOAA Coastal Ocean Program, May 1999.

Goreau, Thomas, et al. "Rapid spread of diseases in Caribbean coral reefs." *Revista de Biologia Tropical,* Vol. 45 (Suppl. 5), 1998, pp. 157–71.

Granéli, Edna, et al., eds. *Toxic marine phytoplankton* (New York: Elsevier Science Publishing, 1990).

Grattan, Lynn, et al. "Learning and memory difficulties after environmental exposure to waterways containing toxin-producing *Pfiesteria* or *Pfiesteria*-like dinoflagellates." *The Lancet,* Vol. 352, 15 August 1998, pp. 532–39.

Haines, Harold, and William Kleese. "Effect of water temperature on a herpesvirus infection of sea turtles." *Infection and Immunity,* Vol. 15, No. 3, March 1977, pp. 756–59.

Hallam, A., and P. B. Wignall. *Mass extinctions and their aftermath* (Oxford: University of Oxford Press, 1997).

Harper, David. *Molecular virology.* (Oxford: BIOS Scientific Publishers, 1998).

Harshbarger, John. "Fibrous tumors in marine turtles in the registry of tumors in lower animals," unpublished paper presented at the December 1997 Marine Turtle Fibropapilloma Workshop, Honolulu, Hawaii, 1997.

Haruhiko, Nakata, et al. "Persistent organochlorine residues and their accumulation kinetics in Baikal seal (*Phoca sibirica*) from Lake Baikal, Russia." *Environmental Science & Technology,* Vol. 29, No. 11, 1995, pp. 2877–85.

Harvell, Drew, et al. "Emerging marine diseases—Climate links and anthropogenic factors." *Science*, 3 September 1999, pp. 1505–10.

Harwood, John, et al. "Workshop on the causes and consequences of the 1997 mass mortality of Mediterranean monk seals in the western Sahara." *IBN Scientific Contributions*, No. 11, Wageningen, The Netherlands: The DLO Institute for Forestry and Natural Research, 1998.

Hendrickson, J. R. "The green sea turtle, *Chelonia mydas* (Linn.), in Malaya and Sarawak." *Proceedings of the Zoological Society of London*, Vol. 130, 1958, pp. 455–35.

———. "Report on Hawaiian marine turtle populations." *Proceedings of the Working Meeting of Marine Turtle Specialists.* IUCN Publications, new series, Vol. 20, 1969, pp. 89–95.

Herbst, Lawrence. "The etiology and pathogenesis of green turtle fibropapillomatosis." Ph.D. diss., University of Florida, 1995.

———. "Fibropapillomatosis of marine turtles." *Annual Review of Fish Diseases*, Vol. 4, 1994, pp. 389–425.

Herbst, Lawrence, et al. "Experimental transmission of green turtle fibropapillomatosis using cell-free tumor extracts." *Diseases of Aquatic Organisms*, Vol. 22, 4 May 1995, pp. 1–12.

———. "Sensitivity of the transmissible green turtle fibropapillomatosis agent to chloroform and ultracentrifugation conditions." *Diseases of Aquatic Organisms*, Vol. 25, 6 June 1996, pp. 225–28.

Hernandez, Mauro, et al. "Did algal toxins cause monk seal mortality?" *Nature*, Vol. 393, 7 May 1998, pp. 28–29.

Hinrichsen, Don. *Coastal waters of the world.* Washington, DC: Island Press, 1998.

Hirama, S., and L. Ehrhart. "Prevalence and severity of green turtle fibropapillomatosis in the Indian River lagoon." *Florida Scientist*, Vol. 62, No. 1, 1999, p. 35.

Hoegh-Guldberg, Ove. *Climate change, coral bleaching and the future of the world's coral reefs.* Sydney, Australia: Greenpeace Australia, 1999.

Holden, Constance. "Reef bleaching spreads in Caribbean." *Science*, Vol. 270, 10 November 1995, p. 919.

Hudnell, Kenneth. "Human vision function in the North Carolina clinical study on *Pfiesteria piscicida*." Research Triangle Park, North Carolina: United States Environmental Protection Agency, 1998.

Hughes, Terence. "Catastrophes, phase shifts, and large-scale degradation of a Caribbean coral reef." *Science*, 9 September 1994, pp. 1547–51.

Indian River Lagoon National Estuary Program. *The Indian River Lagoon Comprehensive Conservation and Management Plan* (Melbourne, FL: Indian River Lagoon National Estuary Program, November, 1996).

Jackson, Maria, et al. "Cooperation between papillomavirus and chemical cofactors in oncogenesis." *Critical reviews in oncogenesis*, Vol. 4, 1993, pp. 277–91.

Jacobson, Elliott. "Mycotic pneumonia in mariculture-reared green sea turtles." *Journal of the American Veterinary Medical Association*, Vol. 175, No. 9, 1 November 1979, pp. 929–33.

———. "Virus associated neoplasms of reptiles." In *Phyletic approaches to cancer*, C. J. Dawe, et al., eds. (Tokyo: Japan Scientific Societies Press, 1981), pp. 53–58.

Jacobson, Elliott, et al. "Conjunctivitis, tracheitis, and pneumonia associated with herpesvirus infection in green sea turtles." *Journal of the American Veterinary Medical Association*, Vol. 189, No. 9, 1 November 1986, pp. 1020–23.

———. "Cutaneous papillomas associated with a herpesvirus-like infection in a herd of captive African elephants." *Journal of the American Veterinary Medical Association*, Vol. 189, No. 9, 1 November 1986, pp. 1075–78.

———. "Herpesvirus in cutaneous fibropapillomas of the green turtle *Chelonia mydas*." *Diseases of Aquatic Organisms*, Vol. 12, 6 December 1991, pp. 1–6.

———. "Pathologic studies on fibropapillomas of the green turtle, *Chelonia mydas*." Unpublished study, 1987.

Kennedy, Seamus, et al. "Mass die-off of Caspian seals caused by canine distemper virus." *Emerging Infectious Diseases*, Vol. 6, No. 6. November–December, 2000.

King, Wayne. "Historical review of the decline of the green turtle and the hawksbill." In *Biology and conservation of sea turtles*, Karen Bjorndal, ed. (Washington, DC: Smithsonian Institution Press, 1981), pp. 183–88.

Knight, Danielle. "Ocean bottom trawling worse than forest clearcutting." Inter Press Service, 14 December 1998.

Kricher, John. *A neotropical companion*. Princeton, NJ: Princeton University Press, 1989.

Kridler, Eugene. "Hawaiian Islands National Wildlife Refuge spring trip, March 19–April 6, 1969." Unpublished report, U.S. Fish and Wildlife Service, Bureau of Spot Fisheries and Wildlife, 1969.

Landsberg, Jan. "Tropical reef-fish disease outbreaks and mass mortalities in Florida, USA: What is the role of dietary biological toxins?" *Diseases of Aquatic Organisms*, 15 June 1995, pp. 83–100.

Landsberg, Jan, and Sandra Shumway. "Harmful algal blooms and their effects on marine and estuarine animals." *Proceedings of the Third International Symposium on Aquatic Animal Health*, Baltimore, MD, 1998.

Landsberg, Jan, et al. "The potential role of natural tumor promoters in marine turtle fibropapillomatosis." *Journal of Aquatic Animal Health*, Vol. 11, No. 3, September 1999, pp. 199–210.

Lessios, H. "Mass mortality of *Diadema antillarum* in the Caribbean: What have we learned?" *Annual Review of Ecology and Systematics*, Vol. 19, 1988, pp. 371–93.

Levitus, Sydney, et al. "Warming of the world ocean." *Science*, 24 March 2000, pp. 2225–29.

Lewis, Bernard. "The Cayman Islands and marine turtle." *Bulletin of the Institute of Jamaica Science Series*, No. 2, 1940, pp. 56–65.

Limpus, Colin, and Jeffrey Miller. "The occurrence of cutaneous fibropapillomas in marine turtles in Queensland." *Proceedings of the Australian Marine Turtle Conservation Workshop*, 14–17 November 1990

(Brisbane: Queensland Department of Environment and Heritage and the Australian Nature Conservation Agency, 1994), pp. 186–88.

Limpus, Colin, et al. "The green turtle, *Chelonia mydas*, in Queensland: Population structure in a warm water temperate feeding area." *Memoirs of the Queensland Museum*, Vol. 35, No. 1, 1994, pp. 139–54.

Long, Edward. *The history of Jamaica* (London: Frank Cass,1774).

Lu, Yuanan, et al. "Detection of green turtle herpesviral sequence in saddleback wrasse *Thalassoma duperrey*: A possible mode of transmission of green turtle fibropapilloma." *Journal of Aquatic Animal Health*, Vol. 12, 2000, pp. 58–63.

Lucké, Balduin. "Studies on tumors in cold-blooded vertebrates." In *Annual Report of the Tortugas Laboratory*. Washington, DC: Carnegie Institute, 1938), pp. 92–94.

Mac, Michael, et al. *Status and trends of the nation's biological resources*, Vol. 1 (Reston, VA: U.S. Department of the Interior, U.S. Geological Survey, 1998).

McAllister, Don. "Status of the world ocean and its biodiversity." *Sea Wind*, Vol. 9, No. 4, 1995, pp. 1–72.

Mclaren, Grant. "Heavy iron, inc." *Professional Pilot Magazine*, November 1984.

Merriam-Webster Medical Dictionary (Springfield, MA: Merriam-Webster, 1995).

Miller, G. Tyler, Jr. *Living in the environment* (Belmont, CA: Wadsworth 1994.

Mlot, Christine. "The rise in toxic tides." *Science News Online*, 27 September 1997.

Moffat, Anne Simon. "Global nitrogen overload problem grows critical." *Science*, Vol. 279, 13 February 1998, pp. 988–89.

Moreton Bay in the balance. Queensland, Australia: Australian Littoral Society, 1992.

Morison, Samuel. *Admiral of the ocean sea* (Boston: Little, Brown, 1942).

Murakami, Yasutaka, et al. "Identification of okadaic acid as a toxic component of a marine dinoflagellate *Prorocentrum lima.*" *Bulletin of the Japanese Society of Scientific Fisheries*, Vol. 48, No. 1, 1982, pp. 69–72.

Nagelkerken, Ivan, et al. "Widespread disease in Caribbean sea fans." *Marine Ecology Progress Series*, Vol. 160, 15 December 1997, pp. 255–63.

National Agricultural Statistics Service. *1997 census of agriculture, ranking of states and counties*, Vol. 2. Subject Series Part 2 (Washington, DC: United States Department of Agriculture, May 1999).

National Office for Marine Biotoxins and Harmful Algal Blooms. "The harmful algae page: Human illness associated with harmful algae." http://www.redtide.whoi.edu/hab/illness/illness.html#Ciguatera Fish Poisoning, 2000.

National Research Council. *Clean coastal waters: Understanding and reducing the effects of nutrient pollution* (Washington, DC: National Academy Press, 2000).

National Research Council. *Decline of the sea turtle* (Washington, DC: National Academy Press, 1990).

New Jersey FishNet/FishNet USA. "Otter trawling." http://www.fishingnj.org/techott.htm, 1999.

Nietschmann, Bernard. "The cultural context of sea turtle subsistence hunting in the Caribbean and problems caused by commercial exploitation." In *Biology and conservation of sea turtles*. Bjorndal, ed. (Washington, DC: Smithsonian Institution Press, 1981), pp. 439–45.

Nietschmann, Bernard. *Between Land and Water* (New York: Seminar Press, 1973).

———. *Caribbean Edge*. Indianapolis: Bobbs-Merrill. 1979.

———. "When the Turtle Collapses, the World Ends." *Natural History*, June-July 1974, pp. 34–43.

Nigrelli, Ross, and George Smith. "The occurrence of leeches, *Ozobranchus branchiatus* (Menzies), on fibro-epithelial tumors of marine turtles, *Chelonia mydas* (Linnaeus)." *Zoologica*, Vol. 28, 1943, pp. 107–8.

Norse, Elliott. "Turning up the heat" (Redmond, WA: Marine Conservation Biology Institute, 1999). http://www.worldwildlife.org/news/pubs/wwf_ocean.htm.

Norse, Elliott, ed. *Global marine biological diversity* (Washington, DC: Island Press, 1993).

Osterhaus, Albert, et al. "Morbillivirus in monk seal mass mortality." *Nature*, Vol. 388, 28 August 1997, pp. 838–39.

Paerl, Hans, and David Whitall. "Anthropogenically-derived atomospheric nitrogen deposition, marine eutrophication and harmful algal bloom expansion: Is there a link?" *Ambio*, 4 June 1999, pp. 307–11.

Parsons, James. *The green turtle and man* (Gainesville, FL: The University of Florida Press, 1962).

Paulay, Gustav. "Diversity and distribution of reef organisms." In *Life and death of coral reefs*, Charles Birkeland, ed. (New York: Chapman & Hall, 1997).

Quackenbush, Sandra, et al. "Prevalence and phylogeny of herpesvirus sequences from normal and fibropapilloma tissues of green and loggerhead turtles sampled at Moreton Bay, Australia." *Proceedings of the Nineteenth Annual Symposium on Sea Turtle Biology and Conservation* (2–6 March 1999, South Padre Island, Texas). U.S. Department of Commerce NOAA Tech. Memo NMFS-SEFSC-443, 2000.

Rabalais, Nancy, et al. "Characterization of hypoxia." *Gulf of Mexico hypoxia assessment*, NOAA Coastal Ocean Program, May 1999.

———. "Nutrient changes in Mississippi River and system responses on the adjacent continental shelf." *Estuaries*, June 1996, pp. 386–407.

Raidal, S., and R. Prince, "First confirmation of multiple fibropapillomas in a western Australian green turtle (*Chelonia mydas*)." *Marine Turtle Newsletter*, No. 74, 1996, pp. 7–9.

Raloff, Janet. "Fishing for answers." *Science News*, 26 October 1996.

Randall, John. "A review of ciguatera, tropical fish poisoning, with a tentative explanation of its cause." *Bulletin of Marine Science of the Gulf and Caribbean*, Vol. 8, 1958, pp. 236–67.

Ranson, Robert. *East Coast Florida memoirs* (Port Salerno, Florida: Florida Classics Library, 1989).

Reaka-Kudla, Marjorie, et al. *Biodiversity II* (Washington, DC: Joseph Henry Press, 1997).

Rebell, Gerbert, et al. "A herpesvirus-type agent associated with skin lesions of green sea turtles in aquaculture." *American Journal of Veterinary Research*, Vol. 36, No. 8, August 1975, pp. 1221–24.

Richardson, Laurie. "Coral diseases: what is really known?" *Trends in ecology and evolution*, Vol. 13, 1998, pp. 438–43.

————, et al. "Florida's mystery coral-killer identified." *Nature*, Vol. 392, 9 April 1998, pp. 557–58.

Ridgway, Sam, and Richard Harrison, eds. *Handbook of marine mammals*, Vol. 2, *Seals* (London: Academic Press, 1981).

Robblee, M., et al. "Mass mortality of the tropical seagrass *Thalassia testudinum* in Florida Bay (USA)." *Marine Ecology Progress Series*, Vol. 71, 30 April 1991, pp. 297–99.

Roberts, Orlando. *Narrative of voyages and excursions on the east coast and interior of Central America* (Gainesville: University of Florida Press, 1965). Reprint of 1827 edition.

Robinson, Robb. *Trawling* (Exeter: University of Exeter Press, 1996).

Ross, Peter. "Seals, pollution and disease." Master's thesis, State University of Utrecht, The Netherlands, 1995.

Russell, Dennis, and George Balazs. "Utilization of alien algal species by sea turtles in Hawaii." *Proceedings of the conference and workshop: Non-indigenous estuarine and marine organisms*, April 1993, Seattle, WA (Rockville MD: National Oceanic and Atmospheric Administration, 1994), pp. 94–97.

Samarrai, Fariss. "Helping urchins may benefit corals." *Sea Frontier*, Winter 1995, pp. 16–17.

Scheffer, Victor. "The last days of the sea cow." *Smithsonian*, Vol. 3, No. 10, January 1973, pp. 64–67.

Schroeder, Barbara, et al. "Ecology of marine turtles in Florida Bay: Population structure, distribution, and occurrence of fibropapilloma." *Proceedings of the Seventeenth Annual Symposium on Sea Turtle Biology and Conservation* (4–8 March 1997, Orlando, Florida). U.S. Department of Commerce NOAA Tech. Memo NMFS-SEFSC-415, 1998, pp. 281–83.

Schroeder, William. "Fisheries of Key West and the clam industry of southern Florida." Report to the U.S. Commissioner of Fisheries, Appendix XII, Doc. No. 962, Bureau of Fisheries (Washington, DC: Government Printing Office, 1924), pp. 50–71.

Sea stats (newsletter of the Florida Marine Research Institute, Department of Environmental Protection), February 1998.

Seagrass Team. "Summary of seagrass workshop." http://www.aoml.noaa. gov/flbay/seagrass.html, 10 December 1998.

Sebastian Area Historical Society. *Tales of Sebastian.* [Booklet.] Sebastian, Florida, 1990.

Shinn, Eugene. "African dust causes widespread environmental distress." *USGS Information Sheet,* United States Geological Survey (Washington, DC: U.S. Department of the Interior, April 2000).

Sindermann, Carl. *Ocean pollution: Effects on living resources and humans* (Boca Raton, Florida: CRC Press, 1996).

Smayda, Theodore. "Novel and nuisance phytoplankton blooms in the sea: Evidence for a global epidemic." In *Toxic marine phytoplankton,* Edna Granéli, et al., eds. (New York: Elsevier, 1990), pp. 29–40.

Smith, Garriet, et al. "Caribbean sea fan mortalities." *Nature,* Vol. 383, 10 October 1996, p. 487.

Smith, George, and Christopher Coates. "Fibro-epithelial growths of the skin in large marine turtles, *Chelonia mydas.*" *Zoologica,* Vol. 23, 1938, pp. 93–98.

———. "The occurrence of trematode ova, *Hapalotrema constrictum* (Leared), in fibro-epithelial tumors of the marine turtle, *Chelonia mydas* (Linnaeus)." *Zoologica,* Vol. 24, 1939, pp. 379–87.

Steidinger, Karen, et al. "Harmful algal blooms in Florida." Report by the Harmful Algal Bloom Task Force Technical Advisory Group, Florida's Harmful Algal Bloom Task Force, 8 March 1999.

Steinbeck, John. *Cannery Row* (New York: Viking, 1945).

Stejneger, Leonhard. "How the great northern sea-cow (rytina) became exterminated." *American Naturalist,* December 1887, pp. 1047–54.

Steller, Georg. "The beasts of the sea." In *The fur seals and fur-seal islands*

of the north Pacific Ocean, part 3 (Washington, DC: Government
Printing Office, 1899), pp. 179–201.

———. *Journal of a voyage with Bering, 1741–1742* (Stanford: Stanford
University Press, 1988).

Stewart, Doug. "Making sense of manatees." *National Wildlife,* April/May
1999, pp. 1–5.

Suganuma, Masami, et al., "Okadaic acid: An additional non-phorbol–12-
tetradecanoate–13-acetate-type tumor promoter." *Proceedings of the
National Academy of Sciences,* Vol. 85, March 1988, pp. 1768–71.

Sundberg, John. "Papillomavirus infections in animals." In *Papillomaviruses and human disease,* K. Syrjanien, et al., eds. (Berlin:
Springer-Verlag, 1987).

Tachibana, Kazuo, et al. "Okadaic acid, a cytoxic polyether from two
marine sponges of the genus *Halichondria.*" *Journal of the American
Chemical Society,* Vol. 103, 1981, pp. 2469–71.

Takacs, David. *The idea of biodiversity* (Baltimore: Johns Hopkins University Press, 1996).

Taubenberger, Jeffery, et al. "Two morbilliviruses implicated in bottlenose
dolphin epizootics." *Emerging Infectious Diseases* [serial online], Vol.
2, No. 3, July–September, 1996.

Taylor, F., et al. "Taxonomy of harmful dinoflagellates." In *Manual on
harmful marine microalgae,* G. Hallegraeff, et al., eds. Intergovernmen-
tal Oceanographic Commission Manual 33 (Paris: UNESCO, 1995),
pp. 283–317.

Teas, Wendy. "Sea turtle strandings and salvage network: Green turtles,
Chelonia mydas, and fibropapillomas." In *Research plan for marine
turtle fibropapilloma,* G. H. Balazs and S. G. Pooley, eds. U.S. Department of Commerce. NOAA Tech. Memo. NMFS-SWFSC–156, 1991,
pp. 89–93.

Tennant, Raymond. "What is a tumor promoter?" *Environmental Health
Perspectives,* Vol. 107, No. 8, August 1999, pp. 390–91.

Terres, John. *The Audubon Society encyclopedia of North American birds*
(New York: Alfred A. Knopf, 1991).

Turner, B. L., et al. *The earth as transformed by human action* (Cambridge: Cambridge University Press, 1990).

Umbgrove, Johannes. *Madreporaria from the Bay of Batavia* (Leiden, the Netherlands: E. J. Brill, 1939).

UNAIDS. *Report on the global HIV/AIDS epidemic* (Geneva: UNAIDS, June 2000).

U.S. Bureau of the Census. *Historical estimates of world population.* http://www.census.gov/ipc/www/worldhis.html, 1999.

————. *Total midyear population for the world: 1950–2050*, http://www.census.gov/ipc/www/worldpop.html, 1999.

————. *World POPclock projection.* http://www.census.gov/cgi-bin/ipc/popclockw, 1999.

U.S. Environmental Protection Agency. "Indian River Lagoon." http://www.epa.gov/OWOW/oceans/lagoon, 1999.

U.S. Congress. Senate. Committee on Commerce, Science, and Transportation. "Coral bleaching." *Hearings.* 101st Congress, 2d session (Washington, DC: U.S. Government Printing Office, 1991).

U.S. Global Change Research Program. "Coral bleaching: ecological and economic impacts." 2001. http://www.usgcrp.gov/usgcrp/seminars/960213SM.html.

Varela, Rene. "The immunology of green turtle fibropapillomatosis." Master's thesis, Florida Atlantic University, 1997.

Visser, I., et al. "Characterization of morbilliviruses isolated from dolphins and porpoises in Europe." *Journal of General Virology*, Vol. 74, 1993, pp. 631–41.

Waller, Geoffrey, ed. *SeaLife: A complete guide to the marine environment* (Washington, DC: Smithsonian Institution Press, 1996).

Watling, Les, and Elliott Norse. "Disturbance of the seabed by mobile fishing gear: A comparison with forest clear-cutting." *Conservation Biology*, Vol. 12, No. 6, December 1998, pp. 1180–97.

Waxell, Sven. *The Russian expedition to America* (New York: Collier Books, 1962).

Weinstein, Anna. "Agriculture." *Monterey Bay National Marine Sanctu-*

ary Site characterization, socioeconomic uses. http://bonita.mbnms. nos.noaa.gov/sitechar/soci7.html, 1999.

―――. "Commercial fisheries." *Monterey Bay National Marine Sanctuary Site characterization*, socioeconomic uses. http://bonita.mbnms. nos.noaa.gov/sitechar/soci3.html, 1999.

―――. "Early uses of resources." *Monterey Bay National Marine Sanctuary Site characterization*, human influences. http://bonita.mbnms.nos. noaa.gov/sitechar/earl.html, 1999.

Wilcox, William. "Commercial fisheries of Indian River, Florida." *Report of commissioner of fish and fisheries* (Washington, DC: Government Printing Office, 1896).

Wilkinson, Clive, ed. *Living coastal resources for southeast Asia: Status and management.* Report of the Consultative Forum, Third ASEAN-Australian Symposium (Townsville, Australia: Australian Institute of Marine Science, 1994).

Wilkinson, Clive. *Status of coral reefs of the world: 2000* (Townsville, Australia: Global Coral Reef Monitoring Network, Australian Institute of Marine Science, 2000).

Wilkinson, Clive, et al. "Ecological and socioeconomic impacts of 1998 coral mortality in the Indian Ocean." *Ambio*, Vol. 28, No. 2, March 1999, pp. 188–96.

Williams, Ernest, Jr., and Lucy Bunkley Williams. "Caribbean marine mass mortalities." *Oceanus*, Vol. 30, No. 4, 1987, pp. 69–75.

Wilson, E. O. *The diversity of life* (Cambridge, MA: Belknap Press, 1992).

Wilson, E. O., ed. *Biodiversity* (Washington, DC: National Academy Press, 1988).

Witherington, Blair, and Llewellyn Ehrhart. "Hypothermic stunning and mortality of marine turtles in the Indian River Lagoon system, Florida." *Copeia*, No. 3, 1989, pp. 696–703.

Witzell, W. "The origin, evolution, and demise of the U.S. sea turtle fisheries." *Marine Fisheries Review*, Vol. 56, No. 4, 1994, pp. 8–23.

Wood, Fern, and James Wood. "Release and recapture of captive-reared green sea turtles, *Chelonia mydas*, in the waters surrounding the Cayman Islands." *Herpetological Journal*, Vol. 3, 1993, pp. 84–89.

Wood, Fern, and James Wood. "Sea turtles of the Cayman Islands." In M. Brunt and J. Davies, eds., *The Cayman Islands: Natural history and biogeography* (Norwell, MA: Kluwer Academic Publishers, 1994), pp. 229–36.

Work, Thierry, and George Balazs. "Relating tumor score to hematology in green turtles with fibropapillomatosis in Hawaii." *Journal of Wildlife Diseases*, Vol. 35, No. 4, October 1999, pp. 804–7.

Work, Thierry, et al. "Immunology of green turtle fibropapillomatosis in Hawaii." Wildlife Disease Conference, Athens, Georgia, 1999, p. 75.

World Bank. *Indonesia: Environment and development* (Washington, DC: World Bank, 1994).

Worldwatch Institute. *State of the world, 1998* (New York: Norton, 1998).

Yasumoto, Takeshi. "Fish poisoning due to toxins of microalgal origins in the Pacific." *Toxicon*, Vol. 36, No. 11, 1998, pp. 1515–18.

Yasumoto, Takeshi, et al. "Finding of a dinoflagellate as a likely culprit of ciguatera." *Bulletin of the Japanese Society of Scientific Fisheries*, Vol. 43, No. 8, 1977, pp. 1021–26.

Zinn, Howard. *A people's history of the United States* (New York: Harper & Row, 1980).

Index

PublicAffairs is a new nonfiction publishing house and a tribute to the standards, values, and flair of three persons who have served as mentors to countless reporters, writers, editors, and book people of all kinds, including me.

I.F. STONE, proprietor of *I. F. Stone's Weekly*, combined a commitment to the First Amendment with entrepreneurial zeal and reporting skill and became one of the great independent journalists in American history. At the age of eighty, Izzy published *The Trial of Socrates*, which was a national bestseller. He wrote the book after he taught himself ancient Greek.

BENJAMIN C. BRADLEE was for nearly thirty years the charismatic editorial leader of *The Washington Post*. It was Ben who gave the *Post* the range and courage to pursue such historic issues as Watergate. He supported his reporters with a tenacity that made them fearless and it is no accident that so many became authors of influential, best-selling books.

ROBERT L. BERNSTEIN, the chief executive of Random House for more than a quarter century, guided one of the nation's premier publishing houses. Bob was personally responsible for many books of political dissent and argument that challenged tyranny around the globe. He is also the founder and longtime chair of Human Rights Watch, one of the most respected human rights organizations in the world.

For fifty years, the banner of Public Affairs Press was carried by its owner Morris B. Schnapper, who published Gandhi, Nasser, Toynbee, Truman, and about 1,500 other authors. In 1983, Schnapper was described by *The Washington Post* as "a redoubtable gadfly." His legacy will endure in the books to come.

Peter Osnos, *Publisher*